Marivaux's Novels

Marivaux's Novels

Theme and Function in Early Eighteenth-Century Narrative

Ronald C. Rosbottom

Rutherford • Madison • Teaneck
Fairleigh Dickinson University Press
London: Associated University Presses

Associated University Presses, Inc.
Cranbury, New Jersey 08512

Associated University Presses
108 New Bond Street
London W1Y OQX, England

Library of Congress Cataloging in Publication Data
Rosbottom, Ronald C.   1942–
  Marivaux's novels; theme and function in early
eighteenth-century narrative.

  Bibliography: p.
  1. Marivaux, Pierre Carlet de Chamblain de, 1688–
1763—Criticism and interpretation.
PQ2003.Z5R58   843'.5   73–8296
ISBN 0–8386–1419–1

PRINTED IN THE UNITED STATES OF AMERICA

For Betty

Contents

Preface   9
Acknowledgments   15
1 Marivaux, Society, and the Novel   19
2 Experiments in Prose: Failure and Success   54
3 Marianne and Society   93
4 Marianne's Other Quest   147
5 *Le Paysan parvenu*   171
Conclusion   223
Bibliography   227
Index   237

Preface

This is a book for the reader who is familiar with Marivaux, but who knows him primarily as a dramatist. Its emphasis is on the major themes of his prose work, and their technical corollaries. During the last decade, prose of the eighteenth century in France has been investigated with increasing success, and most of the efforts have been informed with a desire to discover what were the directions and unifying principles of the novel as a genre. The best critics have recognized that it was important to analyze the novel in terms of the period and the milieu of which it was part, rather than with the misleading retrospective bias—for example, insisting that the novel was either pre-Romantic or pre-Realist—that has characterized so much previous criticism. One of the first important works of this former type was Georges May's *Dilemme du roman au dix-huitième siècle,* which in many ways predicted the current interest in the "sociology of literature" through its emphasis on the influence of extra-literary concerns (in this case, a retardative critical establishment) on the novel's development. However, despite its usefulness and somewhat therapeutic effect, many critics have relied too much on May's thesis, thereby avoiding a broader approach to the history of the early eighteenth-century novel. Peter Brooks, in his recent *The Novel of Worldliness,* uses an intelligent, though again limited, thematic approach to the novels of the Enlightenment; Philip Stewart *(Imitation and Illusion in the French Memoir-Novel)* and René Godenne *(Histoire de la nouvelle française aux XVIIe et XVIIIe siècles)* have studied the novel from an obvious generic viewpoint. Finally, Henri Coulet *(Le Roman jusqu'à la Révolution)* and English Showalter's quite recent study *(The Evolution of the French Novel, 1641–1782)* both treat the traditions from which the eighteenth-century novel evolved. The common denominator of all these works is that for diverse reasons—literary, sociological, historical, philosophical—the novel became a dominant literary genre in the eighteenth century. These critics likewise conclude that it was a genre characterized not only by consistent and imaginative experimentation, but, despite a few unqualified successes, by almost constant failure, at least in post-Jamesian terms.

I do not intend, in the present study, to go over the same ground that Coulet, May, and Showalter have covered. Rather, my purpose is to familiarize the reader with one of the most prolific, and least-known novelists of the first half of the eighteenth century. Since I first began work on Marivaux, less than a decade ago, his critical stock has steadily increased. Witness the numerous editions of his works by Frédéric Deloffre, and the increasingly frequent studies on different aspects of his dramatic and narrative work, especially those by Matucci, Desvignes-Parent, Brady, and Brooks. Yet Marivaux the novelist still remains unfamiliar to many students of the early Enlightenment in France and England. The reasons for this anomaly are perhaps plausible: his two major novels are unfinished; most of his other prose work, until recently, was unavailable; his success as a dramatist has dominated critical interest in him; and, finally, again until recently, there has been a general lack of interest in the pre-Diderotian novel. Earlier critics, such as F. C. Green and André Le Breton, paid some attention, though slight and generally uncritical, to Marivaux's prose, but there has been no major study in French or in English of this aspect of his work.[1]

Why should a student of the literature of the Enlightenment in France and England know of Marivaux the novelist? One reason is that he experimented with the thematic and technical possibilities of the novel at a crucial point in its development as a genre. Marivaux reached his majority and began his career at a time when the basic assumptions of literary and philosophical traditions in Europe were being severely criticized, and often rejected. Of course, one can too easily assume that a writer was influenced by the enthusiasm and movement of ideas that historians have concluded were dominant at a given time. Yet it is clear that a man like Marivaux, moving in the circles he did, laboring under certain distinct social and personal pressures, could not help but be aware of what was happening, intellectually and politically, during the last decades of Louis XIV's reign. For this reason, chapter 1 of the present study recapitulates the intellectual and aesthetic concerns of this period, revealing their effect on Marivaux, and his reaction to them. What biographical information I have presented in this chapter is perforce sketchy, because of a curious lack of details of Marivaux's personal life. Whether this was due to a willful decision on Marivaux's part, or to an accident of history, remains a moot and fascinating question. At any rate, the reader will discover that the formative years of Marivaux's career were intellectually uncertain ones, defined by an astonishing literary versatility. It will be seen how he gradually made aesthetic decisions that would be ultimately successful, as he animated older, established genres, namely the drama and prose fiction, with a vitality and a self-confidence that would set both on their way to becoming the

1. As this book was being edited, I learned that Henri Coulet's thesis, *Marivaux romancier*, will soon be published in France. For an outline of his study, see *L'Information littéraire*, 25ᵉ année, no. 3 (mai-juin 1973): 103–9.

major genres of the latter half of the eighteenth and most of the nineteenth centuries.

In chapter 2 I examine the "minor" prose efforts, that is, those besides *La Vie de Marianne* and *Le Paysan parvenu*. The emphasis here is on the themes and techniques that Marivaux developed in preparation for his two major novels. Marivaux was firmly in the tradition of the *moraliste*, that peculiarly French writer, whose bent was psychological, whose mode was generally satirical, and whose genre was the prose portrait, the epigram, and the apologue. It is my contention that Marivaux saw in the increasingly popular novel a means by which he could satisfy this moralistic tendency, with its detailed emphasis on the subtle chiaroscuro of emotion and expression. The form simultaneously provided him with a canvas broad enough to allow the depiction of his society in all its complexity. Though it would be artificial to insist too heavily on Marivaux's innovations as a novelist, especially given the recent studies that emphasize the genre's very traditional qualities, I do believe that, given the new sensibility, themes, and attitudes of the writers of the early Enlightenment, the novel appeared to them as a most promising genre, and any careful study of what informed fictional prose of the period will substantiate this thesis.

So far, studies of Marivaux's prose have noticeably suffered from a lack of any sustained criticism of his major themes and technical preoccupations. Two works, those of Matucci and Friedrichs, have approached the problem from a general, and thus restricted point of view. Both men emphasize the *development* of themes, rather than using thematics as a means of discovering the originality of Marivaux, both as a novelist and as a *moraliste*. My study of Marivaux's fictional efforts before *Marianne* and the *Paysan parvenu* reveals that he was in quest of a satisfactory, liberating form that could best contain what he saw as the dominant preoccupation of his intellectual circle: the complexity and exhilaration of social commerce. Whether he found such a form in his two best novels, the subjects of chapters 3, 4, and 5, remains a troublesome question. The fact that both novels are formally incomplete, and that Marivaux, from his election to the Académie Française in 1742 until his death in 1763, never returned to the novel, definitely leaves room for doubt about his ultimate success. However, this critic leans toward an affirmative response to the question, for both these novels do succeed in more ways than they fail, and a close thematic analysis of them, buttressed by an awareness of their place in Marivaux's whole corpus, will reveal that he had, at least partially, satisfied the quest for formal certainty that had defined most of his literary life.

There is little doubt that many of the problems that have bothered literary men for centuries similarly bothered Marivaux: how to make money, how to remain faithful to one's art, whom to write for, what to write, when and what to publish, and so on. These are basic questions that must be answered, no matter how immense and tedious the task, if we are ever to understand fully Marivaux the writer. Yet these concerns are not within the domain of this study. My primary interest in writing this book was to discover a thematic unity in Marivaux's prose fiction, to use this unity to explain, at least in part, why Marivaux wrote what he did, the way he did. I also wished to entice readers to read more of Marivaux than *Le Jeu de l'amour et du hasard* and *La Double inconstance*. For this reason, there is not a small amount of textual reference and examples in these pages, for it is important that the reader not only learn of the themes, but that he have some intimation of the stylistic and linguistic originality that makes Marivaux's presentation of them unique. Despite the increasing availability of texts (see my note on editions below), Marivaux's prose work seems to intimidate most students of French and English literature of the period, either because of its style (which, by the way, makes it a thankless translating task), or because of its length. This should not be so, for not unlike Proust, Marivaux demands a certain patience of the reader, a patience that is rewarded as we enter Marivaux's narrative world, wander through it, always under the strict and guiding hand of its creator, and leave it with a new awareness of the subtlety and originality of a prose writer who has intrigued the "happy few" for over two hundred years.

There has been no satisfactory edition of the complete works of Marivaux since the Duchesne edition of 1781. However, Frédéric Deloffre has gone far in rectifying this situation with his own editions of Marivaux's novels, of his complete theater, of his journals and miscellaneous publications in the *Mercure,* and elsewhere. These works are:

> *La Vie de Marianne* (Paris: Garnier, 1957)
> *Le Paysan parvenu* (Paris: Garnier, 1959)
> *Le Télémaque travesti* (Geneva: Droz, 1959), since superseded by
>   *Oeuvres de jeunesse*
> *Théatre complet,* 2 vols. (Paris: Garnier, 1968)
> *Journaux et oeuvres diverses* (Paris: Garnier, 1969)
> *Oeuvres de jeunesse* (Bibliothèque de la Pléiade, Paris: Gallimard, 1972)

All references to Marivaux's works in the present study will be to these editions, and will appear in the text as *Marianne, Paysan, T. C., Journaux,* and *O.J.,* respectively.

Acknowledgments

There are fewer moments more gratifying to an author than when he can publicly thank his colleagues and friends for their advice and support during the composition of his book. In this case, the debts are numerous. Ira Wade inspired, and has sustained my interest in the French Enlightenment; Jeanne Monty and Michel Launay introduced me to Marivaux's novels; English Showalter, Jr., suffered with me through several versions of the present work, always friendly, always with the surest critical eye; Bill Goode patiently read and advised; Clif Cherpack was a peerless devil's advocate; and Gerry Prince put up with more than any friend and colleague should have. Whatever merit this book may have is due in large part to them.

Part of this study was completed thanks to a research grant from the University of Pennsylvania.

Every scholar's spouse should understand why I dedicate this book to my wife, as well as why she has come to think of Marivaux in much the same way as Voltaire did.

Marivaux's Novels

1
Marivaux, Society, and the Novel

I

THE LAST THREE DECADES OF THE REIGN OF LOUIS XIV WERE marked by intellectual audacity and official repression. Recent historical revisions of Louis XIV's "glorious years" have shown that indeed they were limited to the first decade of his own personal rule (1661–1672), and what followed was but an attempt to maintain the status quo. The Sun King, his ministers, and confidants were preoccupied with the centralization and aggrandizement of power and prestige. Versailles was the political and polite center of France as well as of Europe, but although grandiose in design, the court and bureaucracy were stagnant and sclerotic in social and intellectual terms. It was outside the confines of Versailles' deceptive grandeur that new ideas were being formulated and expressed. In the last decades of Louis's reign, old institutions and traditional values were being reexamined and often attacked by such men as Bayle, Fontenelle, Richard Simon, and others. Never before had Europe seen such a discrepancy between social and political reality and intellectual and artistic expression.

The French intellectual was discovering that his world was an uncertain one. New concepts and new tools were

19

needed to confront the new realities he found before him. Voyagers had brought back tales of successful and highly civilized worlds that rivaled France's own. He was told of other religions, which taught truths similar to those of his own faith and which demanded the same fidelity. Scientists were bombarding him with new theories, revealing to him an untold plurality of worlds, infinitely smaller and infinitely larger than his own. The neo-classical aesthetic of the previous generation had vaunted stability. Louis had wanted to control art as he did the state: "All the arts, letters and sciences must come together, as in the time of Augustus, to glorify [Louis's] person and his reign, and all naturally, in perfect order and obedience."[1] But this artificial order was transparent and the intellectual's world was becoming less and less stable as his search for certainty was more frenetic.

It was in this period that Pierre Carlet de Marivaux was born, was educated, and reached his majority (1688–1709). Although essentially a man of the eighteenth century, Marivaux had very strong and lasting ties with the late neo-classical era, and it is this period, its great men and its events, that would continue to influence the writer until his death in 1763. His formation as a dramatist, and especially as a novelist, took place then, and in fact, his introduction to the world of letters came at the climax of the famous Quarrel between the Ancients and the Moderns, an event that made a lasting impression on the young littérateur.

Several good studies have been made of the specific literary side of this multi-faceted quarrel,[2] but little has been written about its nonliterary ramifications. Ostensibly, the Quarrel centered around the argument as to whether Homer and other ancient poets were equal to, better than,

1. Pierre Goubert, *Louis XIV and Twenty Million Frenchmen* (1966; trans. 1970; rpt. New York: Vintage Books, 1972), p. 81.
2. Hubert Gillot, *La Querelle des Anciens et des Modernes en France* (Paris: Champion, 1914) and Hippolyte Rigault, *Histoire de la Querelle des Anciens et des Modernes* (Paris: Hachette, 1856).

or inferior to the poets of the Age of Louis XIV. Such comparative questions had of course been discussed among cultivated men since the Renaissance, but in the last decades of the reign of Louis XIV, they took on special importance. A. Adam has pointed out in an all-too-brief note that the Quarrel was indeed a moment of intellectual crisis which tried to answer the question as to whether the writers of the time were to keep their eyes fixed on the past, or choose to be "modern." Could they ignore the complex revolution that was taking place in the natural sciences? Must they adopt a hostile attitude toward the new styles, manners, and tastes of the "new France?"[3] The extra-literary repercussions were as significant as the literary ones, and both aspects of this famous Quarrel were to have a salubrious effect on the formation of Marivaux the novelist and moralist.[4]

For the most part, the Ancients were a group of socially acceptable, often politically powerful men of letters who were secure in their positions. They were not necessarily reactionaries, but they did support, and often strongly defended the status quo. In the very active years of the Quarrel (1687–1694), their semi-official leader was the respected poet Boileau. But modern critics of the period, and Adam especially, have seen the influential religious orator Bossuet as the true intellectual leader of the group. The Ancients were a numerically smaller group than the Moderns, but their lack of numbers was more than counterbalanced by their prestige. Besides the aforementioned leaders, men such as Racine, La Bruyère, and Malebranche, and the respected female writer, Mme. de Sévigné (a notable exception to the rule that "les femmes sont nées modernes") lent their fame and influence to the party of the

3. Antoine Adam, "Hommage à la mémoire de Fontenelle," *Annales de l'université de Paris* (1957), p. 404. See also Adam's discussion in his *Histoire de la littérature du XVIIe siècle*, 3: 125–31; 5: 80–84.
4. One of the best analyses available on Marivaux and the Quarrel is Lionel Gossman's "Literature and Society in the Early Enlightenment: The Case of Marivaux," *MLN* 82 (1967): 306–33.

Ancients. And, except for the Duc d'Orléans's group at the Palais-Royal, the Court and royal salons of the period were mostly pro-Ancient. Even the Church was involved, with the Jansenists lined up with the Ancients, and the Jesuits siding with the Moderns. As Adam says: "L'opposition revêtait presque l'aspect d'un conflit d'ordre politique."[5]

The Moderns were not helpless underdogs though, even faced with the formidable prestige of the Ancients. As mentioned above, they could count influential Jesuits (and, after 1701, their respected *Journal de Trévoux*) and nobles in their ranks. Also, they were for the most part a young and somewhat iconoclastic group that made up for its lack of prestige with wit and intelligent public relations. Another important source of support was the ever-growing number of newspapers, literary journals, and *gazettes*. These publications were also attempting to confront and defeat the Establishment, and they found that their pages were being filled by more and more adherents to the party of the Moderns. These journals were aimed at a less limited, though of course still quite small public, and this larger audience would be the future supporters of the Moderns in the early decades of the eighteenth century.

The Moderns were generally from less illustrious families than the Ancients, and were not so brilliantly original as their opponents. (It has been suggested that one reason Fontenelle became such an outspoken Modern was his chagrin at being so strongly criticized after his first tragedy, *Aspar* [1680].) But they were much more aware of their public roles as writers, and of the importance of having and catering to a larger reading public than that found in the salons and at court. They cultivated, for instance, the growing audience of women readers, and used this feminine bias to introduce their doctrines into more and larger circles. It is generally conceded that the most damaging strategic mistake made during the years of the Quarrel was that of

5. In his *Histoire . . .*, 5: 81.

Boileau's satire against women (1692). Attacking them as unfaithful, light-headed, and as readers of sentimental and morally corrupt literature, especially novels, the elderly Boileau received an immediate and effective response from his arch-enemy, Charles Perrault, who wrote an *Apologie des femmes* (1694). Not only had Boileau succeeded in alienating a large and potentially useful minority, but he found that in order to quiet the outrage caused by his satire, he had to embrace Perrault publicly at the Academy, an act that formally ended the most virulent part of the Quarrel, which, except for a few skirmishes, would not reignite until the first decade of the eighteenth century.

The lessons of this first part of the Quarrel would be clear to subsequent generations. Although often superficially presented, the pro and con arguments concerning the value of looking to the past for inspiration uncovered some fundamental differences among members of the political, social, and religious establishments of late seventeenth-century France. "L'opposition des deux camps ne portait donc pas sur la valeur proprement littéraire des oeuvres antiques, mais sur la réalité d'un progrès de l'intelligence et de la moralité générale."[6] The Quarrel was one of the symptoms as well as one of the causes of the ethical and artistic revaluation that helped define the early Enlightenment. Ostensibly attacking the sacred cows of the neo-classical literary critics, the Moderns were in fact questioning all traditional values. Being careful to deny any aid from the *libertins érudits,* the followers of Gassendi, the Moderns also successfully avoided any more-than-occasional cries of heresy and free-thinking. They adopted the vocabulary and terminology of the very school they were attacking, and used the more liberal tenets of the traditionalism that confronted them as wedges to force cracks in the theretofore impenetrable façade of neo-classical doctrine. It is perhaps true to say that they were courageous and indignant men

6. *Ibid.*

and women who felt that Providence or fate played little or no part in life, that each individual had the chance to make something of himself, and that this chance should not be thwarted or denied by any arbitrary rules or social barriers.

The Moderns were more optimistic than the Ancients, and their innate faith in the progress of the human spirit and mind would furnish impetus to one of the basic tenets of Enlightenment philosophy. They were not revolutionaries, but they were interested in opening up, or at least loosening, some of the static concepts that characterized most of neo-classical thought. It is perhaps this desire to free social, political, religious, and literary man from the tradition-bound categories of the neo-classical ethic that is the most significant legacy of the Quarrel.

Although of minor importance compared with the Boileau-Perrault quarrel, the flare-up between Mme. Dacier, prose translator of the *Iliad* in 1699, and Houdar de La Motte has especial significance for the present study because it is at this juncture that Marivaux joined in the Quarrel of the Ancients and the Moderns. Contrary to the previous skirmish, this part of the Quarrel found the Moderns in a much better position. The seriousness and bitterness that had been scarcely concealed a few years before was almost absent. And, in fact, the Quarrel ended with a reasonable compromise, drawn up by Fénelon, whose loyalty was to neither party, but whose sympathies were to the Ancients, and graciously accepted by La Motte.[7] The last and most significant victory of the Moderns was the general acceptance by most enlightened critics of the concept that taste was a relative and individual matter. This opinion was codified and widely promulgated through the publication of *l'abbé* Dubos's *Réflexions critiques sur la poésie et la peinture* (first published in 1719, then reedited in 1733). Although still somewhat traditional, Dubos did make two salient

---

7. For details, see Jean Ehrard, *L'Idée de nature en France dans la première moitié du XVIIIe siècle*, 2 vols. (Paris: S.E.V.P.E.N., 1963), 1: 255–57.

points that became the keystones of the new, "modern" aesthetic: that the subjects of art were to be found throughout nature, or reality, and that the elitism of the previous generations had to be modified. The immediate effect was a call to enlarge the artists' potential audience, as well as to enlarge the source of their subject matter. Such an attitude would help to free, at least psychologically, many young writers from the often imposing and restrictive aesthetic of the previous generations. Literature, its art, and its appreciation became a much more personal and self-conscious form of expression.

At this crucial point in the history of modern criticism the young Marivaux made his literary début. Born in Paris in 1688, the son of Nicolas Carlet, a minor functionary, Pierre Carlet spent the first ten years of his life in the capital city.[8] When, in 1698, his father was named *contrôleur contre-garde* of the mint at Riom (later to be its director from 1704 to 1719), in Auvergne, the whole family went to live in the provinces, where the young Marivaux was educated. At about the time he reached his majority, we find Marivaux signing up as a student of law in Paris. This was of course the traditional route followed by most young men of poor but respectable families, and it does not necessarily signify a penchant for jurisprudence. In 1712, at the age of twenty-four, Marivaux wrote and probably produced privately in Limoges, his first work, a weak comedy entitled *Le Père prudent et équitable*. A little later that year, he took the partly finished manuscripts of his first two novels, *Les Effets surprenants de la sympathie* and *Pharsamon, ou les Nouvelles folies romanesques*, to the Parisian authorities for permission to publish. Between 1712 and the early 1720s (with the success of *Arlequin poli par l'amour*), Marivaux would try to evolve his own style and modes, relying increasingly less on imitations of the writers of preceding generations.

8. Most of this and subsequent biographical information is based on the works of Deloffre, Durry, Gilot, and Bonaccorso (see Bibliography for details).

What little we know of Marivaux's early life and origins tells us that he came from a well-respected family of architects on the maternal side. Jean-Baptiste Bullet de Chamblain, his cousin and uncle, member of Louis XIV's prestigious Académie d'Architecture, would provide an entry for the young provincial into the closed circles of Parisian high society. It was there that Marivaux probably first met and became intimate with the group of Moderns headed by Fontenelle and La Motte. The former was the most illustrious man of letters in France at the beginning of the eighteenth century, and he was also the censor who approved Marivaux's first significant works: the above-mentioned *Effets surprenants* (1713–1714) and *La Voiture embourbée* (1713). Having read these works, Fontenelle probably recognized the exuberance, as well as the talent of a young writer who could serve the Moderns well. For Fontenelle was an enthusiastic and serious member of the party of the Moderns, and kept an eye open for new recruits. He introduced Marivaux to Mme. de Lambert's salon, where the young writer came into direct contact with the avant-garde of early eighteenth-century French letters. Although he had probably not made a final decision to become a professional writer, Marivaux surely was influenced, and perhaps intimidated by the style and prestige of this famous salon, and of such frequent guests as La Motte and d'Argenson.

Of course, until the formal truce of 1716, most of the discussions in the salon of Mme. de Lambert centered around the merits of La Motte's verse rendition of the *Iliad* (1713). Rigault tells us that "la société polie des salons, qui commençait à se piquer de philosophie, trouvait de bel air de se moquer de l'*Iliade*. On considérait, a dit Terrason, la cause de La Motte comme celle de l'affranchissement de l'esprit humain."[9] Marivaux participated in these endless discussions, enjoying the fellowship and wit that were a

9. *Histoire de la Querelle des Anciens et des Modernes*, p. 427.

hallmark of the more established salons, while, as Deloffre has intimated,[10] also studying the forms of communication, verbal especially, but most likely nonverbal as well, that were used in these salons. On a more practical level, because many of the Moderns were successful businessmen, Marivaux met important sources of financial information and invested heavily in Law's System, making a comfortable profit. He also managed a successful marriage to a moderately wealthy woman from Sens, Colombe Bollogne, in 1717 (Marivaux was almost thirty, but Colombe was thirty-four years old). One of the ceremony's official witnesses was none other that Prosper Jolyot de Crébillon, probably the most important literary figure in Paris at the time.

These early years were among the happiest of Marivaux's life. But they were not the most successful literarily. Probably in 1714 and early 1715, Marivaux composed two works, one of unequal quality, which would place him firmly, although somewhat belatedly, in the camp of the Moderns. Going even further than La Motte, Marivaux wrote a mock epic entitled *Homère travesti, ou, l'Iliade en vers burlesques* (often referred to as *l'Iliade travestie*). Contrary to recent attempts toward rehabilitation,[11] this poem is of the most mediocre school-boy type, and it is surprising that Fontenelle approved it, without at least suggesting that his young protégé work on it some more. To make matters worse, the work was published six months after the public reconciliation of Mme. Dacier and La Motte. It has been pointed out that although the poem brought notoriety to its young writer, Marivaux eventually gained more enemies than friends because of it, a situation that would do much

10. *Une Préciosité nouvelle: Marivaux et le marivaudage*, 2d ed. rev. (Paris: Armand Colin, 1967), pp. 18–25.
11. See Michel Gilot, "Un étrange divertissement: *L'Iliade travestie*," in *La Régence*, Centre Aixois d'Etudes et de Recherches sur le 18e siècle. (Paris: Armand Colin, 1970), pp. 186–205. Gilot sees the work as well organized and consistently Marivaudian in tone. *"L'Iliade travestie* n'était pas en 1715 un simple divertissement d'homme de lettres, mais une oeuvre réellement subversive" (p 197).

to damage his future literary reputation.[12] It was one of the early events that caused Marivaux's later hypersensitivity to criticism.

The other work he composed at this time was his *Télémaque travesti*, a burlesque novel. In 1714, such a genre was somewhat anachronistic, and Marivaux probably felt so, for he thwarted the book's publication until 1736, when the first three parts were published, and he never admitted to its authorship. Yet the *Télémaque travesti* is, along with his *Voiture embourbée* (1713), one of the best novels of his youth. The title obviously places it in the Modern tradition of scorn for the Ancients and their venerated authors. Although comparison with Fénelon's own *Télémaque* (1699) was inevitable and probably desired, Marivaux's sole aim was not to parody specifically the champion of the Ancients. Rather, he wanted to experiment with the novel form, devise certain comic techniques, and at the same time firmly establish himself as a man of the future, and not an imitator of the past. Given the mode he chose—the burlesque, whose seventeenth-century practitioners, Scarron and Sorel, had set definite precedents—Marivaux came close to weakening his argument that he was in fact a Modern. But, as we shall see in the next chapter, the *Télémaque travesti* is an original and technically significant work of which Marivaux should have been at least satisfied, if not proud.

Besides these two works, which had a certain polemical bias, Marivaux had written and published a mélange of other novels, essays, and plays during those early years of apprenticeship. As previously mentioned, two long and mediocre novels were composed probably in late 1711 and 1712: *Les Effets surprenants de la sympathie* and *Pharsamon, ou les Nouvelles folies romanesques* (later reprinted as the *Don Quichotte moderne*), the latter unpublished until 1737. Other prose pieces include the aforementioned novel *La Voiture embourbée* (1713), and a short prose piece, *Le Bilboquet*

12. Deloffre, *Marivaux et le marivaudage*, pp. 118–19.

(1713).[13] Because of his familiarity with the Moderns, the pages of the *Mercure*, a pro-Modern journal, had been opened up to him, and he published numerous prose pieces there: "Lettres sur les habitants de Paris," subsequently referred to as the "Caractères de M. de Marivaux" (1717–1718); several essays on literary and aesthetic questions (1719); a short story entitled "Lettre de M. de Marivaux contenant une aventure" (1719–1720). Finally two comedies, *L'Amour et la Vérité* (of which only the prologue remains) and *Arlequin poli par l'amour*, as well as a tragedy in verse, *Annibal*, were produced in 1720.

Although Marivaux had not yet committed himself fully to the profession of novelist or dramatist, it is obvious that he was enchanted by the world of letters and found early that he had a certain facility of expression that enabled him to achieve moderate success in almost any genre he tried. But events in the period 1719–1720 would cause him to make a decision about his future career. In 1719, Nicolas Carlet, his father, died, leaving his family in a poor financial state. Marivaux's mother asked to be named director of Riom's mint for a short time, a post her husband had held, and a few months later, Marivaux himself asked for the same nomination, but never received a response.[14] By this time Marivaux had been married two years and had a six-month-old daughter, his only child, Colombe-Prospère. He continued his studies in law, probably more seriously than he had before, but with no impending reason, for, thanks to his wife's dowry and his fortuitous investments, the Marivaux family enjoyed a certain financial ease. However, the next few years brought a series of business and personal misfortunes that would have more than casual effect on Marivaux's artistic future.

First, in July 1720, Law's System collapsed and Marivaux

13. M.-J. Durry has analyzed this piece in the chapter entitled "Le Bilboquet retrouvé" of her book *A Propos de Marivaux* (Paris: Société d'édition d'enseignement supérieur, 1960), pp. 97–102.

14. This significant piece of information was discovered by Giovanni Bonaccorso, and analyzed in his book, *Gli Anni difficili di Marivaux* (Messina: Peloritana Editrice, 1964).

found himself near ruin, having invested his wife's dowry. A short while later, in September 1721, he made a prudent decision, and was admitted as *licencié en droit*. However, since lawyers were numerous and work scarce in Paris, Marivaux decided to become a journalist. Taking the idea from the successful *Spectator* of Addison and Steele (1711–1712; French translation, 1714–1718), he began the publication of his own *Spectateur français*, which would appear on the average of once a month from July 1721 to October 1724. After having published six numbers of the journal, Marivaux declared before notaries that he had officially renounced any claim to his father's inheritance, as well as any desire to serve as manager of the mint at Riom. Soon afterward, his wife, Colombe, died, leaving him alone with a young daughter. It is most likely at this point in his life that, at the age of thirty-four, Marivaux definitely chose the profession of letters as a career.

II

It is somewhat surprising that we know so little of Marivaux's private life. Only the major dates of publication, of presentation, of public acclaim or rebuke are known for certain. In this age of enlightened social commerce, where the private letter had become an art form, and where gossip had joined it, we possess no correspondence to or from Marivaux, and almost no autobiographical references. There is no major figure of that century about whom we know so little. We in fact know more about the civil state of Marivaux's father, a minor provincial functionary, than about his famous son. Thus, any conclusions we draw about Marivaux and his work from secondary, though contemporary sources, are by nature tentative and subject to future revision.

Yet some observations can be made with a small amount of certainty. Meticulous and original detective work by such Marivaux specialists as Gustave Larroumet, Marie-Jeanne

Durry, Frédéric Deloffre, and Michel Gilot, during the past century, have revealed that Marivaux was a very complex man, so much so that a willful desire on his part to hide himself from posterity is not beyond reasonable surmise. For the most part, his contemporaries were wary of him. D'Alembert, in his thorough eulogy of Marivaux, says: "Son caractère n'était guère moins singulier que ses écrits."[15] Marmontel affirms that "il n'y eut jamais, je crois, d'amour-propre plus délicat, plus chatouilleux et plus craintif."[16] And there is the famous anecdote that recounts how two of Marivaux's acquaintances whispered in front of him. Convinced that they were ridiculing him, Marivaux cut off all relations with his friends, until one of them explained later that he had not been the subject of their private conversation.

Everyone knew of Marivaux's sympathy for and largesse toward anyone with a sad tale (a frequent source of anecdotes in his journals). He was somewhat naive when it came to finances, and this characteristic kept him in a relatively impecunious state for most of his life. He treasured friendship highly, and chose his friends carefully. The editor (possibly La Porte) of a collection of Marivaux's writings tells us in a preface (1765) that "simple, attentif, essentiel dans le commerce de l'amitié, M. de Marivaux y portoit également la délicatesse et la sincérité."[17] This basic trust of his fellow man made him an accomplished participant of the social encounters so important in his day. Yet he too retained a certain wariness, which helped to protect him from the dishonesty or hypocrisy of those who were not so *honnête* as he. "Avec un caractere tranquille, quoique sensible, il possédoit encore toutes les qualités qu'exigeoit la société, & qui la rendent sûre et agréable. A une probité

15. Marivaux, *Théâtre complet,* ed. Bernard Dort (Paris Seuil, 1964), p. 24.
16. Cited by Deloffre in his edition of *La Vie de Marianne* (Paris: Garnier, 1957), p. 100, n. 1.
17. *Oeuvres diverses de M. de Marivaux, de l'académie françoise* (Paris: Duchesne, 1765), p. xvi.

exacte, à un noble désintéressement, il réunissoit une candeur aimable, une ame bienfaisante, une modestie sans fard & sans prétention, une affabilité pleine de sentiment, & l'attention la plus scrupuleuse à éviter tout ce qui pouvoit offenser ou déplaire."[18]

This portrait of Marivaux that appears after a careful study of all available sources is an enchanting one, and does help one, despite its sketchiness, to understand better some of the basic themes that he developed and that appear in most of his writings. Marivaux frequently maintained that he was a "spectateur," and only superficially a participant in the society he depicts: "Mon dessein n'est de penser ni bien ni mal, mais simplement de recueillir fidèlement ce que me vient d'après le tour d'imagination que me donnent les choses que je vois ou que j'entends" (*Journaux,* p. 114). Marivaux saw himself firmly in the venerable French tradition of the *moraliste,* a stance that a critic has recently described as "something different from a moralist, not concerned with ethical issues only but with a picture of human behaviour which shall throw into relief its paradox, its complexity, in a word which shall suggest the irony of the human condition."[19] Yet, instead of opting for the epigram, that genre of deceptive clarity which La Rochefoucauld had developed to perfection, Marivaux chose to reveal his themes through the theater and especially through different forms of prose narrative. A close look at some of these recurrent themes will show a consistency of purpose that all too often has been ignored in studies of Marivaux's work.

Marivaux defined all of human existence in social terms, but realized that the forms and rhythms of society were constantly subject to criticism and new definition. Many of his own private concerns regarding social existence would become the major themes of his narrative and dramatic works, and his philosophical modernity would shape those themes into a system of behavior that would serve to define the subject matter of the novel of manners for decades to come. Sincerity, naturalness, social adaptability, and their corollaries of subterfuge and deception (Marivaux's term is *coquetterie*) and moral compromise: these are the themes that haunted Marivaux and that would recur throughout his numerous writings, as he attempted to reconcile the new world view of the Moderns with the tradition and stability that were the legacy of the Ancients. These themes, in the broad outline that follows, reveal the congruence of the private Marivaux that myth and tradition have passed down to us, and the new interests of that group of thinkers and writers known as the Moderns.

Sociability was one of the prime criteria for Marivaux the *moraliste*. His own personal demands on his friends and acquaintances illustrate the role that sincerity and naturalness played in his social ethic. Artificiality always offended him, and his novels, plays, and essays are full of anecdotes that illustrate this. In one telling scene, Marivaux describes how a father had made a polite machine of his son, teaching him all the mechanics of sociability, but none of its naturalness. When his father is out of the room, the boy relaxes and enjoys Marivaux's company, but when he returns, his son changes: "J'ai vu la joie, la confiance et la liberté fuir de son visage; il a changé de physionomie; je ne le reconnaissais plus" (*Journaux*, p. 204). Marivaux understands that most of the "unnaturalness" that he sees around him is learned, and that it must be uprooted if men are going to be able to live comfortably with one another.

The most famous scene in Marivaux's journals occurs in the *Spectateur français* and tells of how, upon returning unexpectedly to his mistress's apartment, he finds her before a mirror, practicing all the expressions and movements that the young Marivaux had, up until then, taken as natural and spontaneous. He shudders at the thought of having fallen for such tricks, and is grateful to have seen the truth: "Je l'avais crue naturelle et ne l'avais aimée que sur ce pied-là; de sorte que mon coeur cessa tout d'un coup, comme si mon coeur ne s'était attendri que sous condition." Confronting her, the disillusioned lover affirms: "Je viens de voir les machines de l'Opéra. Il me divertira toujours, mais il me touchera moins" (*Journaux*, p. 118). Using this scene to open his *Spectateur*, Marivaux asserts that he thus learned how to see behind the masks worn by his contemporaries, and henceforth he will share his discoveries on the lack of sincerity and naturalness with his readers.

Despite the somewhat righteous tone of this and other passages of the *Spectateur*, Marivaux was not an absolutist on questions of morality. Of primary importance in his philosophy was the concept of individuality, and he firmly believed that if society were to work, it must take into account not only the uniqueness of everyone, but also the freedom to be unique. In truth, Marivaux was not an impartial spectator, but rather the champion of a *realistic*—morally and psychologically—view of society. In order to better delineate his concept of individuality in the social context, Marivaux would occasionally use, as a metaphor, his own function as a literary artist. In the eighth number of his *Spectateur*, he writes: "Ecrire naturellement, être naturel n'est pas se mouler sur personne quant à la forme de ses idées, mais au contraire, se ressembler fidèlement à soi-même, et ne point se départir ni du tour ni du caractère d'idées pour qui la nature nous a donné vocation" (*Journaux*, p. 149). This was a defense of his singular style, so often criticized by his contemporaries as being "néologique" or "précieux," yet the defense of the "natural" could be and was extended to his analysis of the role of the individual and his amour-propre in the social context. In another rare commentary on his style, and in defense of its uniqueness, Marivaux told the Académie Française in 1744 that there is "un rapport entre les événements, les moeurs, les coutumes d'un certain temps, et la manière de penser, de sentir et de s'exprimer de ce temps-là" ("Réflexions sur Thucydide," *Journaux*, p. 460). This was a favorite dictum of the Modern camp, which Marivaux had earlier supported in another essay, in 1719, "Sur la clarté du discours" (*Journaux*, pp. 52–56).

The best source we have for what Marivaux felt he was doing that was new is in his "Réflexions sur l'esprit humain à l'occasion de Corneille et de Racine," three lectures given in 1749 and 1750 to the Académie. These essays rank in importance with the famous *avertissement* to *Les Serments indiscrets* (1731), where Marivaux also put down what he was trying to do in his dramatic works. The theme of both these texts is the same: "la science du coeur humain" and how it is learned. In the "Réflexions sur l'esprit humain," Marivaux starts with his continuing feud with the *philosophes* and especially with Voltaire (a feud that, coincidentally, had begun in earnest with the presentation of *Les Serments indiscrets*, which earned Marivaux the favorite epithet of Voltaire: "métaphysique"). In the essay, Marivaux tries to differentiate between the *philosophes* and the "hommes de génie" like Corneille, Racine, and most certainly himself. Yet the polemical nature of these essays is not what interests us here (except that they substantiate the theory that Marivaux was insecure, always looking to include himself in societies or groups of which he was not a part). Marivaux was trying to convince his listeners that though we believe that "la science du coeur humain" is known to us all and is no enigma to any cultivated man, we are in fact in error: "Car cette facilité que nous trouvons à l'apprendre plus ou moins, et qui nous dissimule sa profondeur, ne vient point de sa nature, mais bien de la nature de la société que nous avons ensemble" (*Journaux*, p. 475). That is, the very nature of social interaction prevents the neutrality, "le travail solitaire et assidu," that the careful study of any science demands. So how do we learn this "science"? Not by books; there is another and better school. "C'est la société, c'est toute l'humanité même qui en tient la seule école qui soit convenable, école toujours ouverte, où tout homme étudie les autres, et en est étudié à son tour; où tout homme est tour à tour écolier et maître. Cette science réside dans le commerce que nous avons tous, et sans exception, ensemble" (p. 476). Each and every "citoyen du monde" must know his fellows and their ways or run the real risk of damaging or destroying his fortune, his peace of mind, his honor, and sometimes even his life. At this relatively late date in his career (no further major work would be written before his death in 1763), Marivaux seems to be summing up. From his earliest literary attempts, he had been trying to develop a science of society, a new awareness of the rapidly expanding social contexts that men like Marivaux were facing.

The essential tool of Marivaux's "social science" was compromise, and most of his theater and prose fiction is a literature of compromise. It is difficult to ascertain when this attitude first became prevalent in the early Enlightenment, or why Marivaux chose to spend much of his literary career analyzing it. Yet, as we read the literature of this period, it soon becomes apparent that the good writers were all increasingly concerned with depicting the possibilities of freedom in an apparently rigid social structure. More allowances were being made for individual merit, tastes, ways of expression, and though it was a long way to the frenetic individuality of the late eighteenth century, compromise—moral, intellectual, and emotional—defined the early Enlightenment's attitude toward society.

In Marivaux's world there could be no hypocrisy, in traditional terms, nor could there be complete honesty. Neither extreme was viable. Marivaux illustrated the inefficacy of both in several of his early fictional pieces, concluding that sincerity and naturalness were relative, and no longer absolute terms. In a series of scenes entitled "Le Chemin de la Fortune," which appeared first in *Le Cabinet du philosophe* (1734), Marivaux presents us with an allegorical treatment of the question of compromise (*Journaux*, pp. 355–71). In the first scene, Lucidor and La Verdure appear in a country setting with Fortune's palace in the background.

Around them are several gravestones marking the burial places of virtues. A ditch separates the men from Fortune's palace. In order to reach the palace, they must jump the ditch, leaving behind them some of their virtues, which are weighing them down. Scrupule appears, and warns them against any such action; soon, Cupidité also arrives, and presents them with the alternative: Fortune or nothing.

Suddenly, Fortune herself appears on a throne before La Verdure. She listens to the case of Clarice, a young widow, who cannot find a husband, only lecherous lovers. She asks for help, and is sent away angrily by Fortune, impatient at such virtuous concerns on the part of the young girl. Thus, Marivaux explains that Fortune will help no one who is so virtuous that he is unable to compromise in some way to obtain what he wishes. At this point, La Verdure is questioned as to his own desires, and he explains that he too cannot compromise his virtue to gain riches. Fortune again becomes angry, and warns that compromise is the only means to achieve favors. Marivaux's lesson is obvious: he who would succeed cannot leave honesty and naiveté untarnished.

One of the most "honest" characters created by Marivaux was the nun Tervire, whose story takes up the last three parts of *La Vie de Marianne*. Marivaux had promised his readers this story for several years, and used it to serve an important thematic function. Several critics have seen the story of Tervire as simply another interpolated *histoire* or *nouvelle* in the tradition of the heroic romances that Marivaux knew so well. Even Madame de Riccoboni, who wrote a conclusion to *La Vie de Marianne*, dismissed the story ironically as being boring and superfluous: "Je [Mme. de Riccoboni's Marianne] vous disais donc que, grâces au ciel, la cloche sonna, et que ma religieuse me quitta: je dis grâces au ciel, car en vérité son récit m'avait paru long: et la raison de cela, c'est qu'en m'occupant des chagrins de mon amie, je ne pouvais pas m'occuper des miens" (*Marianne*, p. 586).

Yet the story of the unhappy Tervire has close thematic ties to Marianne's own memoirs. She is the personification of the anti-coquette, and as such adds an important dimension to Marianne's own *coquetterie*. In his analysis of the Tervire sequence, Jean Fabre has offered the theory that there is much more of a contrast between Tervire and Marianne than between Marianne and Jacob.[20] Tervire always thinks of *others* first, before herself; she is open about her feelings, and lacks Marianne's sense of moral irony. Tervire is a victim of society, not one of its successful participants. She is not happy, and never has been, although she had the one thing that Marianne lacked, namely, the knowledge of her origins and of her family. She is also as pretty, as intelligent, and as graceful as Marianne (*Marianne*, pp. 493–94). But as she progresses from one misfortune to another, the reader becomes aware that she will not be so adept as Marianne at extricating herself from misfortune, nor so quick to turn events to her own advantage. Although there are moments when her amour-propre seems to be expressing itself (*Marianne*, pp. 454, 493–94), Tervire is not nearly so careful or aware of this part of herself as is Marianne.

Tervire is very philanthropic, constantly helping others, and giving of herself emotionally. But her goodness only brings her more pain. Those who cannot cope with the subterfuge and hypocrisy of society are doomed to a life of helplessness and frustration, as the metaphor of a cloistered nun so eloquently illustrates. In order to succeed, even to *exist*, in this society, Marivaux believes that one must be born with an innate genius for survival and protection. Tervire does not learn how to compromise, and she ends her life separated from the real world. Marivaux's

20. Jean Fabre, "Intention et structure dans les romans de Marivaux," *Zagadnienia rodzajów literackich* 3 (1960): 5–25. See also Leo Spitzer's article, "A Propos de *la Vie de Marianne*," *Romanic Review* 44 (April 1953): 102–26, for a different view of this sequence. Spitzer sees the two stories as a comparison between "l'héroïsme séculier et l'héroïsme dévot" (p. 115), i.e., Tervire's story is a second approach to the same problem treated in *Marianne*.

story of the nun was not just tacked on to the end of Marianne's because a capricious author lost interest in his original heroine. He had a specific point to make, and succeeded in illustrating the difference between *coquetterie*, that shadowy world where truth and lying become confused, and honesty, which he had previously shown could not long exist in society. It is in this light that Tervire's story should be read.

There are several other anecdotes where Marivaux shows how honesty is not socially viable.[21] As one honest person is told: "Rien ne tarit tant le plaisir de la société, qu'un homme aussi excessivement bon que vous l'êtes à tous égards: son entretien n'a rien de vif, rien qui flatte la curiosité maligne que nous avons tous mutuellement sur ce qui nous regarde" (*Journaux*, p. 185). Honesty is too static, and offers nothing to the variety demanded by the new social philosophy of the Moderns. Like honesty, hypocrisy is also useless, and, for the most part, transparent to the initiates of this realistic social ethic. The hypocrites in Marivaux's last two novels are as distinct in tone and character from Marianne and Jacob as he could make them. Climal, who will be discussed more fully in chapter 3, is a perfect example. Another is that of the prioress of the convent where Marianne meets Mme. de Miran for the first time. Marianne describes the prioress through a study of her gestures, a favorite Marivaudian device: "A voir ces bonnes filles, au reste, vous leur trouvez un extérieur affable, et pourtant un intérieur indifférent. Ce n'est que leur mine, et non pas leur âme qui s'attendrit pour vous: ce sont de belles images qui paraissent sensibles, et qui n'ont que des superficies de sentiment et de bonté" (*Marianne*, p. 149).

Most men and women of the cloth suffer such cynical analyses in Marivaux's novels and essays. The breakdown of traditional religious and moral categories made the

---

21. See in *Le Cabinet du philosophe*, "Le Voyageur dans le nouveau monde," (*Journaux*, pp. 389–437), and in the *Spectateur français*, the story of Anacharsis, from which a passage is cited above (*Journaux*, pp. 179–86).

professional man of religion an obvious and frequent target for even the most devout of the Moderns. Father Saint-Vincent, the priest who introduces Marianne to Climal, is depicted as a naive and somewhat silly man of little worldly experience. The confessor, M. Doucin, in *Le Paysan parvenu*, is also shown to be a religious confidence man, interested only in his own aggrandizement. His victims, the Habert sisters, especially the elder one, are vividly and unsympathetically depicted as *dévotes*, one of Marivaux's favorite targets. "Les dévots fâchent le monde, et les gens pieux l'édifient; les premiers n'ont que les lèvres de dévots, c'est le coeur qui l'est dans les autres; les dévots vont à l'église simplement pour y aller, pour avoir le plaisir de s'y trouver, et les pieux pour y prier Dieu. . . . Les uns sont de vrais serviteurs de Dieu, les autres n'en ont que la contenance" (*Paysan*, p. 47). The hypocrite, according to Marivaux, is interested only in himself, and not in any interaction with others. And he is not criticized for moral reasons, but rather as an impediment to the success of social intercourse.

Obviously, neither honesty nor hypocrisy can ensure the successful functioning of society as Marivaux defines it. A compromise must be made that will permit people to be sincere, without hurting others, and sociable. Since everyone is possessed of a well-defined ego, and since he wishes to present himself successfully in society, compromise is inescapable. Some form of social mask becomes incumbent upon all participants in a given society. Each individual, in his attempt to safeguard his ego, must evolve a science of defense. Marivaux realized the unfortunate consequences of such a world view: it would mean the denial of his belief in the necessity of sincerity in human relations. But, given the social context of the period, it was the only door left open to the Modern moralist.

One of the most prevalent metaphors—and verities—of this period was that of the mask and of mask-wearing. An increasing interest in Venice, and its masked *fêtes*, as seen later in the paintings of Pietro Longhi, Francesco Guardi, and especially Giambattista Tiepolo, had prepared the way for an enthusiastic acceptance of this phenomenon by the Parisian *monde*. As a student of eighteenth-century Venice has said about the mask: "Mieux qu'un déguisement, le masque est un incognito. Il est le secret, l'anonyme, l'impunité assurée, il est la folie licite, la billevesée permise. . . . On ne sait plus qui est personne, et personne ne sait plus qui on est."[22] Another place where the physical act of wearing a mask could be seen, besides at the balls and in the paintings of the period, included, of course, the theater, and especially the Comédie Italienne, back in Paris since 1716. The mask remained an essential dramatic tool of the Italian actors, despite such influential critics of it as Goldoni. However, the good troupes and the great actors knew that without the concomitant art of pantomime to make up for the rigidity of the mask, the use of this device was only partially successful. It is no coincidence that Marivaux produced nineteen of his thirty plays (ten of his first fifteen) at the Comédie Italienne, and that his first success, *Arlequin poli par l'amour* (1720) was performed there. His subject matter demanded the finesse, the implied deception, the ever-present miming that the Italians provided, and it was through such close contact with these foreign actors, as much as through his stories and his "marivaudage," that Marivaux pointed French dramatic writing in new directions.

But I digress. The essential fact to retain as we read Marivaux's prose works is that the century's fascination with the mask—both real and metaphorical—is evident to and emphasized by our writer, the *moraliste*. And the tone and direction of the fascination with this metaphor is summed up no better than by Jean Starobinski:

Seule une civilisation éprise de spectacles et qui accorde la plus grande importance aux plaisirs de la vue, peut cultiver ainsi l'art du travestissement. La fête masquée procure à cha-

22. Cited by Jean Starobinski, *L'Invention de la liberté* (Genève: Skira, 1964), p. 90.

cun l'agrément de voir et d'être vu sans compromettre son
identité, en n'exposant de soi qu'une apparence arbitraire,
variable selon le caprice et l'occasion. Délivré de tout ce qui
l'enchaîne et le définit par sa naissance, par sa condition, par
sa fonction, l'être masqué se réduit à l'image qu'il offre dans
l'instant, à la parole qu'il invente sur le champ. Comme l'ac-
teur, l'homme masqué manifeste une instance instantanée,
dont la liberté, inépuisable mais courte, jouit de la protection
du mensonge.[23]

Marivaux was not the first to use this metaphor, nor indeed
the last. However, the possibilities and forms of disguise—
physical, verbal, psychological—are perhaps the most constant motif of his writings, and any discussion of his prose
and dramatic work must begin with a careful analysis of his
use of them.

In his already classic work, *The Presentation of Self in Everyday Life*[24] (which has as its epigraph a passage from Santayana: "Masks are arrested expressions and admirable
echoes of feeling, at once faithful, discreet, and superla-
tive"), Erving Goffman, one of the most prominent of the
new breed of social psychologists, studies different forms
of the mask (using terms like "performances," "roles,"
"parts," and "fronts") and its effect on social interaction.
Though, as a scientist, he avoids the moralizing of writers
like Marivaux, Goffman's conclusions are quite similar to
those drawn almost two hundred years earlier by the author
of *La Vie de Marianne*. For instance, in a discussion of how
individuals conform to a given social context, Goffman sustains the thesis that absolute harmony is not necessary to
the smooth functioning of society: "Rather, each partici-

23. *Ibid.* See also, for a more specific application to Marivaux, René Pomeau,
"La Surprise et le masque dans le théâtre de Marivaux," *The Age of Enlightenment,*
ed. Barber, Brumfitt, et al. (London: Oliver and Boyd, 1967), pp. 238–51. Pomeau
states that "au XVIIIe siècle le masque était entré dans les moeurs à un degré
qui nous surprend aujourd'hui" (p. 244).
    See also William S. Rogers, "Marivaux: The Mirror and the Mask," *Esprit
créateur,* 1 (1961): 167–77.
    24. 1956; rpt. Garden City, N.Y.: Doubleday Anchor Books, 1959. Page refer-
ences will be found in the text.

pant is expected to suppress his immediate heartfelt feelings, conveying a view of the situation which he feels the others will be able to find at least temporarily acceptable. The maintenance of this surface of agreement, this veneer of consensus, is facilitated by each participant concealing his own wants behind statements which assert values to which everyone present feels obliged to give lip service" (p. 9). The result is "a kind of interactional *modus vivendi*," a "working consensus," not unlike Marivaux's own emphasis on compromise as the only way to a successful society. Toward the end of his introduction, Goffman underlines the reciprocal aspect of social commerce: "Society is organized on the principle that any individual who possesses certain social characteristics has a moral right to expect that others will value and treat him in an appropriate way. Connected with this principle is a second, namely that an individual who implicitly or explicitly signifies that he has certain social characteristics ought in fact to be what he claims to be" (p. 13). The parallels with this thesis and the story of Marianne are obvious to Marivaux's readers, and though Goffman continues to emphasize in his study the interaction of "average" individuals, we can perhaps gain a better, more precise knowledge of the social psychology of *La Vie de Marianne* and *Le Paysan parvenu* from a careful reading of such social anthropology. My purpose is not to use the tools of contemporary sociology to fashion a new interpretation of Marivaux's prose writings, but only to bring to the reader's attention the modernity of Marivaux's themes and motifs, with especial reference to that of the mask, a term that will appear often in these pages.[25]

Marivaux's belief that mask-wearing was a necessary compromise between complete sincerity and blatant hypocrisy is best understood when we study his conception of

25. Coincidentally, as this book was being prepared for publication, Philip Stewart's *Le Masque et la parole: Le Langage de l'amour au XVIIIe siècle* (Paris: José Corti, 1973) appeared in which he too found some of Goffman's theories applicable to Marivaux (see especially pp. 85, 100–102).

amour-propre and his use of the term *coquetterie*. There was little formal "Modern" dogma, and very little group cohesion. Yet eventually, at first informally (in letters, memoirs, conversations, etc.), and later more formally (in essays, prefaces, novels, etc.), there appeared a consistent "Modern" tone with one common denominator: the relativity of opinion, based on an increasing faith in individual judgment. The result was a new moral outlook, with a decided bias toward sociability. This new view of social man was much more optimistic than the seventeenth-century one. In the late seventeenth century, both the traditional values of a closed society and those of a closed religion had come together to deprive civilized man of variety as well as of his individualism. The most eloquent and the most inflexible spokesmen of this world view were Pascal and his Port-Royal colleague, Pierre Nicole. In the latter's *Essais de morale* (1671–78), we obtain a coherent view of his somber morality, "préoccupée de pourchasser l'amour-propre dans ses derniers retranchements," and which contributed "à engendrer, par réaction, une morale fondée sur l'intérêt."[26] The best-known analyst of amour-propre was of course La Rochefoucauld, who, distinct from the Port-Royalist theologians, had tried to secularize the phenomenon in his search for a *modus vivendi*. Whether or not Marivaux and the other Moderns understood La Rochefoucauld's attempts at setting forth a more workable ethic in the *Maximes,* their quarrel with the Ancients demanded that they propagate a new morality, emphasizing the individuality and relativity of judgment mentioned above. (Their often militantly negative reaction to the Jansenist writers of the preceding generation may, in fact, have begun the tendency of interpreting La Rochefoucauld as an intransigent follower of the Port-Royalist theologians, a view that discerning critics, such as W. G. Moore, have recently tried to attenuate.)

26. See, on this distinction, Marcel Raymond's "Du Jansénisme à la morale de l'intérêt," *Mercure de France* 330 (juin 1957), 238–55.

Though Marivaux is a descendant of La Rochefoucauld in many ways—as a *moraliste*, as an analyst of society, as a "loner" who tries to penetrate the mysteries of social commerce—there is no doubt that they differ as well, in tone, in approach, and in ultimate solutions. Perhaps this is most easily seen in the prose genres they chose as their vehicles: La Rochefoucauld, the brilliant, brief, final, and mysterious epigram, and Marivaux, the open, discursive, and adaptable novel. Reacting to the strict, hierarchical, moral, and theological categories of the seventeenth century, the writers of the early eighteenth depicted a new world where sociability became a more important concept. Man's attentions were turned outward—toward other lands, other ideas, other men, and he became less concerned with the negative aspects of self-interest than with the possibilities it offered to form a new freedom. To most of the *philosophes*, "passion, pride, and self-love were the three interconnected vertices of a triangle which confirmed human behavior, self-love being the base." If they were vices, they would be considered "self-correcting vices, and thus, eventually, useful mechanisms of social life."[27] The strict ethic of the seventeenth century had given way to a moral laissez-faire, although still within the bounds of a viable social structure. A natural morality was slowly evolved based on the legitimacy of amour-propre, and where a man's worth, his *vertu*, was defined by his sociability. The individual was respected, but always in terms of his relationship to society.

No writer of the early eighteenth century in France was more sympathetic to this point of view than Marivaux. "Nous avons tous besoin les uns des autres; nous naissons dans cette dépendance, et nous ne changerons rien à cela." This is one of the key phrases of *La Vie de Marianne*, as well as one of the cornerstones of Marivaux's philosophy of social existence. The Moderns, and Marivaux especially,

27. Lester Crocker, *An Age of Crisis* (Baltimore: Johns Hopkins University Press, 1959), pp. 319–20.

were exceptionally social beings. They were comfortable in the company of others, and felt that social forms and social existence were the determining factors in the life of an educated, sensitive man. In a recent study, Peter Brooks analyzes the novelistic production of the eighteenth century in terms of the theme of "worldliness," or *"mondanité,"* a concept that indicates that "one attaches primary or even exclusive importance to ordered social existence, to life within a public system of values and gestures, to the social techniques that further this life and one's position in it, and hence to knowledge about society and its forms of comportment."[28] For the Moderns, knowing how to live in society, that is, in the specific social worlds of their own experience, became a function of determining how best to define the meaning of one's existence. All of Marivaux's heroes and heroines learn to apply this knowledge, within a social context, in their attempts, sometimes futile and other times successful, to discover the truth about themselves. The social structure had become a flexible framework in which the individual could express himself with minimal restraint, as long as he subscribed to a basic law of *honnêteté.*

The other term that appears often in Marivaux's work, and that helps to elucidate more fully his preoccupation with the metaphor of the mask is *coquetterie.* The expression finds its fullest definition in his journals and early essays. For instance, in his "Lettres sur les habitants de Paris," Marivaux tells us that "les femmes ont un sentiment de coquetterie, qui ne désempare jamais leur âme; il est violent dans les occasions d'éclat, quelquefois tranquille dans les indifférentes, mais toujours présent, toujours sur le qui-vive: c'est en un mot le mouvement perpétuel de leur âme. . . . La nature a mis ce sentiment chez [elles] à l'abri de la

---

28. *The Novel of Worldliness* (Princeton: Princeton University Press, 1969), p. 4. See also the article by Roland Barthes on which Brooks bases much of his interpretation, "La Bruyère," *Essais critiques* (Paris: Editions du Seuil, 1964), pp. 221–37.

distraction et de l'oubli. Une femme qui n'est plus coquette, c'est une femme qui a cessé d'être" (*Journaux,* p.
28). And later, in his *Spectateur,* Marivaux affirms: "On ne
peut être femme sans être coquette" (*Journaux,* p. 209).

Coquetterie, as Marivaux used the term, slowly evolved
from a specific form of female play-acting to a more general
and more pervasive form of mask-wearing that could be
discerned in every social being. It becomes both a weapon
to be used on others and a defense to protect oneself from
the *coquetterie* of others. Almost every one of Marivaux's
plays, essays, or novels analyzes, in some way, the perva-
siveness of *coquetterie,* the myriad forms it takes, and its use
as a means to provide social tranquillity. *Coquetterie* is a
science of adaptability—partly innate, partly learned—
which is practiced by all of Marivaux's major characters. It
is the most successful and the most typically Marivaudian
form of mask-wearing, as we will see later.

This then was Marivaux's portrait of society. Since
honesty cannot work, or achieve the desired results, since
amour-propre precludes honesty, then the person who
would succeed must adapt himself to the exigencies of the
social situation in which he finds himself. Sincerity, even
naturalness, then become relative values; they are not ne-
gated by Marivaux's views, but they are reinterpreted in
terms of a new morality. The individual's sincerity to himself becomes the paramount theme of the early eighteenth
century, and this duty has to be worked out in the social
terms of the emerging "Modern" ethic.

III

Although the emphasis of this present study is on the
themes of Marivaux the novelist, the reader should have a
somewhat broader concept of what the novel, as a genre,
was doing in the period 1690–1725. We have already seen
how the evolution of themes had caused a revaluation of
the major fictional genres, yet as one critic has recently

explained: "Most writers [of this period], even rather poor ones, set out to write about their theme, not to illustrate the perfection of some abstract literary form. . . . It is particularly misleading to suppose that a new aesthetic appetite called a new genre into existence."[29] Just as the themes themselves were not entirely new, only more forcefully championed and enunciated, neither was the novel a new genre. And, in fact, aside from the very prolific and imaginative first three decades of the century, and with the rare success of such writers as Rousseau, Diderot, Laclos, and perhaps Sade, the novel during most of the eighteenth century was experiencing a generally unexciting, but important evolutionary process. It would not be until after 1830 that the French novel as a genre really broke cleanly away from the traditions that had served to impede its development.

It is, however, difficult to ignore the fact that the prose writers of the period were questioning some of the restrictions of the romantic ethos, and exploring more frequently the possibilities of contemporary reality. It was a slow development, but a marked one. Increasingly, the most common subject we find in the major prose fiction of the period is the confrontation between an individual and a contemporary and specific *social* situation. Challe developed this new subject in his complicated frame story, *Les Illustres Françaises* (1713), and Lesage approached it somewhat less successfully in his stylized picaresque tale, *Gil Blas* (1715–35).[30] However, both of these works reveal a dilemma that most of the important novelists of the first half of the eigh-

29. English Showalter, *The Evolution of the French Novel, 1641–1782* (Princeton: Princeton University Press, 1972), pp. 350, 351–52. This is one of the best recent works on the development of the novel genre, in both its thematic and technical aspects.
30. It is in fact the picaresque tradition, which seems to have influenced the novelists of this period the most. This is one of the few "noncomic" prose traditions that dealt, although in a unidimensional way, with the problem of an individual in confrontation with society. It is, then, not a coincidence that many of the novels of the first half of the eighteenth century have strong resemblances to the great Spanish picaresque novels.

teenth century faced: how to reconcile their attempts to present a realistic portrayal of their societies with the strictures handed down by tradition and by the unimaginative critics of their chosen genre. For Challe and Lesage, the answer had been to write "nonnovels," but for others of their contemporaries, the answers came less readily.

One of the main impediments was, as I have mentioned, a vocal, powerful, and hostile critical establishment.[31] The novel was considered at best a bastard genre and at worst a corrupting influence on the taste and morals of its readers. Its most ardent defenders often argued from negative assumptions, asserting what the novel was *not,* rather than defending its original qualities. The most famous of these apologies suffers from just such a sense of inferiority and justification. In 1669, Daniel Huet wrote his *Lettre-Traité à M. de Segrais sur l'origine des romans,* and this erudite treatise would serve as the key supporting text for the defense of the novel for a century. Unfortunately, the guidelines laid out by Huet were already outmoded when he wrote his study, and the discrepancy thus established between theory and practice would cause more problems as the novel became increasingly popular. Other justificatory pieces would not be much more help. Du Plaisir's *Sentimens sur les Lettres et sur l'Histoire avec des scrupules sur le Stile* (1683) would be one of the most coherent essays on the "psychological" novel, but would denigrate most other types.[32] Lenglet du Fresnoy's *De l'usage des romans, où l'on fait voir leur utilité et leurs différents caractères* (1734) would know a great vogue, but it too would misunderstand the importance and potential freedom of the novel.

Eventually, in order to find some support for their prose experiments, many writers of the period turned to the

31. Still one of the most perceptive studies of the development of the French novel in this period is Georges May's *Le Dilemme du roman au XVIIIe siècle* (New Haven: Yale University Press, 1963).

32. For an appreciation of this little-known work see Arpad Steiner's "A French Poetics of the Novel in 1683," *Romanic Review* 30 (1939): 235–43.

genre of history. The seventeenth-century idea of the close relationship between the classical epic and the novel (Huet's thesis) was slowly supplanted by the newer history-novel comparison. In order to combat the arguments that the novel was a fallacious and therefore corrupt genre, both to morals and to taste, history was chosen as a legitimatizing companion. May explains that it was not all forms of history that attracted the novelist, but especially "la biographie et la chronique, et, plus particulièrement, l'autobiographie, ou plutôt les mémoires, sortis eux-mêmes des anciennes chroniques. A partir des mémoires authentiques, tels ceux, par exemple, de Commynes ou de La Rochefoucauld, on passe sans solution de continuité aux mémoires apocryphes ou pseudo-historiques d'un Courtilz de Sandras ou d'un Hamilton, puis au roman-mémoires, par exemple à *Gil Blas,* qui commence à paraître en 1715."[33] Thus, early in his association with history, the novelist was selective as to which modes he would use, and first-person narrative, in the form of the memoir novel, the autobiographical novel, the letter-novel and, later, the simple *Ich-Roman* were all used and developed in the eighteenth century.

Although this symbiotic relationship between history and prose fiction had served to give a new respectability to the novel (and, tangentially, had directed more attention to the rehabilitation of history itself, which led to the birth of a new historical awareness and method, exemplified in France by Montesquieu and Voltaire), it had left a cumbersome legacy: the preponderance of first-person narration. Eventually, historiography would free itself from the memoir tradition, but the novel was not so fortunate. The exigencies of narrative verisimilitude would exact their price until the early nineteenth century. Many of the better writ-

---

33. May, "L'histoire a-t-elle engendré le roman?," *RHLF* 55 (1955): 155–76. For an excellent treatment of the corollary of this thesis in England, i.e., how eighteenth-century historians searched for narrative continuity, see Leo Braudy's *Narrative Form in History and Fiction* (Princeton: Princeton University Press, 1970).

ers of prose fiction, such as Challe, Marivaux, Prévost, Montesquieu, and Crébillon, as they became more sure of themselves, would concentrate on the *thematic* use of the first-person narrator, the use of time as a narrative element, and the use of style as an expression of individual personalities. They would push the memoir-novel and the epistolary novel, the predominant forms of eighteenth-century fiction, to their limits of possibility, and the results would be such successes as *Les Mémoires d'un homme de qualité*, *La Vie de Marianne*, *Les Egarements du coeur et de l'esprit*, *Les Lettres persanes*, and later, *La Nouvelle Héloïse* and *Les Liaisons dangereuses*. Yet, for the most part, these technical impediments coupled with certain thematic restrictions would provide few occasions for any but the best writers to succeed.[34]

By the 1720s, we can say that not only had the novel been accepted by many serious men of letters (Fénelon and Montesquieu had used it with success), but it had also begun to free itself from parts of its past—especially from the influence of the romantic, heroic novels of the late Renaissance and first half of the seventeenth century. It was still seen by most writers of the early eighteenth century as a genre associated with a class, a subject matter, and a tone different from what they wanted; they saw in the novel not a new genre, but a new direction in which they could go with their increasingly self-conscious themes. They were uncertain as to the best procedures to follow, but most of

34. One of the most successful of Marivaux's contemporaries was the Abbé Prévost. Jean Sgard and Jeanne Monty (see Bibliography for details) have recently analyzed the themes, techniques, and life of this writer. They both conclude that Prévost was essentially a *moraliste* whose primary interest was to promulgate his own personal social philosophy, a blend of individualism and social responsibility. Like Marivaux, Prévost turned to the novel, and to the memoir-form especially, as his artistic vehicle. And like Marivaux, he experimented with other prose forms, among them his journal, *Pour et contre*. Although their formal quests ended somewhat ambiguously (they both stopped serious work on the novel in the 1740s, twenty years before their deaths), this was the result of increasing frustration on a technical level. Thematically speaking, Prévost, as well as Marivaux, was one of the most successful practitioners of the early art of novel-making, and his legacy cannot be ignored.

the novelists so far mentioned were more and more aware of their publics, and of the potential influence they might have on them. This brought about noticeable changes in literary techniques. For instance, the novelist found that rather than deceive his audience into believing that they were reading a true story, it was better to portray realistically his imaginary world so that they might be able to suspend belief temporarily. *Vraisemblance* was no longer used to dupe, but rather to establish a conspiracy between writer and reader.[35] The hero of the new novel was made to the scale of the novelist and the reader, not to some arbitrary extraterrestrial scale of moral and physical superiority.[36] Individualization, and not generalization, became the rule. The new heroes and heroines—Gil Blas, Des Ronais, Des Frans, Manon Lescaut, Marianne, Jacob, and so on—were more "human" than those of the classical and historical novels of previous generations. The novelist and the reader could relate, in more personal terms, to a sympathetic commoner rather than to a prince. This new process of the individualization of the novelistic hero was another example of the anti-classical bent of the Moderns. They were not only interested in freeing themselves from any tradition—historical, moral, or aesthetic—but also in creating forms and techniques through which to promulgate their new ideas. It was in this atmosphere of negation and re-creation that Marivaux made his debut as a novelist.

In the preface to one of his earliest prose pieces, Marivaux tried to explain to his readers why the format of that particular collection of literary portraits ("Lettres sur les

35. F. Deloffre discusses this problem in his article "Le Problème de l'illusion romanesque et le renouvellement des techniques narratives de 1700 à 1715," *La Littérature narrative d'imagination.* Colloque de Strasbourg, 23–25 avril 1959 (Paris: Presses Universitaires de France, 1961), pp. 115–33. Philip Stewart, in his book, *Imitation and Illusion in the French Memoir-Novel, 1700–1750* (New Haven: Yale University Press, 1969), looks at the same question from another viewpoint, which is debatable, i.e., that novelists really believed that they were deceiving their readers.

36. A. Kibédi Varga, "La Désagrégation de l'idéal classique dans le roman français de la première moitié du XVIIIe siècle," *SVEC* 26 (1963): 965–98.

habitants de Paris") was so unstructured: "Je n'ai point prétendu établir d'ordre dans la distribution des sujets; cela m'a paru fort indifférent. . . . Je continue au hasard, et je finis quand il me plaît. Cet ouvrage, en un mot, est la production d'un esprit libertin, qui ne se refuse rien de ce qui peut l'amuser en chemin faisant" (*Journaux*, p. 8). This declaration of formal independence is a typical statement of a Modern littérateur; it is likewise a protective device used by a young author unsure of himself and of his audience. Later such explanations with their disclaimers would become less ingenuous, and more purposeful. Not unlike many of his favorite characters, Marivaux soon became adept at convincing his readers that in fact he was *not* an artist, but only an honest man who wished to write down some miscellaneous thoughts and impressions. However, in 1717, when he wrote this particular preface, Marivaux was looking for freedom to experiment, and the result was to be a literary apprenticeship of astonishing fertility and variety.

2

Experiments in Prose:
Failure and Success

I

MARIVAUX'S LITERARY APPRENTICESHIP LASTED OVER FIFTEEN years, from 1712 to 1727 (when he most likely began *La Vie de Marianne*). During this period, he experimented with almost every literary form available to him in an attempt to find one—or several—that would satisfy his professional as well as his aesthetic needs. He wrote, or began to write, a comedy in verse, a dramatic allegory, comedies in prose, a neo-classical tragedy, a verse burlesque of the *Iliad*, a semi-fictional essay, an epistolary short story, miscellaneous essays, a series of literary portraits, two journalistic collections of essays, and two philosophical comedies. Most significant for this study, Marivaux composed, between 1712 and 1714, four relatively lengthy works of prose fiction: a romance, two parodies of the heroic romance, and an experimental piece that includes elements of both the romance and the parodic forms. A discussion of certain aspects of these early novels and journalistic efforts will provide us with a portrait of Marivaux's thematic and technical development as a novelist, and help us to understand better the originality and historical significance of *La Vie de Marianne* and *Le Paysan parvenu*.

In his essay on genre criticism, Northrop Frye has some revealing remarks to make concerning the generic and thematic differences between certain fictional forms.[1] It is the distinction he establishes between the romance and the novel that is of interest to us here. Marivaux's transition from the romance (*Les Effets surprenants de la sympathie*) to the novel (*La Vie de Marianne* and *Le Paysan parvenu*) reflects the cautious but steady abandonment, by novelists of the early eighteenth century in France, of the earlier form, although elements of the romance remain prevalent in the novel throughout the Enlightenment. Frye defines the romance as being "nearest of all literary forms to the wish-fulfillment dream" (p. 186). Its heroes and heroines represent an idealized and thus scarcely attainable vision of society. The essential plot radical of the romance is adventure, most often interpreted through the use of the quest theme. On a moral level, the characters are either good or bad, and there is little attempt at subtlety in the definition of the individual. It is in this domain that the novel, a relatively recent genre, can be said to distinguish itself from the romance. The novelist, as Frye explains, "deals with personality, with characters wearing their *personae* or social masks. He needs the framework of a stable society. . . . The romancer deals with individuality, with characters *in vacuo* idealized by revery" (p. 305).

Frye's remarks are substantiated, from a historical point of view, by Ian Watt in his analysis of the "rise of the novel."[2] Watt's study deals with the English novel of the early eighteenth century, and consequently one should hesitate before applying some of his theories to the French novel of the same period. However, in his discussion of the

---

1. *Anatomy of Criticism* (1957; rpt. New York: Atheneum, 1966), pp. 303–14. Subsequent references to this study will appear in the text.
2. *The Rise of the Novel* (1959; rpt. Berkeley, Calif.: University of California Press, 1965). Subsequent references to this edition will appear in the text.

romance tradition and the "new novel" of Richardson, he has touched on a distinction that helps to illuminate the development of Marivaux as a novelist. Speaking of *Pamela,* Watt affirms that "Richardson's novel represents the first complete confluence of two previously opposed traditions in fiction; it combines 'high' and 'low' motives, and even more important, it portrays the conflict between the two" (p. 166). Pamela and Mr. B. are very different lovers from those in the traditional romance. "The barriers between them that have to be broken down are not external and contrived but internal and real" (p. 167). The same pattern can be seen in Marivaux as he moved from the traditional heroical romance form, through the parody of that form, into the "new novel" of the early eighteenth century culminating in *La Vie de Marianne* and *Le Paysan parvenu.*

In his study of Marivaux's style, Deloffre has devised a putative list of the author's literary readings.[3] Given the uncertainty of such an enterprise, it is still quite useful as a scale by which we may gauge Marivaux's awareness of literary tradition. The most striking aspect of Deloffre's conclusions is the predominance of romances and novels on the list. We find that Marivaux knew or had read *Amadis de Gaula, Orlando Furioso,* Cervantes's *Persiles y Sigismunda, Don Quixote,* and *Novelas ejemplares;* novels of Gomberville, Mlle. de Scudéry, La Calprenède, Mme. de Villedieu; burlesque novels of Scarron and Sorel; Lesage's *Diable boiteux* and *Gil Blas,* and Challe's *Les Illustres Françaises;* Montesquieu's *Lettres persanes,* and Fénelon's *Télémaque.* He was likewise familiar with other prose works, not classifiable as novels, such as the writings of Montaigne, Pascal, La Bruyère, La Rochefoucauld, Fontenelle, Dufresny. This list of possible readings easily refutes the standard impression of Marivaux as primarily a writer interested in the theater. He was grounded in the prose tradition of his time (with the

3. *Une Préciosité nouvelle: Marivaux et le marivaudage,* 2d ed. rev. (Paris: Armand Colin, 1967), pp. 74–80.

notable exception of historiography), and, as Deloffre concludes: "Le résultat est qu'il lui faudra longtemps pour se
dégager complètement de la hantise romanesque" (p. 80).

His first novel was *Les Effets surprenants de la sympathie, ou
les aventures de * * ***, most likely written in 1712–1713, and
published, unsigned, in 1713–1714. There was a second
edition published in Amsterdam in 1715. The work is obviously that of a young, inexperienced, but nonetheless
imaginative writer. A brief look at this youthful effort shows
that on both the formal and thematic levels Marivaux was
beginning the long apprenticeship which would carry him
to *La Vie de Marianne* and *Le Paysan parvenu*. This novel was
in the already outmoded tradition of the heroic romances
so popular in the sixteenth and seventeenth centuries, and
was most specifically influenced by Cervantes's *Persiles y
Sigismunda*. The reason why Marivaux chose this form as his
first novelistic effort will probably never be known. Deloffre
has suggested that the work was probably begun while
Marivaux was still living in Riom, and that the provinces
were several decades behind Paris insofar as literary fashion and taste were concerned. There could also have been
a therapeutic reason, that is, the need to begin at the beginning, to examine tradition's possibilities before making his
own.

The novel is essentially a *roman à tiroirs,* made up of seven
major tales. The plot is quite simple: two young lovers,
Clorante and Caliste, meet early in the book, are separated,
have a difficult time trying to get together again, finally do,
and are happily married forever after. The book's length
and the complicated action come from the multiplicity of
events, of story-telling, of subplots that occur. Each principal character, including the narrator himself, who is recounting the story to his mistress, tells his story whenever
he encounters anyone willing to listen. The resultant novel
is at times complicated, but essentially the frame is well
planned. There are several episodes that are reflections of
other similar episodes in the book. The novel as a whole is

a series of mirrored, interpolated plots that give a certain
sophistication to an outmoded form. A gentleman will fall
in love with a young *inconnue,* who tells him her story.
Within *her* story, there will be a tale of a young man falling
in love with a young princess, who wants to tell *her* story.
The effect is vertiginous, but Marivaux almost succeeds
(even he becomes confused at the end), and at least shows
an awareness of the possibilities of storytelling and the
tricks that a narrator can play on his readers.

Some critics have theorized that in reality this novel was
a parody of the very type of work it seems to emulate. The
most convincing evidence for this viewpoint is that Marivaux was in fact writing *Pharsamon,* a parody of the heroic
romance almost simultaneously. Yet this premise is most
certainly false. Marivaux was not parodying Gomberville,
Mme. de Scudéry, and La Calprenède in *Les Effets surprenants de la sympathie.* He was experimenting with form, and
attempting to arrive at a satisfactory marriage of his own
themes and a feasible prose format. Luckily, Marivaux
added a preface to his first novel, which aids us somewhat
in understanding why he wrote it (and why such a Modern
as Fontenelle passed on its publication). Often redundant
and superficial, this little essay is a quite favorable piece on
the possibilities that faced an amateur novelist of the early
eighteenth century. The initial reason for such a preface, as
was so often the case during this period, was a justificatory
one: he wanted to explain his choice of the form and plot
of the heroic romances. However, the result of this explanation was a plea in favor of what was to be Marivaux's own
brand of prose fiction.[4] One of his most important observations is the belief that the world of a novel need not be
verisimilar, in a "rationalistic" sense, so long as its *effect* is
successful, that is, the adventures may be outrageous, but
the telling of them can have a positive, and therefore justifi-

---

4. For the text as well as a more detailed analysis of this preface, see F.
Deloffre's discussion in *O.J.,* pp. 1091–93, a development of his article "Premières idées de Marivaux sur l'art du roman," *Esprit Créateur* 1 (1961): 178–83.

able effect on the reader. The important thing is to have "une expression naïve et vraie, . . . un goût de sentiment . . ." (*O.J.*, p. 7); the reader's credulity will follow naturally. Thus, it is to the emotions and not to the intellect that Marivaux directs his first novel, and he believes that he is renewing the form: "Je trouve à mon gré qu'on a retranché des romans tout ce qui pouvait les rendre utiles, et souvent même intéressants. Ceux qu'on compose à présent ne sont que de simples aventures racontées avec une hâte qui amuse le lecteur à la vérité, mais qui ne l'attendrit, ni ne le touche; il est simplement curieux, et rien de plus" (*O.J.*, pp. 8–9).

From a thematic point of view, there are several elements in *Les Effets surprenants de la sympathie* that presage some of Marivaux's more serious preoccupations in his later works. Of these themes, three especially attract our attention: the psychological complications of initial love, the more specific motif of the young orphaned girl, uncertain of her past as well as of her future, yet pretty, intelligent, and quite capable of existing in an initially hostile society,[5] and, the major theme of all of Marivaux's prose work, the role of disguise and subterfuge in social relations. Love, the most traditional of themes, was of especial interest to Marivaux, but for untraditional reasons. It has been said that he was primarily interested in "l'amour naissant," and not in the vagaries of mature love. This is basically correct, for Marivaux was fascinated with the psychological implications of one person's surrender to another. He rightly saw love as a mental state that demanded sacrifice on the part of both lovers. This sacrifice was the subordination of one's amour-propre to a level that would allow him to say "je vous aime," words that in fact appear very rarely in Marivaux's

---

5. Examples of this last motif are those of Clorinde (*O.J.*, pp. 41ff.), Dorine (*ibid.*, pp. 96ff.), and Parménie (*ibid.*; pp. 131ff.). Although Matucci especially has traced the major themes of Marivaux's prose works in his *L'Opera narrativa di Marivaux*, I intend to insist on those which will form the basis of my thematic analysis of *La Vie de Marianne* and *Le Paysan parvenu*.

work. When uttered, these words meant that I recognize that you exist, that you are at least as important as I, and that I am hoping that you will reciprocate by giving yourself to me. This is the moment for which most all of Marivaux's so-called comedies aim: he who says "je vous aime" first has lost the game.

Elements of this initial confusion and self-protection may be found in *Les Effets surprenants de la sympathie*. Before Clorante realizes that he has fallen in love with Clarice, he feels "reconnaissance" for her, an initial step in the process. "Il est mille occasions où la reconnaissance ressemble à l'amour. Clorante avait trop peu d'usage pour en démêler la différence; il crut qu'il aimait Clarice" (*O.J.*, p. 25). Later, Clarice will accuse Clorante of being ungrateful, not unfaithful, when he admits that he may still love another woman (p. 108). So gratitude, one form of recognition, engenders love, another form, and both forms demand a sacrifice on the part of the lover. (Another treatment of this problem will be seen in chapter 3 of this study, concerning Marianne and Mme. de Miran.) "Il est des moments, quand on aime, où le coeur, oubliant son propre intérêt, aime à tout sacrifier à l'objet aimé: mais quand un mal présent nous accable, ce coeur n'a d'attention qu'à ce qui le touche; et ce serait peut-être un défaut de tendresse, que d'être capable de délicatesse en certaines occasions" (p. 111). Only Marianne would be better able to analyze the intricacies of love and amour-propre.

One of the most common traditions of the prose romance was that of physical disguises. Marivaux's novel is no exception, but, as with the question of love, their occurence takes on added significance because of Marivaux's later use of them. As was mentioned in chapter 1, mask-wearing, at first physical, and later increasingly psychological, is one of Marivaux's most typical metaphors. In his first novel, many characters disguise themselves, and, as one of them says, the world of this novel is marked by "la nécessité de feindre" (p. 124). The protagonists disguise themselves to deceive their lovers, their rivals, their captors, their friends.

When Clarice puts on peasant dress to test her rival, she does so with such excitement that one would say that "son bonheur était attaché à son déguisement" (p. 110). The heroine of one story especially, the young and virtuous Parménie, gives us a portrait of the "fourberie fine et secrète" that underlies social commerce. The passage can serve as a thematic introduction to most of Marivaux's major prose and dramatic works, and for this reason is quoted in full:

> L'éducation du monde ne donne à ceux qui la reçoivent presque toujours qu'une apparence vertueuse; on apprend ce qu'il faut faire pour paraître ou généreux, ou vertueux, et l'on apprend rarement ce qu'il faut faire pour le devenir véritablement: on s'attache à l'air et aux manières, et quand on sait l'art de les rendre aimables, on se croit tel qu'il faut être. Le monde ne connaît que cette perfection superficielle, et toute sa sagesse n'est enfin que plus ou moins d'hypocrisie d'autant plus dangereuse, que ceux qui la possèdent le plus finement ne s'en aperçoivent pas. Ils se croient bons, parce qu'ils font par habitude une action qui a l'air de la vertu. C'est cette apparence qui les séduit, leur délicatesse ne s'étend pas jusqu'à vouloir être bons par sentiment; leur coeur ne connaît que le plaisir d'avoir trompé, il n'en sent point la honte; et l'estime qu'on a pour eux est le fruit d'une fourberie fine et secrète, ressemblante à la vertu, que l'éducation leur a inspirée, et dont ils sont, à la vérité, comme innocents, parce qu'il s'abusent en abusant les autres. (p. 135)

Marianne's character, as well as her dilemma, were already taking shape in Marivaux's active imagination.

Although we can find there fascinating glimpses of Marivaux the moralist, a close reading of *Les Effets surprenants de la sympathie* reveals that he, not unlike many other contemporary novelists, was uncomfortable with the limitations of the form. Deloffre has recently pointed out many of the chronological, geographical, and even linguistic anomalies of the text.[6] It is especially revealing to note as well that although the novel is in the third person, fully two-thirds

6. In his *notice* to the novel, *O.J.*, pp. 1095–1101.

of it is made up of first-person narration, that is, oral recapitulations of a character's life. In fact, there are two major *récits* within the novel, those of the heroines Caliste and Parménie, which actually compose the majority of the novel's structure. Marivaux's interest in female narrators was taking shape in this novel, an understandable development given his interest in the potentially large and sensitive female readership he mentions in his "avis au lecteur." This is the first example we have of Marivaux's use of the memoir form; later, in his journals and two most famous novels, it will become his dominant narrative format.[7] Not a great novel, nor even a good one, *Les Effets surprenants de la sympathie* was a significant step in Marivaux's literary apprenticeship.[8]

Almost simultaneously with the composition of *Les Effets surprenants de la sympathie* in 1712, Marivaux probably began *Pharsamon, ou les Nouvelles folies romanesques,* a travesty of this very form of sentimental novel. And though, for reasons still unclear,[9] the novel was not published until 1737, it did serve another important therapeutic function for the young novelist. This work is the first example we have of Marivaux as a writer of "comic" fiction. Hereafter, with rare exception, this would be his dominant mode. The influence of Cervantes and Sorel on *Pharsamon* are obvious, and the story itself is not very new. A young man, Pierre Bagnol, has read too many heroic romances and wishes to model his life thereafter. His servant, Cliton, agrees to do so with him, and they set out to find their princesses. They have numer-

7. For a fuller treatment of this question, see my article "Marivaux and the Possibilities of the Memoir-Novel," *Neophilologus* 56 (1972): 43–49.

8. The critical reaction to the novel was almost nonexistent, with one curious exception. In June 1713, a lengthy plot recapitulation appeared in the *Journal des savants.* It is Deloffre's contention that Marivaux's influential friend, Fontenelle, wrote it himself. Such attention and praise ("L'ouvrage est écrit avec politesse et d'une manière fort attirante") must have reaffirmed Marivaux's shaky commitment to literature, impelling him to write other prose narratives.

9. See Deloffre's notes, *O.J.,* pp. 1163–68, for the unusual publishing history of this work. One more obvious reason that Marivaux did not insist on *Pharsamon*'s publication could well have been his awareness of its mediocrity.

ous adventures, most turning out badly for them, until the end of the novel when, through a mysterious process known as a "fumigation," they are cured of their extravagant ideas. In Marivaux's story, Bagnol-Pharsamon has the misfortune to meet a girl who is also suffering from a Quixote complex. This complicates Marivaux's novel somewhat, but does not save it from its basic mediocrity. As Deloffre has stated in his *Marivaux et le marivaudage:* "Pharsamon est écrit . . . dans une langue sans recherche, et qui dénote encore une assez forte empreinte des romans précieux" (p. 96).

Yet there are elements in the novel that reveal Marivaux's preoccupation with the evolution of a new form and style conducive to the successful expression of his themes. More so than in his first novel, Marivaux interrupts his narrative often to pass judgment both on his story and his hero. There are many examples; a few will suffice: "Je ne vous dirai pas ce qui se passa pendant quelques jours" (*O.J.*, p. 413); "Laissons-le là pour le moment; car il me semble que le lecteur me demande déjà compte de l'oncle que j'ai laissé. . . . Le lecteur aurait bien pu le conduire chez lui, quand j'aurais oublié de le faire" (p. 451). "J'ai mal fait de m'embarquer dans cette aventure" (p. 457).

Halfway through the novel, he introduces "mon critique," whose function will be to keep Marivaux to the point: "Hé vite, me dit mon critique; vous avez laissé vos amants transis; ils sont pâles comme la mort, et vous vous amusez à faire un traité de la cause de leurs mouvements et de leur nombre; cela vient bien à propos! Que deviennent-ils?" (p. 529), and so forth. The technique is neither subtle nor very original; we find examples of it from Cervantes up to Marivaux.[10] Yet it is an important step in

10. Wayne C. Booth has examined this phenomenon in his article "The Self-conscious Narrator in Comic Fiction before *Tristram Shandy,*" PMLA 67 (1952): 163–85. See as well Jean Rousset's article, "Comment insérer le présent dans le récit: l'exemple de Marivaux," *Littérature* no. 5 (1972): 3–10, which owes much to Booth.

Marivaux's awareness of himself as a novelist, and the technique of authorial intervention may be said to have had a salutary effect on this young novelist as he tried to free himself from a stagnant tradition. There is a note of serious purpose underlying the use of this already hackneyed device, as Marivaux examines the basic premises of prose fiction itself in his attempt to discover a new mode of expression.

Marivaux of course parodies all the traditional elements of the prose romance as Pharsamon's adventures continue. For instance, when, after a long separation, the four lovers meet, there is an instant recognition scene between two of them: "Ils se reconnaissent tous deux, se regardent dans cette entrevue inopinée, avec ces regards si touchants que nos romanciers donnent à tous les illustres amants qui se rencontrent par hasard" (p. 529). Again, Marivaux was not so much criticizing the romance, which so many had done before him, as he was trying to find out what made a particular type of prose fiction work. At one point, "Pharsamon cherchait la raison du comique éternel qui se mêlait à ses aventures" (p. 521), in contrast to the more "serious" adventures of his idols. Marivaux explains that the romancer was concerned mainly with the "merveilleux" and not with the "aventures comiques" of their protagonists, and seems to imply that the two modes cannot be mixed, at least as far as contemporary fictional possibilities allowed. However, in this basically comic novel, Marivaux inserts a story, "l'histoire du solitaire" (pp. 463–500), which is different in tone and subject matter from the romance parody that *Pharsamon* is. And though this interpolation of a serious story in a work of comic fiction was not a new phenomenon, its use most likely expressed a desire on Marivaux's part to combine somehow the "serious" and "comic" modes into which prose fiction had been arbitrarily divided for centuries.

The story not only catches our attention because of its serious tone and style, but also because of what it is about.

The "solitaire" is in reality a young girl, orphaned at an early age, yet recognized as being noble by a marquise, and adopted by her. She falls in love, and the two lovers act out a play in order to reveal their love for each other. Yet the girl cannot marry her lover, a nobleman, because of her obscure birth and lack of a dowry. The remainder of the tale deals with the obstacles, mostly social and financial, that forbid the marriage of these two young people. Although Clorine, the heroine, suddenly finds her father again, and learns that she is indeed of noble birth, the story ends without a marriage. Marivaux had not only analyzed a situation that is an obvious preview of *La Vie de Marianne*, he had also tried to create a new and more realistic tone than neither the comic nor sentimental novel had provided the novelist of the early eighteenth century. The modern novel is primarily interested in the psychology of the individual as he moves in a specific historical and social context. Although this interpolated story still remains closely tied to the romance tradition that Marivaux was parodying in *Pharsamon*, it does possess certain of those thematic elements which define the European novel after Defoe and Richardson in England, and Lesage and Prévost in France.

Before he broke completely with the prose tradition that he had followed in *Les Effets surprenants de la sympathie* and *Pharsamon*, Marivaux wrote two other works (again, most likely during the same two-year period, 1712–14, that he had written the others) which dealt, on the artistic level, with the question of new forms and ideas. They were *La Voiture embourbée* and *Le Télémaque travesti*. Although the latter was probably written after *La Voiture embourbée*, it is a more traditional piece. The occasion for the composition of this parody is obvious: the Quarrel of the Ancients and Moderns. Marivaux, having already written *l'Homère travesti*, a verse parody of the *Iliad*, wished to continue his attacks on the Ancients, thereby assuring his acceptance by the Modern camp. The Preface to the *Télémaque travesti* was a polemical piece, aimed at the most recalcitrant of the Ancients, and was embarrassingly dated already in 1713, and even more so in 1736 when it first appeared. His goal was obvious: "Ah! messieurs, faites donc grâce à un homme qui, du merveilleux, du sublime et de l'héroïque d'*Homère*, a fait ses efforts pour en tirer du comique!" (*O.J.*, p. 718). And yet, at this early date and even in such an ebullient and self-indulgent exercise, Marivaux's seriousness of purpose is evident. Concluding his Preface, he refers to his novel as "un livre qui démasque ses [Homer's] héros" (p. 719). Later, when he would write *Marianne* and the *Paysan parvenu*, he would be interested less in unmasking heroes than in exposing the foibles of his fellow men. The literary parodist would become the social satirist.

Continuing one of Marivaux's favorite motifs, the story of the *Télémaque travesti* is about a young peasant, Brideron, and his uncle, Phocion, who become so imbued with Fénelon's *Télémaque* (1699) that they decide to live their lives by it, planning each step according to its outline. ("On trouvera dans cette histoire même liaison et même suite d'aventures que dans le vrai Télémaque," p. 722). Again, we have a tale of people whose lives are governed by the fiction they read, and by the subsequent misapplication of the ideas received from these books. The heroes of the *Télémaque travesti* have considerable difficulty distinguishing between appearance and reality, even on the most obvious level. (Later, but treated much more subtly and seriously, Marianne and Jacob will have the same problem.) This story differs somewhat from the more diffuse *Pharsamon* in that both heroes intentionally plan to direct their lives according to the exact story of Telemachus. Says Brideron at one point to a sympathetic friend: "Madame, il faut que vous sachiez que je cherche mon père, tout comme ce jeune prince cherche le sien; que c'est lui que j'imite, que nous avons les mêmes aventures" (p. 743). And later, "j'ai mon chemin tracé; il faut que je mette le pied où Télémaque a mis le sien" (p. 765). Such characters are comic because they are inflexible, and in the *Télémaque travesti* this inflexibility is compounded by the fact that their lives are to be geared to only *one* book, and a heroic, idealistic romance at that.

Both Phocion and Brideron transform this book into a bible; it becomes the most important of their possessions: "[Brideron] baisait son livre de joie: Bénis soient l'imprimeur, le relieur, et le papier de ce livre, disait-il, j'y vois ma vie comme on voit un poisson dans l'eau, c'est un cordeau qui me conduit" (p. 927). Both characters have little apprehension about the future since they know exactly what will happen to them because of the book. And although, as with Don Quixote, their adventures become burlesque, Marivaux cheats somewhat by allowing all of their expectations to come true. (The role of chance in the novel's formula is quite extensive.) When laughed at by others because of their folly, they laugh secretly in return, because "nous savions bien que tout arriverait à la lettre, à cause de ce qui arriva jadis chez Aceste" (p. 745).

This novel shows a much more confident Marivaux at work than is evident in his other novels of the same period. He had changed the formula of the burlesque novel somewhat; he had presented characters who were slightly more developed morally than we saw in the earlier prose works; and, he had shown himself aware of yet another novelistic genre, the historical novel, which he uses to some advantage in this work.[11] Likewise, Marivaux had begun to develop in the *Télémaque travesti,* for the first time in prose, a linguistic device that would become his most important legacy to the narrative literature of France: the use of language as a determinant and as a means by which a character's personality may be understood, both by the readers as well as by his fellow protagonists. Marivaux was obviously enchanted with the possibilities of dialogue in this novel, and since much of the story is made up of conversations between Phocion and Brideron, centering around daily,

11. For an analysis of this aspect, see Deloffre's notes, pp. 1257–61.

mundane matters, their language becomes a significant sign for the comprehension of their characters.

Another difference between this novel, and the comic novels that had preceded it, centers around Marivaux's depiction of reality, that is, of the exterior world and of its effect on his protagonists. Of course, the realistic re-creation of local color was one of the hallmarks of the comic novels of the seventeenth century, yet a careful reading of the *Télémaque travesti* reveals an awareness on the author's part of the importance of the "real" world to the fictional atmosphere that he was trying to create. Two examples will suffice to illustrate this phenomenon. As Phocion and Brideron set out on their ridiculous adventure, they come to the château of a widow who had entertained Brideron *père* ten years before. Marivaux gives a long and detailed description of the château, its rooms, and its surroundings, as he prepares his readers for the transition that Brideron is about to undergo (pp. 733–35). It is not an ostentatious château, but obviously a great house. "Les chambres du château brillaient d'une beauté naturelle qui ne devait presque rien à l'art; l'or, l'argent et le marbre étaient exilés de ces lieux; mais la fraîcheur, beaucoup de propreté, et le sage arrangement des meubles, remplaçaient une inutile magnificence" (p. 733). The narrator describes carefully the furniture of one of the rooms: "On voyait des chaises de paille artistement travaillées, et mêlées par un beau désordre entre quelques chaises de tapisserie dont le dessin était antique et curieux; dont le siège, durci par le long service sans être endommagé, témoignait l'habileté de l'ouvrier, qui semblait, avec les clous, y avoir attaché une éternelle durée" (p. 733). Such minute description will be found nowhere else in Marivaux's work, not even in *Le Paysan parvenu*. Likewise, it differs from the burlesque descriptions found so prevalently in the great comic novels of the seventeenth century in that it is "serious" here, used to establish an atmosphere that will help to determine the fictional destinies of Brideron and Phocion.

By the time they reach their rooms, Brideron and Phocion have been thoroughly impressed by the appearance of good living that permeates the château. They look out their windows, and see "l'humble et petite retraite d'une fermière, qui, entourée de trois ou quatre enfants . . . raccommodait . . . à l'un un petit sabot partagé en deux; elle chaussait l'autre d'un bas grossier un peu crotté, mais utile" (p. 734).[12] The view of this scene of poverty has its effect on Brideron when he turns around to find a collection of fine clothes laid out for him on his bed. The contrast is evident, and Brideron "crut qu'il allait être couvert de tout l'or des Indes; et ne pouvant modérer son impatience, il le [the most beautiful suit] mit et se regardait alors; il se déboutonnait, incertain de la manière dont il le laisserait" (p. 735). Through such a passage, Marivaux wanted to show his reader that Brideron's actions, expectations, and opinions had been influenced by the experience of looking at the château and its surroundings; his awareness of "reality" had conditioned his response.

The remainder of the novel is full of such scenes, as Marivaux examines the relationships between a character's thoughts and his perception of reality. Later, both Marivaux and Prévost would include such descriptions in their more serious works, thereby creating the "intermediate reality" that Auerbach has shown to be the dominant mimetic tendency of the literature of the early Enlightenment.[13] Still somewhat self-conscious here, such scenes show that Marivaux understood that reality could be, and often was problematic for literary characters, and the conjunction of the exterior world and the interiority of many

12. This same passage has also been cited by J. von Stackelberg in an all-too-brief article (see Bibliography for details) on the *Télémaque travesti*, which sustains my own thesis that this novel is a departure from the *roman comique* of the seventeenth century. Von Stackelberg likewise contends, and justly so, that despite F. Deloffre's opinion, Marivaux was in fact parodying Fénelon's own *Télémaque*, a novel that had almost singlehandedly retarded the development of realistic fiction in France.

13. See especially his chapter "The Interrupted Supper" in *Mimesis* (1953; rpt. New York: Anchor Books, 1957), pp. 347–82.

of his characters' personalities would be one of Marivaux's most serious preoccupations in the years that followed. With the *Télémaque travesti*, Marivaux had wanted to purge the genre of some of its parodic and burlesque tendencies in an attempt to recreate the image of contemporary reality that he felt the novel should treat.

In *La Voiture embourbée*, written almost contemporaneously with the *Télémaque travesti*, Marivaux not only parodied all types of prose fiction, he also specifically parodied himself. With the composition of this work, Marivaux seemed to have come to some important conclusions concerning writing in general. This short novel would be the last formal prose piece that he would publish for seventeen years when, in 1731, Part I of *La Vie de Marianne* would appear. (The *Télémaque travesti* would not be published until 1736, and then only partially, without Marivaux's permission and despite his denial of authorship.) There would be published in the interim short prose anecdotes and stories, and two of his journals, but none of these efforts belonged to any established prose tradition. The composition of *La Voiture embourbée* definitely served a therapeutic function in Marivaux's attempts to define a new prose style, both on the technical as well as thematic levels.

The novel (and that is what it must be called, although because of its length and format, it could also be called a *nouvelle*[14]) is a frame story. The passengers of a mired coach —the narrator, a middle-aged woman, her beautiful young daughter, an old financier, and a nobleman who prides himself on his wit ("un bel esprit")—decide, at the narrator's instigation, to while away the time composing "un roman impromptu." Each passenger will take up the story where the previous one left off, and continue until he wants to stop. The originality in Marivaux's use of this traditional format lies in his setting of the scene and in the self-conscious parody of his own contemporary prose efforts.

14. This is how Deloffre describes it in his *La Nouvelle en France à l'âge classique* (Paris: Didier, 1967), pp. 74–77.

The narrator addresses his preface to a friend who asked him to recount what happened on a recent trip. The preface sets the tone of the rest of the novel: "Je ne sais si ce roman plaira; la tournure m'en paraît plaisante, le comique divertissant, le merveilleux assez nouveau, les transitions assez naturelles, et le mélange bizarre de tous ces différents goûts lui donne totalement un air extraordinaire" (*O.J.*, p. 313). It is "le mélange bizarre" that makes this work so important to the student of early eighteenth-century prose realism. Marivaux was aware that he was crossing boundaries, mixing genres, and shading differences in critical terms; he wanted the *Voiture embourbée* to be read not only for amusement but also for instruction in the possibilities of prose narrative. And he is proud of his work, refusing to act humble as other writers did in more traditional prefaces: "Je ne puis souffrir cette humilité fardée, ce mélange ridicule d'hypocrisie et d'orgueil de presque tous messieurs les auteurs; j'aimerais mieux un sentiment de présomption déclaré, que les détours de mauvaise foi" (p. 314).

Marivaux's narrator takes his time as he subtly and indulgently establishes the right atmosphere before the "roman impromptu" begins. The first quarter of this short novel concerns the description of events and the presentation of the narrators who will fabricate the novel. A critic has recently said that it is in fact in these pages where Marivaux's modernity and originality as a novelist are first discernible.[15] The narrator tells us that "j'examinai dans cette conversation les différents caractères de nos voyageurs" (p. 319), and like Marivaux's other *personnages-spectateurs*, he soon knows his fellow passengers well: "Comme j'avais pénétré son caractère [of the older lady], vous pouvez vous imaginer que je m'y conformais, et je lui répondis d'un langage assortissant au sien" (p. 321). In this way, he is especially equipped to reproduce the individual styles of

15. Morten Nøjgaard, "Le Problème du réalisme dans les romans de Marivaux. Réflexions sur l'introduction de la *Voiture embourbée*," *Revue Romane* 1 (1967): 71–87.

the other characters as they participate in the telling of the story. Marivaux is vaunting, through the narrator, his own stylistic virtuosity. In this early work, we see an excellent example of an author's self-consciousness, of his awareness of himself as a fabricator of fiction. More than any other example of his juvenilia, *La Voiture embourbée* shows Marivaux in the midst of the exhilaration that young and confident authors often betray.

This somewhat rudimentary psychological realism is well complemented by an atmospheric realism. There is an interesting preoccupation with food and drink (pp. 322–23; 332–33), with time (pp. 323, 351–52, 370, 385), and with the physical description of the inn (pp. 322–23). A brief vignette will illustrate how careful Marivaux was in this short piece to emphasize the mundane. Speaking of the village curate's elderly maid, the narrator describes her bleak room: "A droit [*sic*] elle avait un escabeau qui lui servait de table, où elle mettait son lard et son pain quand elle avait mordu une bouchée de l'un et de l'autre; à gauche était un banc d'environ trois pieds, chargé de l'attirail de son humble toilette: attirail composé de deux gros peignes, dont l'antiquité et les cheveux avaient entièrement changé la couleur jaune en noir" (pp. 325–26). In effect, this is gratuitous information, for the curate's housekeeper will not play a significant role in the novel's main story. However, through such scenes as these, Marivaux treats one of the basic problems confronting the writer of serious prose fiction of the early eighteenth century, namely, how to deal with "reality" and fiction simultaneously and seriously. As the narrator says, addressing his reader at the end of this long introduction: "Peut-être, mon cher, aurez-vous trouvé trop long le sujet qui conduit à notre histoire [the "roman impromptu"], mais le sujet est une petite histoire aussi, et comme je n'ai eu dessein que de vous divertir, peu m'a dû importer que ce soit, ou par le sujet, ou par l'histoire" (p. 334–35). Both parts of *La Voiture embourbée* were equally important to Marivaux the novelist. This is a novel about

the composition of a novel, and therefore Marivaux felt that
he should show awareness of some of the questions confronting a prose writer.

The "roman impromptu" itself shows Marivaux at his
best as a parodist. It is in this work that he finally rids
himself of the "hantise romanesque" that Deloffre has
mentioned. *La Vie de Marianne* and *Le Paysan parvenu* would
be totally new efforts in the domain of the novel, made
possible in large part by his fictional exercise in the *Voiture
embourbée*. There are in fact six co-narrators in this work,
and their contributions are of unequal length: the narrator
himself (pp. 336–57), the middle-aged lady (pp. 357–70),
the *bel esprit* (pp. 371–78), the lady's young daughter (pp.
378–85), the financier (pp. 385–87), and finally the curate's
nephew, who brings a rapid end to the novel (p. 387–88).
The narrator sets the ground rules. It will be a novel of
love; "au reste," he continues, "comme il ne s'agit ici que
de nous réjouir, rendons l'histoire divertissante, et pour
cela, j'imagine un sujet qui pourra fournir des traits plai-
sants; chacun à son tour pourra continuer le roman suivant
son goût; cependant il ne faut gêner personne, et il sera
susceptible de comique, de tendre, de merveilleux, et
même si l'on veut de tragique. C'est bien dit, répondit la
dame, car chacun a son caractère" (p. 324). It is here that
the most original aspect of the novel appears: each addition
will depend for its tone and its direction on the individual
personality of the teller. Not only will we get different stories, but we also will receive valuable insights into the characters of the tellers. To make the game more interesting,
we have already been introduced to the narrators in the
first twenty-five pages of the novel, and, as readers, are
curious to see how each of their contributions will turn out.

The "roman impromptu" is entitled "Les Aventures du
fameux Amandor et de la belle et intrépide Ariobarsane."
Interestingly enough, the narrator begins and gives a very
successful parody of the romantic, heroic adventure novels
that Marivaux had himself parodied, less successfully, in

Pharsamon. Amandor and Félicie (who later changes her name to Ariobarsane) are two middle-aged novel readers, caught up in the world of irreality and anxious to become like the characters of the novels they adore. They fall in love, but cannot marry, because such action would belie the difficulties replete in the novels of love. And so, not unlike the hero of the *Télémaque travesti,* Amandor and Ariobarsane have a series of humorous escapades, joined often by their burlesque servants, Pierrot and Perrette.

When Marivaux's narrator finishes his part of the story, the middle-aged lady continues, admonishing her predecessor for the lightness with which he treated the serious passion of love. Her effort is typical of the romances of the previous century, full of disguises, kidnappings, separations of lovers, and so forth, with no hint of humor or authorial irony. Shepherdesses hide in caves, and there is even an interpolated story about a 260-year-old magician who disguises himself as a young prince. The lady stops her addition to the "roman impromptu" without finishing this story, adding: "Je ne sais comment vous avez trouvé ce que j'ai dit; mais vous m'avez demandé du tragique, du merveilleux, de l'étonnant; je vous ai servi le mieux que j'ai pu" (p. 370). In a few pages Marivaux had captured the essence of most of the popular romantic fiction of the period, and just as effectively had dismissed it. The *bel esprit* picks up the thread now, and gives the reader an early example of the *roman noir,* complete with murder, prisons, torture, and the like. At this point, the young girl continues the story, and makes of it a joke as Ariobarsane awakes from a dream and "vit disparaître tous ces fantômes de magie, d'esclaves, de tourments que lui avait peints son imagination" (p. 379). Thus, finally, does Marivaux make fun of the whole question of storytelling. The entire group laughs at this action by the young girl, and although she continues the story with the financier and the curate's nephew, it really ends there. Just as suddenly, the narrator ends the *Voiture embourbée* itself, explaining that the coach had been repaired, and ironically concluding: "J'arrivai à Nemours, je quittai mes voyageurs, et je fis résolution de vous faire le récit de nos plaisirs; vous me le fîtes promettre, ma parole est acquittée, serviteur" (p. 388). And so ends one of Marivaux's most original pieces.

Marivaux would not return, after 1713–1714, to the form that he so successfully parodied in *La Voiture embourbée* until he began *La Vie de Marianne* about fifteen years later. Through parody (and this was the *third* parody of prose fiction written by Marivaux in two years), Marivaux liberated himself formally from the prose tradition that was still so prevalent in the early Enlightenment. In a few short years, he had analyzed and experimented with the possibilities of narrative fiction. This period culminated in the composition and publication of *La Voiture embourbée* (since he had chosen *not* to publish the *Télémaque travesti*, probably written contemporaneously). This little piece was a condensation of the parodic tendencies of Marivaux, as well as an affirmation of his belief in the effectiveness and validity of realistic prose fiction. Clearer than a poetic treatise would have been, this work consolidated the premises that Marivaux would develop over the next decade and a half: a need for a formal and thematic restructuring of prose fiction, to be obtained through more experimentation in a looser, less formal genre.

II

First, with short prose pieces, published occasionally in the *Mercure* (1717–20), then with the publication of his journalistic works, *Le Spectateur français* (1721–24) and *l'Indigent philosophe* (1726–27), and later, of *Le Cabinet du philosophe* (1734), Marivaux was to solve positively some of the problems that he had treated negatively, through parody, in his earlier works. The two *Mercure* pieces that are the most significant for present purposes are the "Lettres sur les habitants de Paris" (August 1717–August 1718) and the

"Lettres contenant une aventure" (November 1719–April 1720).[16] These are still the works of a young prose writer, yet one more confident of himself than he had been in his earlier novels, and ready to experiment with new forms and themes. However, neither of these short pieces was really new. The "Lettres sur les habitants de Paris" were obviously influenced by La Bruyère's *Caractères*. In this work, Marivaux looked for and found types of Parisians who, through their particular moral make-up, reflected more universal types. Again, Marivaux the spectator and moralist who deciphers appearances in order to penetrate to reality is present in this short collection of "lettres." The form of the work is very loose, and the style conversational, as if the author were trying to free himself from any formal necessities. In another "modest" preface, Marivaux contends that he is claiming nothing for the work, that it was written for himself and with little regard for an audience. All of his "petits ouvrages sont nés du caprice" (*Journaux*, p. 22), and this one is no exception. Yet his very awareness of the formlessness of his piece is an indication of his artistic concerns at the time. He had found himself capable of writing more than adequate narrative prose since 1712, and he was now determined to discover an adequate form in which to use it. "Les Lettres sur les habitants de Paris" is one of his first efforts in this direction, and, significantly, it was the first of his works to be signed "de Marivaux," instead of only Pierre Carlet.

His favorite themes of the role of self-interest in social relations and the need for some sort of social mask are examined in this work, and treated even more successfully in "Les Lettres contenant une aventure," a short epistolary story that was a new format for him. These were supposedly "real" letters, rather than the "literary" letters on the citizens of Paris, and were written by a young man, M.

16. The first may be found in *Journaux*, pp. 8–39 and the latter in *Journaux*, pp. 76–100.

de M***, to a friend. The young writer had been an eaves-
dropper on an extraordinary conversation between a relatively naive girl and her more worldly friend, an experienced coquette. The thematic significance of these
letters lies in the development of the concept of *coquetterie.*
The coquette (the piece was later republished under the
name "L'Apprentie coquette") is nameless, but she is one
of Marivaux's most fascinating female characters, and definitely is a precursor of Marianne. Not unlike Mme. de Mer-
teuil, in her famous Letter 81 of the *Liaisons dangereuses,*
Marivaux's coquette explains to her youthful pupil how and
why she became initiated into "les plaisirs de la coquetterie" (pp. 79ff.). She learned early of the power of her
charms, of the uses of a pretty dress or a well-placed rib-
bon, of the psychological support one may receive from a
mirror. Love became a game that had to be played, and
when the game ceased, so did love: "Tu ne le croiras peut-
être pas: mais rien ne nuit tant à l'Amour que de s'y rendre
sans façon" (p. 87). This is one of Marivaux's most penetrating observations, and a favorite theme in his best plays,
*Le Jeu de l'amour et du hasard, La Double inconstance, Les Serments
indiscrets.* The portrait that we receive of this coquette is a
sketch of Marianne: she is very aware of herself; she is
constantly in conflict with love, because it demands some
element of self-sacrifice. She says at one point: "Je n'étais
pas d'humeur à ruiner les plaisirs de ma vanité, en faveur
de ceux de mon amour" (p. 88). She becomes more and
more accomplished at *coquetterie,* and less and less aware of
the difference between truth and lying, until at one point
she can say that "la nature n'est pas plus vraie que mon art"
when it comes to duping others (p. 94).

As Marivaux's coquette reconstructs her past for her eager pupil (referred to now as "la convertie"), one becomes
aware that she enjoys not only telling her story to someone
else, but also reliving it herself. It is an oral memoir, but not
unlike the written memoir that Marianne will leave for posterity a few years later. As her story ends, Marivaux's co-

quette reaches a paroxysm of self-revelation and self-justification as she moralizes on why she had led such a life of sexual conquest and subterfuge. As well as she can judge, she says, she believes that her "souplesse de coeur et d'esprit," her audacity at making several conquests at once, her ability to surmount unexpected reverses, "ce talent d'être impunément coquette, de faire soupirer mes amants sous le joug d'une coquetterie actuelle, dont aucun d'eux ne m'accuse, qu'ils ne devinent point; je crois . . . ne devoir ces avantages qu'à l'insatiable envie de sentir que je suis aimable, et qu'à un goût dominant pour tout ce qui m'en fait preuve" (p. 96). And later, her entire moral perspective turns inward, as she exults over her story: "Mes conquêtes présentes et passées s'offrent à moi; je vois que j'ai su plaire indistinctement, et je conclus, en tressaillant d'orgueil et de joie, que j'aurais autant d'amants qu'il y a d'hommes, s'il était possible d'exercer mes yeux sur eux tous" (p. 97).

Her story, and the letters, end here. (This is one of the first of many unfinished prose pieces left by an unsatisfied Marivaux.) In this piece, Marivaux had not only analyzed profoundly one of his favorite themes, he had also made a tentative move toward the memoir format. He had noticed the close relationship between first-person narration and the themes of *coquetterie* and amour-propre. This conjunction of theme and technique will be further refined in his last two novels. But, in the interval, his subsequent prose works would continue to explore the possibilities of different types of narration and the few themes outlined in these literary letters.

Marivaux's best nonnovelistic prose work, and perhaps his most ambitious narrative project, is the *Spectateur français* (*Journaux*, pp. 114–267). The unstructured format of the journal (a form he had copied from Addison and Steele) finally afforded him the freedom for which he had been searching. Unlike his English predecessors, and more like his compatriot Prévost, Marivaux was less interested in "cultivating and polishing human life by promoting virtue and knowledge," as Addison claimed his aim to be. He was

more concerned with formal and thematic experimentation. He imitated the *Spectator* only superficially (occasional
letters seeking advice, anecdotes of domestic life and strife,
etc.); on the whole, Marivaux's vision of social commerce
was much more complex, and more subtle psychologically
than that of Addison. Without any doubt, this work served
to outline in detail the major themes and techniques that
he would use so well in *Marianne* and *Le Paysan parvenu*. Just
as the earlier novels had served a tonic function in allowing
him to develop his talents in terms of several traditions, so
the *Spectateur français* served a further therapeutic need in
allowing him to dispense with the remaining vestiges of
these traditions.

One of the most revealing coincidences in the literary
history of the early Enlightenment is that Prévost was un-
dergoing, contemporaneously, the same formal and thematic crisis as Marivaux. In his recent excellent studies of
this writer,[17] Jean Sgard has shown that Prévost too was a
much more serious narrative artist than we have been led
to believe. And as early as 1731, he had seen as well the
possibilities of a new form, treating new ideas, contemporary and mundane, in the journal. "Prévost ira jusqu'à faire
de son tome V des *Mémoires et avantures* [*d'un homme de qualité*]
une sorte de chronique, une somme de reportages, d'anecdotes, de comptes rendus de spectacles, dans laquelle il
nous livre son opinion pour et contre le gouvernement, la
religion, les moeurs de l'Angleterre: tout le livre dixième
du roman peut passer pour une première ébauche du *Pour
et contre*."[18] And in 1733, he began his journal, which was
a potpourri of philosophical observations, real and imaginary anecdotes, short stories, translations of English essays, and so forth.[19] It is in fact in one of the numbers of

17. *Prévost romancier*, and *Le "Pour et Contre" de Prévost* (Paris: Nizet, 1969).
18. Sgard, *Le "Pour et Contre"* . . . , p. 10.
19. Sgard tells us that "le dessein de Prévost sera de faire du journal un mode
complet d'expression, axé sur la vie contemporaine, accessible à un vaste public;
. . . une sorte de chronique, une somme de reportages [et] d'anecdotes . . . (*Le
"Pour et contre" de Prévost*, pp. 9, 10). The same could just as easily have been said
of Marivaux's plans.

Pour et contre that we may find one of the most sympathetic and perspicacious observations made of Marivaux's own journals.[20]

More than his two other journalistic efforts, Marivaux's *Spectateur* is a rich and complex mixture of forms, tones, styles, and themes. In its twenty-five *feuilles*, all of about equal length, there are three main stories, numerous shorter stories and anecdotes, moralistic essays, literary criticism, and literary portraits in the style of La Bruyère. In his first number, Marivaux establishes unquestionably the major themes of the rest of his literary writings, both narrative as well as dramatic, that is, those of subterfuge and deception, and of their necessity in social commerce. Marivaux's narrator is the "Spectateur," who writes as an average man, looking, scrutinizing his fellow men in order to find some specific social truths that will enable him to exist more successfully in society. Again, Marivaux uses the technique of apparent modesty and authorial disinterest, a stylistic *coquetterie*, in order to persuade his readers that he is not concerned with false rhetoric, but rather with describing events and things as they affect us. "Je ne suis point auteur, et j'aurais été, je pense, fort embarrassé de le devenir" (*Journaux*, p. 114).

We have already seen in chapter 1 that Marivaux set the tone of the *Spectateur* in the first number with the anecdote about the girl who was practicing her charms before a mirror. He had decided to accept a stance of moral relativism after this event: he will no longer judge men, but rather analyze them and their actions in social terms. In subsequent numbers (nos. 5, 10, 13, 22, 24), Marivaux analyzes the discrepancy between physical appearance (clothes, physiognomy, the company one keeps) and reality (one's basic moral character, intelligence, talent), another of his favorite themes, since he felt often that he was misjudged by those who were no better than he. He likewise tells

20. Vol. 2, no. 30 (1734): 340.

several anecdotes about the innumerable "porteurs de visages" (p. 124) that he sees around him (nos. 3, 8, 10, 12,
16, 22); discusses the importance of amour-propre to all
men (nos. 3, 8, 13, 15, 16, 17–19, 23); amuses himself with
other instances of the *coquetterie* of women (nos. 1, 3, 8, 9,
10, 16, 17–19). He begins several long pieces, interrupts
them when he feels that they are too monotonous, and
leaves all three of them unfinished. In this way, he shows
his awareness of the formal freedom that the journal had
afforded him. At the same time, he perfected the stylistic
self-consciousness referred to earlier, and which would
make his contributions to the birth of narrative realism so
critical. "Je ne sais point créer," he says at one point, "je
sais seulement surprendre en moi les pensées que le hasard
me fait naître, et je serais fâché d'y mettre rien du mien"
(p. 114). The narrator's mask is at times just as obvious as
those of the people he describes.

The three main stories that are included in the *Spectateur
français* give witness to Marivaux's fascination with the possibilities of narrative expression. All three stories are in the
first person: one is a journal or diary of a young Spaniard's
visit to Paris (nos. 15–16); the second is a memoir of an old
woman (nos. 17–19); the last uses a semi-epistolary, semi-
memoir format, treating the adventures of an "inconnu"
(nos. 21–23, 25). The first piece is a "story" in only the
most general way, since there is little or no plot; it is rather
the musings and observations of another spectator.
Through this self-conscious reproduction of a journal
within a journal, Marivaux draws his readers' attention to
his own virtuosity and originality in the *Spectateur français*
itself. The Spaniard's diary (which Marivaux tells us he had
translated from Spanish) begins *in medias res,* and even has
the dating one would expect to find in a diary (p. 193). The
narrative perspective vacillates between the reconstruction
of the day's events, and the instantaneous "writing to the
moment" made so popular later by Richardson ("On
frappe à ma porte; c'est une visite qui me vient. . . . Me voilà

seul . . .," p. 195). Marivaux is again experimenting and discovers that first-person narrative, despite its formal limitations, does provide various possibilities to a novelist.

The "histoire de l'inconnu" is the memoir, in the form of a letter to Marivaux, of a well-born young man whose family loses its fortune, forcing them to go to the country to live. Previously an influential member of the court, the memorialist's father educates his son in the ways of the world and its uncertainties. He inculcates in his young son a love of virtue and honesty, two rare commodities in Parisian society. Soon, both the narrator's mother and father die, leaving the youth, alone and poor, to fend for himself and his sister. The one advantage they both have is their virtue, and they repulse all attempts, no matter how advantageous financially, to compromise this virtue. Eventually, the young people decide that the boy should go to Paris to seek both their fortunes, and he leaves, just as Jacob and Marianne had done, to find success and happiness. As he draws closer to the great city, a subtle change overcomes him, and he becomes imbued with an "esprit de défiance et de courage, qui me rappela tout entier pour moi-même, et me rendit l'objet unique de toutes mes attentions" (p. 263). The story ends here, unfinished, before Marivaux's hero reaches Paris. However, Marivaux had again managed to sketch one of his favorite character types, another preparation for his two major novels: the young person, born of a good family, conscious at an early age of his superiority —moral, intellectual, and otherwise—vis-à-vis others, and confident of his eventual success in Parisian society. In fact, Jacob's story would take up, with obvious changes, where that of the *inconnu* stopped.

The most significant narrative piece of the *Spectateur français*, both technically as well as thematically, is that composed of the memoirs of an old lady. In a friendly scuffle, Marivaux's narrator manages to obtain half of the lady's "mémoire de ce que j'ai fait et vu pendant ma vie." (Typically, Marivaux gives only half, just as he had found only a fragment of the Spaniard's journal. It is an obvious trick to explain away some of his uncompleted narratives.) The author is seventy-four years old, and she has decided to reconstruct her past, in writing, but not unlike the oral recapitulation of the coquette in the "Lettres contenant une aventure." This is the first serious exploitation of the memoir-form, on a psychological as well as formal level, by Marivaux, and it was written about five years before he began *La Vie de Marianne.* Marivaux's "dame âgée" carefully reconstructs her initiation into the sociosexual world, "le monde" (pp. 208–11). She explains how she became a co-quette: "J'étais femme, et on ne peut être femme sans être coquette" (p. 209). Slowly, her whole existence begins to revolve around her ability to draw attention to herself: "Je recevais tous les jours tant de preuves que j'étais aimable, et ces preuves-là me faisaient tant de plaisir, que je n'ou-bliais rien pour en recevoir toujours de nouvelles" (p. 213). And there follows an explicit description of the education of a coquette (pp. 214–15).

However, and it is here that Marivaux showed his aware-ness of the thematic possibilities of the memoir form, Mari-vaux's heroine becomes conscious of her advancing years: "Mes années commençaient à m'inquiéter; leur course me semblait plus rapide qu'à l'ordinaire. J'étais jeune encore, mais je ne me voyais pas loin de ce terme où la jeunesse d'une femme devient équivoque" (p. 214). Later, she reit-erates that "ma jeunesse continuait à se passer" (p. 217), and, eventually, "l'âge enfin me gagnait; . . . mon visage . . . n'était plus disciplinable" (p. 219). Instead of retiring from social activities and of feeling sorry for herself, Mari-vaux's heroine decides that the only way open to her in her present situation is to work to convince others of how beautiful she *used to be,* so that they could "voir au vrai ce que j'étais" (p. 220). And so she sets up a new system of subterfuges to replace the old. Her *coquetterie* becomes more psychological and less physical. In the end, though, the task becomes too great, and she becomes a *dévote,* retir-ing to the country.

And yet, she had written the memoirs that Marivaux's

narrator found in her apartment. They were written in order to convince us of her past claims to respect and admiration. She uses the same artificial modesty as evidence of her sincerity that many of Marivaux's narrators use ("je n'écris l'histoire de ma vie que dans l'espérance qu'elle pourra servir à l'instruction des autres," p. 213), and yet we know that there is much more to it than that. Like the older Marianne, the "dame âgée" has lost her physical charms, and must now rely solely on her wit and stylistic "naturalness" in order to work her web of deception. Her memoirs become proof to her of her glorious past, and simultaneously serve as rhetorical affirmation of the same for her readers. The same will be true of Marianne's own autobiography.

It is evident that the *Spectateur français* served to develop those skills which would place Marivaux in the first rank of the French novelists of the early Enlightenment. Searching for a new prose form in a period that was marked by philosophical and aesthetic uncertainty, Marivaux used the formula afforded him by the journal to strengthen his weaknesses as well as to discover new ways of expressing his "Modern" ideas. He removed many aspects of the romance tradition from his repertory; he experimented with the reflective qualities of first-person narration; he developed a narrative self-consciousness that allowed him to be more subtle and insinuating in his analysis of character. All of these new directions, coupled with the linguistic refinements that would cause him to be accused of preciosity by contemporaries, but eventually to be admired for his sensitivity by more perspicacious critics, enabled Marivaux to begin the most ambitious project of his career: a detailed psychological analysis of the life of one woman, recounted by herself.

For the next two years, Marivaux wrote very little prose fiction. We may surmise that he was trying to decide in which direction to go, artistically speaking. It is almost certain that he began both the first part of *La Vie de Marianne* and his second journal, *L'Indigent philosophe,* at about the same time, late 1726 or early 1727. If a crucial point in the artistic biography of any writer can be said to exist, this was most certainly such a moment in Marivaux's life. The experience of his *Spectateur français* had enabled him to begin two works simultaneously, which proceed, at least on a formal level, in two different directions. The *Indigent philosophe* is a short piece written ostensibly by a "philosophical bum,"[21] living in the provinces, and in the form of *journal-mémoires* (*Journaux,* pp. 275–323). It is quite literally a formal bridge between the *Spectateur français* and *La Vie de Marianne.* Unlike his other two journalistic efforts, the narrator of this piece is well developed psychologically and more distinctive physically. He is supposedly a happy-go-lucky person who had suffered a certain amount of social injustice because of his appearance and low station in life. He is the best delineated of one of Marivaux's favorite character types, the honest, sensitive, intelligent man who suffers because he does not *appear* to be so. It has already been shown how this motif fascinated Marivaux; in fact, this journal is the closest Marivaux himself ever came to writing an autobiography.

On the stylistic level, the narrator continues one of Marivaux's favorite games, that of affecting aesthetic disinterest, thereby allowing for a more "natural" style, concomitant with his own personality and way of life. "Pour moi, je ne sais comment j'écrirai: ce qui me viendra, nous l'aurons sans autre cérémonie; car je n'en sais pas d'autre que d'écrire tout couramment mes pensées" (p. 276). However, the polished and finished product will give the lie immediately to this stylistic mask. In fact, in the sixth number of the *Indigent philosophe,* Marivaux gives one of his most sensitive treatments of this question of style in narrative. Writing as a Modern, he asserts that his new subject matter

21. This is E. J. H. Greene's term, used in his article "Marivaux's Philosophical Bum," *Esprit Créateur* 1 (1964): 190–95.

demands a new style, and not that of the logic and order of the preceding generation (p. 310). In a wonderful *raccourci,* the "philosophical bum" reveals the core of Marivaux's experiment in this journal: "D'abord on voit un homme gaillard qui se plaît aux discours d'un camarade ivrogne [part of the story is the musings of the "bum" and his drinking companion], et puis tout d'un coup ce gaillard, sans dire gare, tombe dans les réflexions les plus sérieuses; cela n'est pas dans les règles, n'est-il pas vrai? Cela fait un ouvrage bien extraordinaire, bien bizarre: eh! tant mieux, cela le fait naturel, cela nous ressemble" (p. 310). Caught up in the excitement of what he is proposing, Marivaux's narrator continues, asserting his desire to copy the "beau désordre de la nature": "Je me moque des règles. . . . Ma plume obéit aux fantaisies [de mon esprit] . . . , car je veux qu'on trouve de tout dans mon livre. . . . Bref, je veux être un homme et non pas un auteur, et ainsi donner ce que mon esprit fait, non pas ce que je lui ferais faire" (pp. 310–11).[22] In the second number of the same journal, he had also written: "Quand j'ai mis la plume à la main, je ne voulais vous entretenir que de moi, je vous l'avais dit; mais ne vous fiez pas à mon esprit, il se moque de l'ordre, et ne veut que se divertir" (p. 283). And so the "style" and "form" and the subject matter are joined together in this work to create a new genre. Marivaux was at last free enough to be original, and the remaining two decades of active literary production would witness to this new freedom.

On the thematic level, Marivaux continued to explore in *L'Indigent philosophe* the question of amour-propre and social commerce. Although he had been scorned by society, ignored because of his powerlessness in a world predicated

22. Cf. this passage to another, longer one in the second number of the *Cabinet du philosophe,* (*Journaux,* pp. 346–51), where Marivaux writes again of the necessity of dispensing with static forms, and gives an allegory concerning one man's search for "Beauté" and "le je ne sais quoi," the latter concept much more acceptable to Marivaux, the Modern.

on moral and psychological power, Marivaux's hero asks only that he not be humiliated, and he continues to preach the rules of compromise and accommodation in a social context. "Il faut que l'amour-propre de tout le monde vive," he says (p. 492). We all have a "sentiment de notre excellence," which is natural and inescapable. Should we abuse this feeling, we become too proud, but should we understand it and consult it occasionally, we can "tirer bien des pressentiments d'une haute destinée" (p. 306). Thus, careful modulation of this characteristic will lead us to gain the most of life; however, such success depends on the actions of others as well as on our own. This is the great dilemma of social commerce, and, in a world where "tout le monde est bourgeois gentilhomme, jusqu'aux gentils-hommes mêmes" (p. 323), it is very difficult to effect a viable social system.

L'Indigent philosophe, like so many of Marivaux's narratives, ends suddenly. Yet it reveals that the author had subtly remodeled the format of the *Spectateur français,* and had treated more boldly some of the themes of the preceding journal. However, he still had not really perfected the form, and chose to try once again to accommodate the looser journalistic formula to his themes. At the same time that he was writing Part II of *Marianne,* and right before he began work on *Le Paysan parvenu,* Marivaux wrote his last journalistic work, *Le Cabinet du philosophe* (*Journaux,* pp. 335–437). Published in early 1734, and probably written in the summer of 1733, this journal differed from the previous efforts in an important way: it was most likely conceived as one unit, and not as an open-ended work to which the author planned to add subsequent numbers. A final claim to virtuosity, this short piece experimented once again with comic, philosophical, even frivolous tones, with different subjects, with different narrative techniques. There are in the eleven numbers a dialogue ("Le Chemin de la Fortune"), a short story ("Le Voyageur dans le nouveau monde") and an apologue ("La Veuve et le magicien"), as well as further examples of his fascination with women in the form of literary portraits ("Réflexions sur les coquettes"). In many ways, this work is the perfection of the journalistic formula that Marivaux had been using in *l'Indigent philosophe* and *Le Spectateur français*, although it is not nearly so ambitious and brilliant an effort as the latter. It is a satire, to borrow Northrop Frye's distinctive use of the term, that "deals less with people as such than with mental attitudes" (p. 309). Although Marivaux's journals do not belong *formally* to this tradition (that is, they are not encyclopedic or erudite, nor are they characterized by a central plot around which the author builds his satiric system), they do belong to the tradition *intellectually*. Just like the satire, as Frye explains, this form is not "primarily concerned with the exploits of heroes, but relies on the free play of intellectual fantasy and the kind of humorous observation that produces caricature" (pp. 309–10). The satire also favors an episodic form, and Marivaux's special artistic temperament naturally led him to adopt the journal for this reason. On this subject, Ronald Paulson has shown that the *Spectator* of Addison and Steele was a variation on the satirical tradition: a modern attempt at adapting an ancient form to contemporary moral and aesthetic exigencies.[23] Marivaux's *Le Cabinet du philosophe* is the similar application of a perfected form—the literary journal—to the demands of the early Englightenment's search for moral and psychological realism.

The three fictional pieces found in the *Cabinet du philosophe* once again reveal those themes which Marivaux emphasized in most of his writings. We will see later how La Verdure, the hero of the short dialogue, "Le Chemin de la Fortune" (nos. 4–5), prefigured Jacob, who also had to learn moral equivocation in order to attain his fortune. The story of the widow and the magician (no. 10, pp. 419–26)

23. *The Fictions of Satire* (Baltimore: Johns Hopkins Press, 1967), pp. 3–73, 210–20 especially.

treats allegorically the theme of the coquette's psychological inability to accept advancing age and, with it, the loss of her charms. The widow of the story has been jilted by her lover and goes to a magician to ask why. She is so beautiful and witty, how can any man forsake her? Who is her rival, she demands? By means of a magic mirror, the magician shows her a portrait of her rival. The widow unfairly and egotistically criticizes the young girl, concluding that such a creature could not possibly be her rival. The magician concedes that she is correct, and promises her that now he will conjure a portrait of her *true* rival. Again, the widow viciously attacks the new portrait, until the magician tells her that, in fact, the portrait is one of her when she was only twenty-one. The moral is clear, and Marivaux had allegorized a theme that we have already seen treated in the story of the old coquette's memoirs in the *Spectateur français,* and that will be repeated in Marianne: the intellectual blindness imposed on people by their amour-propre, and the inability of certain types to accept the loss of those advantages which had made them admired by others. Although superior in many ways, these women define themselves in terms of others, and when their appearance becomes less controllable, they can no longer deceive as well as before. Soon they are trying to convince others of their *past* successes, and the memory of their younger selves haunts them incessantly.

It is, however, in "Le Voyageur dans le nouveau monde" (intermittently appearing in nos. 6–11) that Marivaux nears perfection as a writer of short fiction, and where he makes an irrevocable commitment to a rational society in which mask-wearing plays a significant role, but as a civilizing force used to protect all our ticklish egos, and not as an aggressive weapon to help win a battle of social superiority. The story is typical of an eighteenth-century writer, ready to compromise on the question of honesty and sincerity, but only if it will help in making social commerce easier. In this short piece, Marivaux wanted to make us aware, ever so subtly, of the social mask, of its necessity, as well as of the danger of allowing it, and not what lies behind it, to become the essence of existence.

At the beginning of his tale, Marivaux's narrator claims that he is about to show us "un Monde vrai" quite different from our own world. In this new place, "en vivant ensemble, [les hommes] se montrent toujours leur âme à découvert, au lieu que la nôtre est toujours masquée" (p. 389). Perhaps in reading his tale, he continues, we will be able to apply what we learn to better our relationships with others and to "voir clair," so that instead of fleeing the company of men, we will in fact seek it. Briefly, the story concerns a young man who has been jilted by his mistress and his best friend. Determined to leave all behind him, he sets forth for a self-imposed exile. On his way, he meets an older and wiser man to whom he takes an immediate liking. He recounts his story, observing that "les hommes se contrefont si bien qu'il n'y a rien de sûr avec eux" (p. 395). His companion offers to show him men who are *not* mask-wearers. The stranger convinces the young man that they are indeed going to a new, strange land, but, in effect, they are only returning to France. Learning from his reading, the young man realizes that "les hommes sont faux: mais ce qu'ils pensent dans le fond de l'âme perce toujours à travers ce qu'ils disent et ce qu'ils font" (p. 397).

The narrator finds himself, on his arrival in "le monde vrai," able to discern the truth under the veil of deception thrown up by his fellow men. He realizes that men say one thing and mean quite another, but the initiate can learn to discern the truth because it is "dans la tournure de leurs discours, dans l'air qu'ils ont en parlant, dans leur ton, dans leur geste, même dans leurs regards; . . . des paroles prononcées ne seraient pas plus claires. Tout cela forme une langue à part qu'il faut entendre" (p. 401). The narrator has described here what has become known as *marivaudage:* that special way of saying one thing while implying another, of playing with words, not to be witty, but to hide from one's opponent in order to better attack him. Through this "nouvelle préciosité," Marivaux managed to give a firm, serious underpinning to the light wit that would characterize the early Enlightenment.

After several humorous episodes where people innocently converse but the narrator "hears" what they are actually thinking (which today is a favorite technique of film cartoons and comedies), Marivaux's hero becomes more "philosophic" toward his fellow man, and less anxious to castigate him for his hypocritical inconsistencies. Such a change illustrates the different attitudes toward social man that we find in the seventeenth and eighteenth centuries. Man was a complex of egocentric tendencies whose problems were compounded, in the eyes of Pascal and La Rochefoucauld, especially because he was so socially oriented. But, in Marivaux's time, after the "Modern revolution," it was thought that sociability, if properly practiced, should be the *sine qua non* of the educated gentleman. And Marivaux's narrator has been educated, as his companion says: "Et à présent que la lecture des livres que je vous ai donnés, et que les réflexions que vous avez faites en conséquence, vous ont appris à connaître les hommes, et à percer au travers du masque dont ils se couvrent, vous les verrez toujours dc mêmc, ct vous serez le reste de votre vie dans ce Monde vrai, dont je vous parlais comme d'un Monde étranger au nôtre" (p. 419). At this point, the wise friend tells Marivaux's hero that in fact they had never left France, and that there was no such thing as a "monde vrai," except intellectually.

Like so many of his narratives, this one too is left unfinished, yet Marivaux had succeeded in saying what he wanted, through the use of a reflective first-person narrator. And, except for *La Vie de Marianne* and *Le Paysan parvenu*, this was the last piece of narrative fiction that he would write. With the conclusion of the *Cabinet du philosophe*, Marivaux leaves the journal format, satisfied that he had exploited it fully. His last effort was marked by a stylistic control that he had not attained in either of the two previous journalistic pieces. He seemed to have reached that point of confidence in his own abilities that would enable him to continue with *La Vie de Marianne* and to write *Le Paysan parvenu*. Marivaux's experience with this rather untraditional genre had allowed him to effectuate a smooth transition from the romances and parodies of his youth to the more realistic and "modern" novels of the 1730s. For fifteen years he had experimented with almost every prose form (as well as with poetic and dramatic ones), and was now ready to begin another adventure in the possibilities of narrative fiction.

3

Marianne and Society

I

TO THOSE WHO ARE WELL ACQUAINTED WITH MARIVAUX'S prose work from 1712 to 1727, it is clear that his master-piece, *La Vie de Marianne, ou les Aventures de Madame la comtesse de * * ** (published serially between 1731 and 1741), was not a radically new departure for him. He had been experimenting with its major themes and techniques for years. However, his decision to write *La Vie de Marianne* is of importance to those who would understand the development of the modern novel in France. At a crucial point in his career, after he had already made a good reputation as a dramatist and essayist, Marivaux chose to write a memoir-novel. The result was one of the first of Europe's "modern" novels: it treated, seriously and minutely, a subject drawn from the middle echelons of contemporary society. Coincidentally, 1731 also saw the appearance of Prévost's *Manon Lescaut*. Both novels treat young women of uncertain social backgrounds in serious conflict with their societies; one succeeds, the other loses, and their examples would continue to inspire novelists for the next century and a half.

Not only was the subject matter of *La Vie de Marianne* modern (and more will be said on this point later), but so

was the format. All of those elements which had characterized prose fiction in France since the Renaissance are still
present in *Marianne,* although muted. There are vestiges of
the romance (the lost princess in search of her parents), of
the picaresque story (the protagonist wanders through and
describes the different social strata), of the sentimental
novel (a central love story that is characterized by obstacles
impossible to overcome), of the memoir form (an older
person who writes her life history for the edification and
amusement of others), of the epistolary form (Marianne's
memoirs are in the form of a long letter to a close friend),
and finally, even of the parody itself (as Marianne's adventures are often ironic comments on all the foregoing types
of prose works). Yet *La Vie de Marianne* is likewise a new
type of novel, with its emphasis on the rapport between
language and psychological knowledge, with its original
use of first-person narration, and with its presentation and
analysis of a morality predicated on a new concept of social
existence. This chapter will examine *La Vie de Marianne* in
terms of its innovations, with some emphasis on Marivaux's
development of the themes and techniques he had first
used in his earlier works.

The ostensible subject of *La Vie de Marianne* concerns the
heroine's attempts to establish herself in the upper echelons of society. From the beginning of the story, the reader
is made aware of her beauty and superior intelligence, as
well as of her extreme sensitivity. These are qualities that
presuppose that Marianne was not the daughter of the
nurse whose body had been found in the coach that had
been held up by brigands, but rather the child of the well-
dressed man and woman also found there. The description
of this scene (pp. 10–11) is a key passage for several reasons. First, it sets the mood of uncertainty concerning Marianne's birth that pervades the entire novel. This theme
was not new to Marivaux. He had used it in an episode that
appears in his first novel, written some fifteen years before,

Les Effets surprenants de la sympathie. There is, among the many episodes of the novel, the story of a young girl, Dorine, who aids the heroine, Clarice. Dorine is first believed to be of low birth, but she is only the adopted daughter of a peasant woman, Fétime, who explains to Clarice: "L'accident qui me l'a donnée a cependant quelque chose de singulier, et quand vous le saurez, vous croirez comme moi que la naissance de Dorine doit être illustre et extraordinaire" (*O.J.*, p. 94). Dorine was thrust into the arms of a group of peasants by a frightened nurse being chased by armed men. The nurse died immediately, saying only that "je meurs contente, puisque cet enfant vit encore; je n'en suis pas la mère; sa naissance est illustre" (p. 96). But we do not know even this much about Marianne's origins. Marivaux obviously felt that interest in the progress of his story would be heightened if he only hinted at Marianne's noble birth.

The interplay of appearance and reality—an important aspect of all of Marivaux's works—is also introduced through this episode: "Si l'une des deux [femmes] était ma mère, il y avait plus d'apparence que c'était la jeune et la mieux mise" (p. 11), says the narrator. No one is sure of Marianne's birth, and she soon learns the advantages that mysterious origins provide, including the use of her story to impress others. Later she says, in reference to this point: "Il y a de certaines infortunes qui embellissent la beauté même, qui lui prêtent de la majesté" (p. 80). Deciding early to be something more than a shopgirl, and realizing, as we see above, that appearance is often more efficacious than reality, Marianne uses all the advantages at her disposal to achieve this end, and one of the most effective will be the "mystère de sa naissance."[1]

The motif of "naissance" serves other functions in the

1. For an intelligent discussion of this question, especially in Marivaux's theater, see André Séailles, "Les Déguisements de l'amour et le mystère de la naissance dans le théâtre et le roman de Marivaux," *Revue des sciences humaines* 65 (1965): 479–92. See also my article, "Marivaux and the Significance of 'naissance'," *Jean-Jacques Rousseau et son temps,* ed. Michel Launay (Paris: Nizet, 1969), pp. 73–92.

novel. It continues the idea of disguise and subterfuge and keeps the reader's attention centered on the novel's outcome: is Marianne really a noblewoman, or not? The book's title *(La Vie de Marianne, ou les Aventures de Madame la comtesse de * * *)* tells the reader that Marianne becomes a countess, but we still want to know *how* she obtains her title. Yet another purpose that Marianne's mysterious birth serves is to emphasize the theme of rootlessness. Marianne is uncertain of her origins, and therefore of her identity, and it will be shown later how the search for self-identification is an important subplot of *La Vie de Marianne.* So although she uses the obscurity surrounding her birth as a weapon against society, the fact that she does not know her family is a constant concern for the young heroine. The irony of this situation may be seen in the passage where Marianne is defending herself to the abbess of the convent to which she was brought after having been kidnapped. "Je ne sais que trop ce que je suis, je ne l'ai caché à personne, on peut s'en informer, je l'ai dit à tous ceux que le hasard m'a fait connaître. . . . On ne saurait me mettre plus bas. . . . Je suis la dernière de toutes les créatures de la terre en naissance, je ne l'ignore pas, en voilà assez" (pp. 298–99). Although she uses her unfortunate state to gain the abbess's sympathetic aid, the tone of Marianne's self-defense is obviously pathetic as well as humble. She realizes that she is speaking the truth about herself, no matter what end she hopes to attain. The use of the mystery of her birth as a means to arrive is a double-edged weapon.

Besides having a mysterious birth, Marianne's "legend" comes from her having been told in her earliest years—and subsequently convincing herself—of her own superiority in terms of beauty, intelligence, and style. Received in the home of a parish priest and his sister, Marianne soon becomes the talk of the whole area. "On venait pour me voir de tous les cantons voisins. . . . On n'aurait pas caressé une petite princesse infortunée d'une façon plus digne; c'était presque du respect que la compassion que j'inspirais" (p. 13). This is of course second-hand knowledge on the part of Marianne the narrator. The priest's sister had undoubtedly kept the young Marianne continually aware of her singular history and beauty. After fifty-five years of worldly experience, the older Marianne can now analyze and draw conclusions from what she knows about the effect she had on those around her even at such a tender age. As we have noticed, this theme of romantic fantasy and its confusion with reality appears everywhere in Marivaux's narrative fiction. The women who come to see the young Marianne create the fanciful image of a young, lost princess, and impose this image on Marianne. She will use this tendency of people to confuse reality and appearance in her quest for acceptance, but at the same time she herself will fall victim to such inventions. As the novel progresses, Marianne becomes more and more convinced that she is superior in every way to all those around her. This belief does not change as she rises through the social strata, and the mask that she puts on at first voluntarily will eventually become stuck.

This theme of the confusion of fantasy and fact was most clearly treated in Marivaux's earlier work, *Pharsamon, ou les Nouvelles folies romanesques*. It will be recalled that this was the story of a young man who becomes imbued with the fantasy of the novels he read so assiduously. He confused reality and fantasy and the comedy of the novel results from the depiction of this confusion. The same theme is repeated in *Le Télémaque travesti* (1714), the comedy of the inflexible hero who locks himself in the world of dreams, and cannot leave. In *La Vie de Marianne* and *Le Paysan parvenu*, the formal differences between fantasy and reality found in these earlier works have disappeared, and, as one critic has shown, an ambiguity is evident that makes much more complex the worlds of Marianne and Jacob.[2] Ma-

2. Jean Parrish, "Illusion et réalité dans les romans de Marivaux," *MLN* 80 (1965): 301–6.

rianne tells us, however, that interest in her soon waned; she observes cynically that "tout s'use, et les beaux sentiments comme autre chose" (p. 14). People stopped coming to see her, and no longer brought her gifts: "Quand mon aventure ne fut plus si fraîche, elle frappa moins l'imagination" (p. 14). The women speak of charity and good works now, and Marivaux's narrator concludes that "la religion de ces dames ne me fut pas si favorable que me l'ait été leur folie; je n'en tirai pas si bon parti" (p. 14). Marianne was a perceptive child, and what she saw around her remained in her mind for the years that followed. She tells us, for instance, in speaking of her first foster mother, that "souvent, en me regardant, les larmes lui coulaient des yeux au ressouvenir de mon aventure" (p. 15). Such scenes will recur often as Marianne makes her way through society. It would seem that Marivaux used the very brief account of the first fifteen years of Marianne's life mainly to let us know that from her earliest days she had made a significant impression on those around her.

These are but a few, and the most obvious, of the correlations that one can establish between *Marianne* and Marivaux's other narrative works. Several critics have shown that in fact there is a long, thematic filiation from Marivaux's first novel to his last.[3] The remainder of this chapter, however, will be an analysis of those themes and techniques which characterize *La Vie de Marianne* as typical of the emerging novel of the early eighteenth century.

II

Most of Marianne's adventures in high society revolve around the Climal family: Climal himself, Valville, and Mme. de Miran. All of these relationships are closely linked, and each has its effect on the others. The element

3. See especially Mario Matucci, *L'Opera narrativa di Marivaux* (Naples: Pironti, 1962).

of chance (a significant narrative device of the period) is of course evident. Indeed, the action of the novel rests on the fact that Valville, Climal, and Mme. de Miran are related, and this forms one of the most obvious weak points of Marivaux's ability as a novelist. However, an argument may be made that he uses it adroitly to establish the impression of a closed universe. The disquieting effect of Marianne's intrusion into this restricted society is thus much more acutely felt by the reader.[4] In many ways, the depiction of an elitist society was necessary for Marivaux to analyze, in a concentrated way, the subtle variations of social commerce that make up much of his dramatic and narrative themes. As recent critics have told us, it is misleading and not very useful to examine Marivaux's novels in retrospective, anachronistic terms of "realism." His novels were "modern"; they dealt in minute psychological detail with a specific, recognizable contemporary society. The fact that this society was "closed" should be of little concern to us when we discuss Marivaux's "modernity." In fact, with *Le Paysan parvenu,* Marivaux would show himself more than capable of widening his fictional universe, but the emphasis in this latter novel is on physical rather than psychological manipulation, and this fact, plus the sex and social origins of Jacob, would provide for a much more "realistic" work. All such questions of literary terminology must be asked in relative terms if we are to give valid answers. It is in such a way that we will try to understand Marianne's own world.

The episode treating Marianne's relationship with M. de Climal is perhaps the most revealing of her character and her strategies. Spanning in the main Parts I–III, it serves the dual purpose of attacking hypocrisy in its more obvious manifestation, and of providing Marivaux with a means of developing Marianne's personality. By the end of Part II of the novel, the reader has a clear portrait of the young

4. This idea of a closed society and of its effect on the literature of the period is thoroughly examined in the works, already mentioned in chapter 1, of Barthes and Brooks. See Bibliography for details.

coquette, and the action that follows only illustrates the qualities of Marianne's personality that we have seen developed in the first two parts.

M. de Climal, a rich religious hypocrite, takes Marianne under his lecherous wing and places her in Madame Dutour's linen shop as an apprentice—an occupation that Marianne does not particularly relish, but that is better than being a chambermaid, the alternative offered her. It is not long before she becomes aware of a change in M. de Climal's previous solicitous and charitable attitude. "J'étais étonnée des choses dont il m'entretenait; je trouvais sa conversation singulière; il me semblait que mon homme se mitigeait, qu'il était plus flatteur que zélé, plus généreux que charitable; il me paraissait tout changé" (p. 30). Sure enough, Climal, teasing her about her beauty, tricks Marianne into offering him her love: "Hélas! vous le méritez bien, lui dis-je naïvement. A peine lui eus-je répondu cela, que je vis dans ses yeux quelque chose de si ardent, que ce fut un coup de lumière pour moi; sur-le-champ je me dis en moi-même: il se pourrait bien faire que cet homme-là m'aimât comme un amant aime une maîtresse. . . . Tout d'un coup les regards de M. de Climal me parurent d'une espèce suspecte" (p. 37).

Although the narrator has most likely telescoped into one scene a series of subtle maneuvers on the part of Climal, and even of Marianne herself, it is within these few sentences that Marianne grows into a full-fledged woman, a real coquette. Climal, like the women who came to visit Marianne as a child, shows himself to be susceptible to her beauty and charms, and Marianne is aware of this. The word *naïvement* at the end of the first sentence above is the last time it can be honestly applied to Marianne. Where heretofore she had acted—and reacted—through instinct, Marianne now becomes much more aware of her options and methods of action. "Tout d'un coup," "sur-le-champ," she takes the initiative. She no longer has to play the simple games of affected politeness; things are now much clearer.

For the first time, Marianne has come face to face with hypocrisy and deception. She asserts that since Climal has presented himself to her under the guise of a charitable man of piety, she has no inclination for him (p. 38). Her amour-propre has been injured, and that is a serious matter. It is evident that her entire relationship with Climal has undergone a fundamental change. It is at this point that the famous incident concerning the dress begins. This episode, perhaps more than any other in the novel, serves to outline the theme of subtle, but purposeful deception that will become such an integral part of Marianne's character. M. de Climal had offered to buy Marianne some clothes, among them a new dress. Marianne of course wants the dress, but she is uncertain as to whether she should let him buy it for her. It would tend to limit her freedom of action, because she would then be indebted, in no matter how slight a manner, to M. de Climal.[5]

She analyzes her reasons for allowing him to buy her the dress—even after she suspects he is in love with her (p. 38). The fact that Marianne is not *completely* convinced that Climal loves her, she figures, will allow her to benefit from his apparent kindness in wanting to buy her the dress in question. Such deceptively subtle reasoning on the part of the young coquette will become one of Marianne's hallmarks. "L'habit fut acheté: je l'avais choisi; il était noble et modeste, et tel qu'il aurait pu convenir à une fille de condition qui n'aurait pas eu de bien" (p. 38). At the age of fifteen, she knows already what she needs and what becomes her best. Then Climal offers to buy Marianne some underwear. She tells us that "ce fut ce beau linge qu'il voulut que je prisse qui me mit au fait de ses sentiments" (p. 39). There is no longer any doubt—on her part or on the reader's—

---

5. Cf. a similar passage in Richardson's *Pamela, or Virtue Rewarded* (Letter XXIV), where a dress takes on similar symbolic importance. The perennial question as to Richardson's debt to Marivaux (*Pamela* was published in 1742; Part I of *Marianne* in 1731) has been adequately answered by F. C. Green in his *Minuet* (New York: Dutton, 1935), pp. 365–98.

that Climal has ulterior motives. In one of those instances when Marianne the narrator separates herself from Marianne the young heroine, we get a frank appraisal of how the latter begins her apprenticeship as a subtle coquette: "Je consultais donc en moi-même ce que j'avais à faire; et à présent que j'y pense, je crois que je ne consultais que pour perdre du temps: j'assemblais je ne sais combien de réflexions dans mon esprit; je me taillais de la besogne, afin que, dans la confusion de mes pensées, j'eusse plus de peine à prendre mon parti, et que mon indétermination en fût plus excusable. Par là je reculais une rupture avec M. de Climal, et je gardais ce qu'il me donnait" (p. 39).

Through such a scene of self-analysis, Marianne the narrator is making it clear to the reader that the younger Marianne was aware of her predicament—whether or not to accept the clothes—and equally conscious of the consequences of her decision. The introductory "par là" of the last sentence is comparable to the adverb "ainsi" in the preceding passages cited. It ends the rationalization process and introduces the foregone conclusion, which is itself expressed with the imperfect tense, indicating that the decision had actually already been made.

This incident is illustrative of the fact that Marianne realizes the value of remaining outwardly naive and innocent. Only in this way can she hope to gain the attention and favor of those whom she wishes to impress, or conquer. She likes the clothes that have been given her and realizes that they will set off her charms to an even greater degree. But she does not want to dwell on this happy prospect, "car j'aurais rougi du plaisir qu'il me faisait, et j'étais bien aise apparemment que ce plaisir fît son effet sans qu'il y eût de ma faute: souplesse admirable pour être innocent d'une sottise qu'on a envie de faire" (p. 40). Marivaux often uses the word "rougir," as he does here, to indicate that someone has let the mask slip for a moment, and thus has dangerously exposed himself. Marianne was already adept enough in her relationship with M. de Climal to realize that he was watching her closely, so she is especially careful not to let her mask slip. She must retain her apparent naiveté before her anxious suitor. The older Marianne, again with that touch of nostalgic pride which allows us to pierce *her* mask of narrative objectivity, recognizes that Marianne's reasonings are specious (notice use of adverb "apparemment") and based on the pride of keeping one's virtue intact. "Ce petit cas de conscience ainsi décidé, mes scruples se dissipèrent et le linge et l'habit me parurent de bonne prise" (p. 40).

However, Marianne quickly discovers that she has begun an inexorable process of gradual moral disintegration. M. de Climal becomes more and more obvious in his advances, and, no matter how many arbitrary standards of behavior the young Marianne sets, she is forced to abandon them one by one. She soon finds herself in one of those moral fencing matches, so common to Marivaux's protagonists, where, if they are to retain their superiority over those who wish to use them, they must succeed decisively. And, in a series of movements, she successfully parries M. de Climal's advances: "Je feignis donc de ne rien comprendre aux petits discours que me tenait M. de Climal. . . . Je fis semblant d'être distraite pour me dispenser d'y répondre. . . . En feignant de prendre le baiser qu'il m'avait donné pour le choc de sa tête avec la mienne . . ., je crois qu'il fut la dupe de ma petite finesse" (pp. 41, 42). It is hard to believe that such an accomplished hypocrite was so easily gulled by the young girl. Yet she is proud of her apparent success. All of Marivaux's heroes and heroines seek to dupe others and to keep themselves from being similarly deceived. One must be ever on the alert against being deluded. Mme. Dutour recognizes this phenomenon when she says to Marianne at one point: "Vous êtes d'un naturel soupçonneux, Marianne; vous avez toujours l'esprit au guet" (p. 99). This is a necessary characteristic for survival in the Marivaudian universe.

These scenes bring into question another problem: the

sincerity of Marianne the narrator. Why does she reveal so carefully the birth of gentle deception and subterfuge in Marianne the young heroine? The question can only be partially answered at this point, but it is evident that Marivaux's narrator wishes to establish a rapport of sincerity with her reader. Through the "honest" re-creation of the younger Marianne's deceptive rationalizations, the narrator hopes that her whole story will thereby receive a sympathetic reading. The problem that the narrator faces, however, is that when she describes the younger Marianne as making "un consentement [au] mensonge" (p. 44), the reader must ask himself whether she has changed in the intervening years. It is an ever-present question in the novel, of which Marivaux was aware, and which he exploits fully through his original use of the memoir format, as well as of the epistolary structure. A letter to a friend, as *La Vie de Marianne* really is, should be the most sincere of documents, a fact that Marivaux's narrator adroitly exploits.

Marianne finally recognizes the fact of Climal's love, after Mme. Dutour not so subtly suggests why Climal had bought the clothes for Marianne in another shop rather than in hers, but the young girl continues to rationalize her actions, affirming that although he may love her, she does not want his love. If she took his gifts, "c'était par un petit raisonnement que mes besoins et ma vanité m'avaient dicté, et qui n'avait rien pris sur la pureté de mes intentions. Mon raisonnement était sans doute une erreur, mais non pas un crime" (p. 45).

These fine distinctions between "erreur" and "crime," between lying and affected innocence will become more and more exemplary of Marianne's actions in her attempt to find acceptance. Her exaggerated protestations of innocence are but the results of another "petit raisonnement," and lead to an expected conclusion. Absolutely certain of Climal's attentions, she is still not going to return his gifts, but decides to be "honest" with him, telling him that she will accept his favors, but not his love. "Après quoi, je prendrais sans scrupule tout ce qu'il voudrait me donner; c'était là mon petit arrangement" (p. 49). This hypothetical situation, of course, never occurs, but the passage does reveal the complexity of the young Marianne's character. She shows herself to be at the same time naive enough to believe that M. de Climal's largesse would continue after she told him that she would not return his love, but she remains the coquette in the subtle quality of her own rationalization—and new set of demands. She is always willing to negotiate. Even though she is sure of Climal's intentions, he must openly, and with no nuances, commit himself before she feels any need to pass judgment on the propriety of her own actions.

The final stage in Marianne's relationship with M. de Climal occurs in Part III (pp. 127–33). Valville had surprised Climal at Marianne's feet and, like Mme. Dutour, had drawn embarrassing conclusions. Climal, in a panic, had abruptly severed his relationship with Marianne. At this juncture, Mme. Dutour advises Marianne to give up the dress that Climal had given her, arguing that it is too beautiful a dress for a poor and virtuous young girl to wear. Mme. Dutour not only reminds Marianne of her unfortunate situation vis-à-vis Climal, but she also reminds her that she is once again an orphan in the care of a seamstress. The young girl's pride has suffered a terrible blow. Moreover (for this episode occurs after the famous scene in the church where Marianne had made her social debut), she had already learned the effect that beautiful clothes coupled with her charms could have on those people whom she wished to impress. Her wardrobe is one of her most useful weapons, and she does not want to surrender it. There follows a detailed series of arguments (again reminiscent of Richardson's Pamela) as she attempts to discover some way to reconcile her "vertu" with her desire to keep Climal's gifts.

The entire scene takes place in her apartment. As she is preparing the packet to send back to M. de Climal, she congratulates herself on her sincerity and high ideals. But the older Marianne, who is narrating, enters the story to tell us that all is not as it seems: "Cependant le paquet s'avançait; et ce qui va vous réjouir, c'est qu'au milieu de ces idées si hautes et si courageuses, je ne laissais pas, chemin faisant, que de considérer ce linge en le pliant, et de dire en moi-même (mais si bas, qu'à peine m'entendais-je): Il est pourtant bien choisi; ce qui signifiait: c'est dommage de la quitter" (p. 131). The narrator has decoded for us the thoughts of her subject, and draws us into her confidence. Through such a process, which occurs frequently in the first three parts of the novel, Marivaux cautions his reader against trusting too much Marianne the narrator. The reader must be wary of this memorialist, for she too is capable of deceiving us through apparent sincerity, as her younger self was able to deceive others.

By this time, Marianne has wrapped up the undergarments, but she is still wearing the dress. Here her resolve leaves her. She will even return Climal's money, but she cannot give back the dress: "Je n'étais point avare, je n'étais que vaine; et voilà pourquoi le courage ne me manquait que sur la robe" (p. 132). And she finally arrives at a satisfactory reason for keeping the dress. She will go to the priest, Saint-Vincent, who had placed her in Climal's hands, and ask his advice. How will she dress? She will wear Climal's gift as proof of her intentions: "Je la gardai donc, et sans scrupule, j'y étais autorisée par la raison même: l'art imperceptible de mes petits raisonnements m'avait conduit jusque-là, et je repris courage jusqu'à nouvel ordre" (p. 133). Her rationalizations are obvious and reminiscent of those she employed to obtain the clothes from Climal in the first place. There is a certain attempt at logic, which serves to adumbrate the speciousness of her arguments, and the narrator draws our attention to this. She is smiling in spite of herself at this young, beautiful, intelligent girl. She attempts to explain to her reader that Marianne should be excused because of her youth and impetuosity, but she does not, and cannot, succeed in winning completely the reader's sympathetic understanding. Marivaux had succeeded too well in establishing a mood of deception.

The whole Marianne-Climal episode is the vehicle that Marivaux uses to establish the fact of Marianne's education and success in mask-wearing. It is in this episode, spread throughout the first three parts of the novel, that we see the emergence of several Mariannes. On the purely narrative level, there is the naive, yet increasingly coquettish young girl. Through the narrator's interventions, we become more and more aware of the young heroine's aptitude for mask-wearing. In her brief relationship with Climal, the younger Marianne establishes a method of operation that will carry her successfully through the rest of her adventures. She has learned through the experience of one of the most basic of human relationships that subterfuge and deception pay off handsomely. At the same time, Marivaux, through the older narrator, lets the reader see that his young heroine has an unwitting tendency to deceive herself as well as others through the intricacy of her endless rationalizations.

The episode also presents us with at least two other Mariannes: the disinterested narrator, and the very interested narrator. Through his adroit use of authorial intervention on the part of the older Marianne, Marivaux constantly reminds his readers to question, at least partially, the motivations of his memorialist. Is she always telling the truth, and if so, *why* is she doing do? One of the fundamental themes of the novel, as we shall see later, is the quest for self-knowledge, and this quest is as much that of Marianne the narrator as it is of Marianne the heroine.

The role of Valville, Climal's nephew, and of love in *La Vie de Marianne* once again points up the originality of Marivaux as an early eighteenth-century novelist. This novel is not the love story that most Marivaux criticism has attempted to make it; it is the story of how a young girl, with neither money nor family, yet convinced of her superiority, rises to the social rank of countess solely by means of her beauty and intelligence. Everything else is a function of this basic theme. In fact, the love affair between Marianne and Valville is complex and disturbing. The reader at first admires the refined sentiments of Marianne, but soon realizes that something other than passion is at the base of her actions. Subtly, Marivaux was parodying some of the most sacred tenets of the long prose fiction of his predecessors.

Marianne's liaison with Valville has a threefold significance for her, and she uses masks for different reasons and in different ways so as to gain the most benefit from the relationship. First, Valville introduces Marianne to love and all its tribulations. This was, of course, Marivaux's central theatrical theme, and he uses it to full advantage in his novel. A young girl's use of the mask, as she falls in love, is the most common of all Marivaudian motifs, but it should still be emphasized here, for Marianne was as successful in this respect as she was to be (and had been) in others. Secondly, Marianne's affair with Valville provides her with a certain amount of security. If she can keep Valville's attentions, she is aware of the advantages—social as well as financial—that may befall her. Also, although she does not know of this at first, Valville is Mme. de Miran's son, and will thus serve an important function in establishing a close relationship between the two women. As a consequence, Marianne has to mask herself in order to convince Mme. de Miran of her worth, while being careful not to lose Valville until she succeeds with his mother. As a result of this complicated maneuvering, there will come a time when Mme. de Miran becomes much more important to Marianne than Valville ever was.

Lastly, the love that Marianne experiences for Valville enables her ego to better define itself. It is an essential stage in her quest for self-identification. The mask comes into play here when Marianne uses it primarily for defensive instead of offensive action, that is, to protect herself while she searches for some stability in an ever-changing and hostile environment. When Marianne first experiences the sensation of love, she also becomes more acutely aware that her *moi* must have her full and constant attention.

One of the pertinent questions concerning this love affair revolves around the problem of the sincerity of Marianne's love for Valville. The affair, and possible marriage, of the two young people forms one of the unifying subplots of the novel. Marianne herself admits that, at least in the beginning, there was an element of sincerity in her feeling for the young nobleman: "Apparemment que l'amour, la première fois qu'on en prend, commence avec cette bonne foi-là, et peut-être que la douceur d'aimer interrompt le soin d'être aimable" (pp. 63–64). The result is that she even temporarily forgets about the success of her appearance before the other women who are in the church when she first sees Valville. She is so preoccupied with this surprising turn of events that, on leaving the church, she fails to notice an approaching coach and is almost struck by it (p. 64). As the reader learns later (p. 350), Valville has a penchant for damsels in distress, and is very solicitous to the young orphan. Their eyes meet, and Marianne blushes. "Je n'ai de ma vie été si agitée. Je ne saurais vous définir ce que je sentais," she tells us (p. 64). In the paragraphs that follow she explains, in curious terms, the "surprise of love" that she felt: "C'était un mélange de trouble, de plaisir et de peur." Love was something that frightens a young girl, "qui la menace, qui l'étourdit, et qui prend déjà sur elle." With the appearance of love, "l'âme . . . sent la présence d'un maître qui la flatte, mais avec une autorité déclarée qui ne la consulte pas, et qui lui laisse hardiment les soupçons de son esclavage futur" (p. 66).

This is the second stage in Marianne's initial experience with love. After the first confrontation, she begins now to consider the effect it has on her *moi*, and how it causes her to lose some of the power she previously believed she had over herself. Georges Poulet has best described what happens when the Marivaudian character finds himself in love, and incapable of situating himself in what has become a confusing universe of different values and emphases,[6] but I must take exception to one conclusion that Poulet seems to draw. Marianne does not remain passive, even in the face of such a destructive, disconcerting force as love. At first, she is completely disarmed, but soon rallies, and by the time Valville has brought her to his home to be examined by a doctor, she has regained, to a large extent, her composure and savoir-faire. Although still a novice in this new game of love, and still somewhat uncertain, she rises to the occasion when the doctor asks her to show her injured foot (p. 67). She blushes, at first, "honestly." Then, still blushing, but for a different reason (pleasure, excitement, fear), Marianne begins to understand the possibilities of what is about to happen. She can show Valville her "joli petit pied" without any danger to her virtue. It is not her fault, and the others are completely unaware of the happiness she experiences at this turn of events.

Yet there is a certain "honesty" in Marianne's dishonesty. She is very definitely aware of the subterfuge that surrounds her, as well as of her own participation in it. Reflecting on her secret pleasure in showing her foot, she asks: "Combien dans le monde y a-t-il d'honnêtes gens qui me ressemblent, et qui, pour pouvoir garder une chose qu'ils aiment, ne fondent pas mieux leur droit d'en jouir que je faisais le mien dans cette occasion-là! On croit souvent avoir la conscience délicate, non pas à cause des sacrifices qu'on lui fait, mais à cause de la peine qu'on prend avec elle pour s'exempter de lui en faire" (pp. 67–68). Marianne is young and relatively inexperienced as far as her worldly education is concerned, but almost from the beginning of the novel, it is evident that she has an innate

6. "Marivaux," in his *Etudes sur le Temps humain*, II, *La Distance intérieure* (Paris: Plon, 1953), pp. 10–11 especially.

ability (as did her creator) to decipher the gestures and
remove the masks of her fellow men. Although we suspect
this element in Marianne's character, it is the older Marianne who constantly reminds us of it.

By the time Marianne leaves Valville to return to Mme.
Dutour's shop, she has conquered his heart, and he has at
the same time been completely unmasked by Marianne's
affected modesty (p. 73). This is, of course, an age-old
game between lovers, but it takes on added significance
when we realize that the mask and what lies behind it form
the main theme of Marivaux's novel, and that in every situation, Marianne is always prepared to put on the mask in
order to dupe others. But what of Marianne herself? Has
she too been conquered by love? Marianne tells us in a
subsequent passage (p. 73) that she definitely experienced
the sensations of first love. She is confused and temporarily
at a loss for words and thoughts ("Je demeurai étourdie,
muette et confuse; ce qui était signe que j'étais charmée.")
It is at this moment that she experiences her existence for
the first time, thereby becoming a complete woman. This
"coming of age" and her experience of love are more significant than the fact that it is Valville whom she loves. As
Poulet has emphasized, the object or cause of falling in love
is of no more than secondary importance to the effect that
it has on the person experiencing love, especially for the
first time. Marianne becomes extremely sensitive to the
truth of her own existence, and becomes even more convinced that she is the only one who counts in the universe.
Somewhat paradoxically, Marivaux's world of masks and
lies demands that each person become more and more
self-sufficient; all his main protagonists learn that the only
truth is one's feelings, one's own being. The mask is still
needed, however, to protect oneself. Marianne realizes
this, and almost immediately assumes the mask again,
thereby reestablishing her superiority over this new and
frightening situation: "Je me retrouvai pourtant; la présence d'esprit me revint, et la vapeur de ces mouvements qui

me tenaient comme enchantée se dissipa" (p. 73). Marianne is ever alert not to allow herself to be overcome with emotion.

Marivaux had a somewhat cynical view of love. He saw it as a game of masks and deception between two people whose amour-propre would not allow them to be honest with each other. Most of his theater is based on the disguises and stratagems of young people as they attempt to force their opposite number to admit their love first. This motif is also present in Marianne's relationship with Valville, especially in the beginning. Marianne is at a double disadvantage because of her social status, and this becomes clear, for instance, when she has to parry with Valville at his home concerning her address. (Valville wished to have her sent home and Marianne was unwilling to let him know that she worked in Mme. Dutour's linen shop [pp. 76ff.].)

Perhaps the most illustrative example of Marianne's abilities to meet all contingencies is her attempt to regain the initiative that she feels she lost when Valville surprised his uncle, Climal, at her feet, kissing her hand. Marianne, confident of her innocence, was nonetheless conscious of the compromising situation in which Valville had caught her. Before she can explain, Valville says "Voilà qui est fort joli, mademoiselle," and leaves as quickly as he entered (p. 120). Marianne is temporarily speechless with embarrassment and frustration. The best way to continue a Marivaudian love affair is to make certain that each participant's amour-propre remains intact. But should it be threatened, the game becomes more serious.

In yet another long passage of rationalization, Marianne concludes that Valville scorns her now, that he no longer respects her virtue. Such an opinion is outrageous to her, and she ends her reflection with a self-righteous dismissal of both Climal and Valville: "L'un est un misérable, et l'autre croit que j'en suis une; ne sont-ce pas là des gens bien regrettables?" (p. 130). Yet her self-vindication rings hollow, for it remains obvious to Marianne that Valville had not been aware of her nobility of soul, of her own virtuous character, or he would not have so abruptly walked out on her. This, plus the fact that Valville was her lover, does not allow for any but the most drastic action. She must regain the psychological primacy she had established over Valville, or else her very being will be in danger. She puts it quite bluntly: "L'objet qui m'occupa d'abord, vous allez croire que ce fut la malheureuse situation où je restais; non, cette situation ne regardait que ma vie, et ce qui m'occupa me regardait, moi" (p. 129).

As the first step in her campaign to regain the initiative, Marianne resolves to return the clothes Climal had given her, but the question is to whom will she return them? Obviously, to the man who doubts her virtue, and not to the man who asked her to forsake it! Although she does not return the clothes until after her fortuitous meeting with Mme. de Miran, she does instruct Mme. Dutour to send them "chez le neveu de M. de Climal" (p. 157), and she adds a note to go with them. In this note, Marianne uses honesty (or its appearance) as a weapon, elaborating somewhat on the truth, as she explains how she came by the clothes ("Il m'avait dit qu'il me les donnait par charité, car je suis pauvre"), and why she sent them to Valville: "Je n'aurais pas recours à vous dans cette occasion, si j'avais le temps d'envoyer chez un récollet, nommé le père Saint-Vincent, qui a cru me rendre service en me faisant connaître votre oncle, et qui vous apprendra, quand vous le voudrez, à vous reprocher l'insulte que vous avez fait à une fille affligée, vertueuse, et peut-être votre égale" (pp. 157–58).

Within the few lines of this note, Marianne manages not only to justify her acceptance of Climal's gifts, but also to play on Valville's sympathies. She also lies about not being able to send these clothes directly to Climal. We know it is a lie because she has previously told us that she *wants* to send them to her lover rather than to the old man who had attempted to seduce her (p. 130), also it is highly unlikely

that Mme. Dutour would not know Climal's address, because he was her customer. She ends her note with a tempt-
ing reference to her mysterious origins, hoping thereby to
entice Valville into reconsidering their relationship. The
letter is a masterpiece of ingenuousness, deception, and
honesty which, when combined, form a mask that will draw
Valville almost immediately back to Marianne.

After these initial episodes of the affair between Valville
and Marianne (falling in love, Marianne's loss and regain-
ing of Valville's respect), the relationship goes through two
more trials: the proposed marriage and Valville's infidelity.
Henceforth, the narrator begins to place emphasis not so
much on the love affair itself, but rather on what its advantages may be to Marianne. Early in the novel, then, Marianne succeeds in obtaining a proposal of marriage from
Valville, even though he had already promised himself to
someone else of an equal social and financial status. Marivaux sustains interest in the potential union through a series of contrived obstacles—from Mme. de Miran's initial
objections to Valville's infidelity. The novelist knew that
the suspense generated over the marriage possibilities
would help keep his readers interested down to the last
page. (And since the book's publication took over ten
years, he needed something to sustain that interest.)

First, Marianne convinces Mme. de Miran that she is
worthy of her son's affections. At one point, she tells her
story to mother and son, emphasizing the pathetic aspects
of her solitude. Her two listeners are "émus jusqu'aux
larmes;" Valville, his head bowed, cannot speak, and finally
"ses pleurs coulèrent," causing his mother to cry with him.
"Nous nous taisions tous trois, on n'entendait que les sou-
pirs" (pp. 195, 197, 198). Eventually, such strategies bear
fruit, and Mme. de Miran willingly assents to the union,
although she reiterates the opposition of the "usages éta-
blis" and the "maximes du monde" to such a marriage.
However, Marianne's superior virtue and personal characteristics, and Valville's honorable intentions absolve Mme.

de Miran of any social wrongdoing in condoning the marriage. Significantly, the virtuous Marianne and the virtuous Mme. de Miran are now allies against the prejudices of an unjust society. Marivaux has the reader's attention where he wants it. Will Marianne marry Valville or will she not? Marianne herself is continually uncertain as to whether or not the marriage will take place (pp. 208, 240, 241, 278, 295). Clearly, Marivaux used the episode of the projected marriage to sustain interest in his story as well as to keep Marianne in that perpetual state of uncertainty and agitation which best brings out those elements in her psychological make-up which distinguish her from her fellows.

The famous scene that takes place between Marianne and the court minister (Parts VI-VII, pp. 313–38) ends with the latter saying "faites comme vous pourrez, ce sont vos affaires." There is no longer any obstacle to the marriage of Marianne and Valville. But it is here that Valville begins to lose interest in Marianne. Using as an excuse a business deal that necessitated his presence at Versailles, Valville continually postpones the intended marriage. He becomes more and more gallant and witty, thereby convincing Marianne, by now grown more knowledgeable in the ways of her world, that he has changed in his feelings toward her. At this juncture Mlle. Varthon, a young Englishwoman, appears on the scene. Before Marianne's eyes, Valville becomes infatuated with her (pp. 350ff.). Psychologically, it would seem that Marivaux had created in Valville a young *galant* who is much more interested in falling in love than in establishing any lasting relationship. Marianne becomes aware of this as she reflects on the attentions her lover gives to the ill Mlle. Varthon (pp. 352–53).

At first, the thought that Valville is no longer interested in her is so difficult to accept that her mind refuses to do so. Only her subconscious amour-propre causes her to take notice of, and regret, the little attentions that he is paying Mlle. Varthon. Slowly, she comes to the conclusion that their relationship was boring Valville, who thrives on change and adventure (had he not fallen in love with a shop assistant?). He had grown too sure of Marianne's professed affection for him: "Hélas, sûr! Peut-être ne l'était-il que trop" (p. 353). No longer anxious to win her love, his vanity no longer at stake, the game is over for Valville. This is another lesson that Marianne learns. Also, we must not overlook that the Valville-Marianne affair had also served its thematic purpose in the novel, and that Marivaux had found a convenient way of ending it. The relationship between Marianne and Mme. de Miran had already taken precedence in his scheme of things.

Part VII of the novel ends on a note of desperation as it becomes inescapably clear to Marianne that Valville has lost all interest in her, "L'indigne! Est-il possible qu'il ne m'aime plus! . . . Ah! mon Dieu, où en suis-je, et que ferai-je? Hélas! ma mère, je ne serai donc point votre fille!" (p. 367). And when Mlle. Varthon shows Marianne a letter that Valville had written her, she cries: "Il écrit, mais ce n'est plus à moi, dis-je, mais ce n'est plus à moi!" (p. 370). Marianne seems to be at a loss for new stratagems as she contemplates her unexpected misfortunes. But Part VIII, published about six months later, begins on an entirely different note: "J'ai ri de tout mon coeur, madame, de votre colère contre mon infidèle. . . . Valville n'est pas un monstre comme vous vous le figurez. Non, c'est un homme fort ordinaire, madame. . . . C'est qu'au lieu d'une histoire véritable, vous avez cru lire un roman. Vous avez oublié que c'était ma vie que je vous racontais: voilà ce qui a fait que Valville vous a tant déplu" (p. 375). In this paragraph, Marivaux, on one level, replies to those who had vehemently criticized Valville's infidelity.[7] On a second level, he is letting his readers know that it is not Valville's infidelity in itself that is important, but rather Marianne's reaction to

---

7. "Marivaux . . . s'était brouillé avec tout Paris en faisant Valville infidèle." This observation is cited by Deloffre in his edition of *Marianne*, p. xli, n. 1. Another indication of the reaction to this episode is that Mme. Riccoboni based her continuation of *La Vie de Marianne* on the heroine's reaction to Valville's infidelity.

it, the primary subject of Part VIII. Finally, Marivaux is
again presenting the idea that we are not reading a novel,
but rather memoirs. He asserts that fiction in fact "lies"
when it depicts men as being forever faithful to their mis-
tresses. It is much more difficult and realistic to show men
as they really are. Marivaux is therefore breaking with the
popular romantic tradition in his belief that novels (although *La Vie de Marianne* is claimed by him to be true
memoirs) should relate the truth. "Je vous récite ici des
faits qui vont comme il plaît à l'instabilité des choses humaines, et non pas des aventures d'imagination qui vont
comme on veut. Je vous peins, non pas un coeur fait à
plaisir, mais le coeur d'un homme, d'un Français qui a
réellement existé de nos jours. Homme, Français, contem-
porain des amants de notre temps, voilà ce qu'il était. Il
n'avait pour être constant que ces trois petites difficultés à
vaincre: entendez-vous, madame?" (p. 376).[8] This is the
older Marianne, who is again reminiscing, and who serves
the more important purpose of reminding the reader that
there is still a benevolent force directing the heroine's actions.

Marianne must once again regain a psychological advantage over Valville, thereby repeating what she did in the
first part of the novel when Valville suspected her virtue.
The parallel between these two episodes should not be
overlooked: Marivaux frames the Valville-Marianne love
story with two similar instances of Marianne's victory over
Valville. Yet the second time even more than the first, she
is less concerned about Valville's love than about his opinion of her. She must not allow him to think that he has
outsmarted her. She will change and make him see her as
a new, more exciting mistress: "Il me reverra, pour ainsi

8. Cf. this passage to Challe's preface to *Les Illustres Françaises* (1713), where he
says of his characters: "A l'égard des noms que je leur ai donnés, j'ai cru les leur
devoir donner françois, parce qu'en effet ce sont des François que je produis, &
non pas des étrangers," ed. F. Deloffre (Paris: Société d'édition "Les Belles-
lettres," 1959), 1:lix.

dire, sous une figure qu'il ne connaît pas encore. Ce ne sera plus la même Marianne" (p. 377). She has become much more confident, and realistic, about her ability to manipulate others.

There are two scenes in this final part of Marianne's story where she faces Valville after having learned of his infidelity. At first, she finds it difficult to hide the fact that she knows, but she soon is aware, by virtue of that uncanny knack of Marivaux's characters, that Valville is even more ill at ease than she (p. 397). Such expressions as "je m'aperçus que Valville rougissait," and "l'inquiet et coupable Valville" (p. 399) tell the reader that Marianne is once again in full control of the situation, no longer ill (it was Marianne's protracted illness that gave Mlle. Varthon and Valville the chance to get together), and anxious to regain the initiative.

That evening Marianne finds herself alone with Valville. Obviously wearing a mask of innocence and disinterest (Valville is still unaware that she knows anything of his liaison with Mlle. Varthon), Marianne plays with her former lover unmercifully. She asks him when they will be able to get married, why they must wait so long, and so forth. Then Marianne shows him the letter that her rival had given her from Valville in which he stated his love for her. "Comme je la lui présenta ouverte, il la reconnut d'abord. Jugez dans quelle confusion il tomba; cela n'est point exprimable; il eût fait pitié à toute autre qu'à moi; il essaya cependant de se remettre" (p. 403). But he is incapable of continuing the masquerade, and from here on, Marianne is in absolute control of the situation.

Her victory is complete: Valville is astounded by her presence of mind and control of events. He capitulates completely: "Mademoiselle, comme il vous plaira. J'ai tort; je ne saurais parler" (p. 406). Marianne is pleased with the success of her plans, but does not wish to appear so. She must convince Valville of her superiority, and, she hopes, leave him in sorrow that he has lost such a virtuous and

courageous girl. At this point, Mlle. Varthon interrupts the
conversation, and Marianne leaves them whispering together. She happily contemplates the "dignité de sentiments que je venais de montrer à mon infidèle" and the
"supériorité que mon âme venait de prendre sur la sienne."
Confidently, she challenges him: "Je le défiais de m'oub-
lier" (p. 407). Her revenge ("La vengeance est douce à tous
les coeurs offensés") is based on the fact that Valville will
be sorry that he has lost *her*. Her scheme had been to affect
a mixture of nobility and gentleness that would underline
the fact that she is of a superior race, leaving Valville
ashamed and humiliated by the sincerity and gentility that
she has shown. Such a scene would have been impossible
in one of Marivaux's comedies; there is no way for Valville
to save face, and thus no way for the spirit of accommodation and reconciliation, which is the hallmark of traditional
comedy, to occur. In several ways, Marivaux, in *La Vie de
Marianne,* crosses the narrow boundary between comedy
and pathos that he so carefully respects in his best dramas.

Let me conclude these remarks on Marianne's relationship with Valville (the second member of the Climal family
with whom she has difficulties) by reiterating the threefold
purpose of the episode as regards the novel's structure. It
has already been explained that the entire sequence serves
to unify the themes and action of the novel. Most of the
novel's suspense is based on whether or not there will be
a marriage between Marianne and Valville, and on the obstacles, interior and exterior, that would impede the union.

On a second level, the love affair between Marianne and
Valville was entirely within the novelistic tradition of the
period. Marianne's story would have been of little or no
interest to anyone without the question of love. In fact,
Marivaux's audience was so accustomed to love stories
similar to Valville's and Marianne's that they were truly
shocked, as we have seen, when Valville, "héros de roman," showed himself to be not only unfaithful, but unfaithful to the heroine. But this critical reaction was not

unexpected by Marivaux, for he had obviously intended this love story to achieve different ends from those such stories had traditionally treated. It was not the game itself that interested Marivaux, but how it was played.

Marivaux's originality as a moralist and storyteller is best seen when the Marianne-Valville episode is analyzed on the third and final level. Marianne never specifically tells her reader that she will use Valville to attain the social status that she feels is rightfully hers. Yet she has shown herself to be extremely perceptive when it comes to analyzing the potential value of her relationships with others (for example, her affiliations with Climal and Mme. Dutour). Her primary concern is to justify her own existence (the very act of falling in love is significant in this respect, as we have seen) and to attain her desired place in society. Only the most insensitive person would be unaware of the advantages that a marriage to Valville would bring. (After all, had she not introduced herself into his world at the church?) At the same time, her union with Valville would be proof to herself as well as to others that Marianne belonged to the social world that had been previously closed to her.

Marianne consistently plays two roles in her relationship with Valville: she hides, as any Marivaudian heroine would, her love for him until she feels secure enough in his love to expose her own; at the same time, she hides from Valville the sentiment that propels her to advance and nurture the relationship. Her innate desire to vindicate herself in the eyes of those who scorn her origins is the motivational factor that keeps both her and her story vibrant and fascinating. Marianne is not a simple coquette who desires success more than love, but a complex young woman who is attempting to establish herself in a world that wants to reject her. Her love affair with Valville is an important part of this attempt.

The third member of the Climal family with whom Marianne is involved is Valville's mother, Climal's sister, Mme.

de Miran. Besides being the last member of the Climal family that Marianne meets, she also represents the third "mother" that Marivaux's heroine has found. The first was the curate's sister, who died after bringing Marianne to Paris from the provinces. On her deathbed she gives Marianne some advice to which she listens carefully and which she tells her reader she still remembers: "Son discours et les idées de sa mort m'avaient bouleversé l'esprit" (p. 21). In these final instructions, Marianne's foster mother warns her to always be good. "Je vous ai élevée dans l'amour de la vertu; si vous gardez votre éducation, tenez, Marianne, vous serez héritière du plus grand trésor qu'on puisse vous laisser. . . . Les gens vertueux sont rares, mais ceux qui estiment la vertu ne le sont pas. . . . On ne veut se marier qu'à une honnête fille" (pp. 19–20). The priest's sister goes on to say that a girl who has lost her virtue is treated in a cavalier fashion by all those men who make fun of the very virtue that they want in their wives. Only a little reflection is necessary to keep a girl virtuous. "Car, en y songeant, qui est-ce qui voudrait cesser d'être pauvre, à condition d'être infâme?" (p. 20). This passage crystallizes what this provincial lady had been telling Marianne for the fifteen years that she had raised her.[9] It also outlines a significant part of Marianne's strategy vis-à-vis the society she wishes to enter (this is especially true with Mme. de Miran and Valville). Not unlike Richardson's Pamela, Marianne's primary weapon will be her virtue in a world unaccustomed to it.

9. It also reminds us of a similar scene in *La Princesse de Clèves*, where a dying mother leaves formative instructions to her daughter. Because of the Princess's extra-marital love for Nemours, Mme. de Chartres warns: "Vous êtes sur le bord du précipice: il faut de grands efforts et de grandes violences pour vous retenir. . . . Pensez que vous allez perdre cette réputation que vous vous êtes acquise et que je vous ai tant souhaitée. Ayez de la force et du courage, ma fille, retirez-vous de la cour" (Paris: Garnier, 1961), pp. 277–78. Calling on the heroine's "vertu" and "devoir," Mme. de Chartres's advice will lock the Princess in a moral box, thereby ruining her life. Because of her moral, social, and psychological positions, Mme. de Clèves has little freedom to control her destiny. This is obviously not the case with Marianne, who will use her "mother's" advice, not as a moral guide, but as a means to control the responses of those she wishes to deceive.
For an intelligent analysis of this episode in Mme. de Lafayette's book, and of its overall importance, see William O. Goode's "A Mother's Goals in *La Princesse de Clèves*: Worldly and Spiritual Distinction," *Neophilologus* 56 (1972): 398–406.

Marianne's foster mother's advice also prefigures that given her by Mme. Dutour regarding Marianne's relationship with M. de Climal (pp. 46–48, 99–100). Mme. Dutour is the second "mother" that Marianne has in the novel. Her "adoption" by Dutour can be considered a step up the social scale, since the seamstress is a Parisian as well as a bourgeoise. But more important than her social position is Mme. Dutour's morality. She is a better-delineated character than was the curate's sister, and as such, her words of advice to Marianne take on added weight for Marivaux's readers. And Marivaux's heroine is just as aware of their meaning as she was of those of her first guardian. The first time that Mme. Dutour gives Marianne a lesson in morality occurs after she has scolded her for allowing M. de Climal to buy her linen in someone else's shop. She also insults the girl by inferring that a young orphan must go a long way to please a man such as Climal. Marianne, shocked and embarrassed, retaliates by crying and threatening to leave. "Mme Dutour fut effrayée du transport qui m'agitait; elle ne s'y était pas attendue, et n'avait compté que de me voir honteuse" (p. 46). (This is one of the first instances where Marianne's apparent virtue, honesty, sincerity, etc. convince a second person that he is dealing with an extraordinary girl.) Mme. Dutour is immediately sorry and concerned that she has misjudged Marianne. It is at this point that she gives Marivaux's heroine some worldly advice. Again, the narrator tells us: "Je n'ai jamais oublié les discours qu'elle me tint" (p. 46). Her guardian tells her that were she in Marianne's place, she would take all that Climal had to offer, materially, that is. But she would retain her virtue, because "il n'y a rien de tel que d'être sage, et je mourrai dans cet avis. Mais ce n'est pas à dire qu'il faille jeter ce qui nous vient trouver; il y a moyen d'accommoder tout dans la vie" (p. 47).

Somewhat later, after Mme. Dutour hears that Marianne is still concerned over taking clothes and money from Climal, she repeats what she said earlier, but in a more urgent and harsh tone. "Eh! pardi! oui, on vous donne, et vous

prenez comme de raison: à bien donné, bien pris" (p. 98).
And, "dans le monde, on est ce qu'on peut, et non pas ce
qu'on veut. . . . Il est vrai [que M. de Climal] ne va pas droit
en ce qu'il fait pour vous; mais qu'importe? . . . Si l'homme
n'en vaut rien, l'argent en est bon, et encore meilleur que
d'un bon chrétien, qui ne donnerait la moitié tant. Dem-
eurez en repos, mon enfant: je ne vous recommande que
le ménage. On ne vous dit point d'être avaricieuse" (p.
100). Although Marianne ostensibly refuses this advice as
being grounded in avarice, she does use some of Mme.
Dutour's reasoning to develop her own plan to thwart Climal's sexual interests, while still accepting his gifts. Thus,
in the final analysis, the bourgeois and somewhat charming
advice of Mme. Dutour is an important lesson in Marianne's worldly education ("La naïveté et l'affection avec laquelle Mme Dutour débitait ce que je vous dis là valaient
encore mieux que ses leçons," p. 48). Both of Marianne's
foster mothers had inculcated in her the importance of
virtue and "sagesse," but they had also shown her that
besides the peace of mind a virtuous girl has, she can also
gain from her honesty ("Les gens vertueux sont rares, mais
ceux qui estiment la vertu ne le sont pas"). Both women
had played important roles in the moral development and
education of Marianne. It is at this point that Marianne
meets Mme. de Miran.

In many ways, Mme. de Miran is the epitome of all that
Marianne searches for in her world: love and stability. For
although her affair with Valville is not so normal nor so
passionate as it appears on the surface, this does not mean
that Marianne is a dispassionate, completely self-sufficient
person. As an orphan, she had found charity, pity, concern,
and a certain amount of love (in the case of the curate's
sister), but never the attention and concern that a loving
mother gives to her child. It is Mme. de Miran who will
provide this element, and Mme. de Miran's relationship
with Marianne serves the purpose of normalizing somewhat Marivaux's extraordinary young heroine.

On another level, Mme. de Miran represents the highest

social level that Marianne attains within the pages of the novel as Marivaux left it. Marivaux also uses her to represent the sensible and honest part of the world, which will judge Marianne on her own merits. The other side of the coin is, of course, that Marianne, through her association with Mme. de Miran, becomes aware that apparent honesty and frankness on her part are her greatest attributes. As we have seen in the analysis of the liaison between Marianne and Valville, she uses Mme. de Miran as she uses everyone else, but at the same time, she feels closer to her than to anyone else in the novel.

Mme. de Miran is perhaps the most gently treated of Marivaux's major female characters, and is described in one of the reflective portraits for which Marivaux was so unfairly criticized (pp. 167–71). F. Deloffre has aptly shown that this is a description of Mme. de Lambert whose salon Marivaux had frequented, and who had died in July 1733 (Part IV, where the passage appears, was written in 1735–36). It cannot therefore be ignored that an element of "reconnaissance émue" on Marivaux's part is present. But Marivaux's artistry would not allow this portrait, unjustly attacked as being entirely gratuitous, to break the progression of the theme he was emphasizing. In this literary portrait, one of Marivaux's best,[10] we are confronted with the coquetry of Marianne the narrator, as she explains how Mme. de Miran's goodness precluded the game-playing to which Marianne had grown accustomed. Perhaps this is why the two women eventually became so close.

> Ma bienfaitrice, que je ne vous ai pas encore nommée, s'appelait Mme de Miran, elle pouvait avoir cinquante ans. Quoiqu'elle eût été belle femme, elle avait quelque chose de si bon et de si raisonnable dans la physionomie, que cela avait pu nuire à ses charmes, et les empêcher d'être aussi piquants qu'ils auraient dû l'être. Quand on a l'air si bon, on en paraît moins belle; un air de franchise et de bonté si dominant est

---

10. See Brooks's analysis of this passage in *The Novel of Worldliness* (Princeton: Princeton University Press, 1969), pp. 107–10,

tout à fait contraire à la coquetterie; il ne fait songer qu'au bon caractère d'une femme, et non pas à ses grâces; il rend la belle personne plus estimable, mais son visage plus indifférent: de sorte qu'on est plus content d'être avec elle que curieux de la regarder. (pp. 167–68)

This is an extremely well-turned passage that underlines the importance that Marivaux gave to the question of mask-wearing, and to the difficulty of penetrating to the essence of others. He sets up the opposition of "franchise," and "bonté" versus *coquetterie*, and hints that although Mme. de Miran was possibly a beautiful woman when younger, she lacked that element which would have made her beautiful *in the eyes of others*. And Marianne is very aware of this:

On ne prenait pas garde qu'elle était belle femme, mais seulement la meilleure femme du monde. Aussi, m'a-t-on dit, n'avait-elle guère fait d'amants, mais beaucoup d'amis, et même d'amies; ce que je n'ai de peine à croire, vu cette inno-cence d'intention qu'on voyait en elle, vu cette mine simple, consolante et paisible, qui devait rassurer l'amour-propre de ses compagnes, et la faisant plus ressembler à une confidente qu'à une rivale.

Les femmes ont le jugement sûr là-dessus. Leur propre en-vie de plaire leur apprend tout ce que vaut un visage de femme, quel qu'il soit; beau ou laid, il n'importe: ce qu'il a de mérite, fût-il imperceptible, elles l'y découvrent, et ne s'y fient pas. (p. 168)

There are three levels on which these passages should be read. First, Marianne is quite obviously describing Mme. de Miran as a good and sensible woman. In any other uni-verse, these virtues would suffice to define a woman and give her existence meaning. But Marivaux is careful to point out that, although admired, Mme. de Miran is not feared or envied by her peers, and this is reflected in their attitude toward her, a "beauté sans conséquence." This is not to say that she is a weak character, only that she is not a *complete* woman. Marivaux had, after all, said that when a woman ceases to be a coquette, she ceases to be.

This introduces the second point of the passage: the

description of the people (mostly women) who frequent Mme. de Miran's salon. They have all appeared elsewhere in Marivaux's writings: women conscious of their own worth, and anxious to substantiate it through the effect they have on those around them. The fact that Mme. de Miran does not take any interest in this game-playing serves to lessen the impact or influence she has on her social circle —no matter how good she may be, no matter how many friends she may have. Although the remainder of the portrait is more laudatory, these first few paragraphs definitely belong to the general tone and thematic content of the whole novel.

Finally, this portrait of Mme. de Miran furnishes the reader with an intriguing and revelatory glimpse of Marianne the narrator. We already know that the age of Marivaux's narrator is around fifty years, and he establishes a comparison between the older Marianne and Mme. de Miran in the first sentence of the portrait. They are both middle-aged women, but with an essential difference in character: one is a coquette, while the other is not. From the beginning of the novel, we are aware of the older Marianne's enjoyment in recounting the exploits of her youth. She was a beautiful young girl, and still retains remnants of that beauty; and she remains a coquette, still desirous of the attention of her reader(s), as she once was of the attention of her lovers. The insistence on her lack of a narrative style ("où voulez-vous que je prenne un style?"; ". . . je parlais tout à l'heure de style, je ne sais pas seulement ce que c'est."; etc.) is an example of the affected ingenuousness of the "sincere" and accomplished coquette. The portrait itself becomes a literary device for understanding and controlling Mme. de Miran, just as Marianne's powers of penetration had served her when she was younger. As Peter Brooks has said: "The verbal style of the narrator stands as the end term in the evolution of Marianne's personal social style."[11]

11. *Ibid.*, p. 100.

The scene that brings out best so many of the intricacies of the relationship between Marianne and Mme. de Miran is that in which the two women see each other for the first time. Marianne, after her conversation with Saint-Vincent where she denounces Climal and again asks the priest's aid, goes to a nearby church and weeps at her misfortunes. Mme. de Miran comes upon the crying Marianne and notices immediately, as the narrator tells us, that the young girl is pretty, well-dressed, worthy of her sympathy (p. 146). Two similarities between this and Marianne's earlier meeting with Valville are apparent: she is wearing the same beautiful clothes, and the meeting occurs in a church. However, the passage that relates how they faced each other for the first time reveals much more interesting parallels: "Nos yeux se rencontrèrent. Je rougis, en la voyant, d'avoir été surprise dans mes lamentations; et malgré la petite confusion que j'en avais, je remarquai pourtant qu'elle était contente de la physionomie que je lui montrais, et que mon affliction la touchait" (pp. 146–47).

The expressions that Marivaux uses to depict this meeting and the atmosphere he thus creates could easily refer to the first meeting between two lovers. Most of the elements are there: the first look, the blush, the coyness. And, in fact, a similar scene had occurred when Marianne and Valville had first looked into each other's eyes after the carriage accident: "Aussi le regardais-je, toujours en n'osant, et je ne sais ce que mes yeux lui dirent; mais les siens me firent une réponse si tendre qu'il fallait que les miens l'eussent méritée. Cela me fit rougir, et me remua le coeur à un point qu'à peine m'aperçus-je de ce que je devenais" (p. 65). In the scene under discussion, Marianne, typically, is instantly aware of the reaction she had caused in Mme. de Miran, and she is scarcely at a loss for a response. She is also careful not to let any emotion show other than surprise, and a little embarrassment. She instantly dons a mask.

Marianne first converses with Mme. de Miran when she is brought before the prioress of the convent, a hypocritical and socially conscious woman. She tells her story to Mme. de Miran and the prioress, noting carefully the effect it has on both women (p. 153). This is the first of six times that Marianne recounts her entire story to an audience. The others are to Valville and Mme. de Miran again (pp. 194–99); to Mlle. de Fare and Valville (pp. 266–67); to the abbess of the second convent to which she is brought after being abducted (pp. 298ff.); to the minister and others, including Mme. de Miran (pp. 328–29); and finally to Mlle. Varthon (pp. 355–56). Each of these instances will be discussed in turn, but it should be remarked that Marianne learns early that her story is a tearjerker, in a very literal sense. As she tells her story, she adapts it each time, ever so slightly, to her audience. By the time she tells it to Mlle. Varthon, she is quite open as to how she relates it, and the reaction she expects: "Je parlai en déplorable victime du sort, en héroïne de roman, qui ne disait pourtant rien que de vrai, mais qui ornait la vérité de tout ce qui pouvait la rendre touchante, et me rendre moi-même une infortunée respectable" (p. 356). She had told the story so much, and with such success, that it was now a matter of instinct and inspiration as to how and why she would relate it. ("Mon sentiment me menait ainsi sans que j'y pensasse.") Marivaux had adapted a stock novelistic device—the interpolated story of a damsel in distress—to the exigencies of his basic theme of social subterfuge.

Mme. de Miran's reaction upon first learning Marianne's story was almost immediate, and she not only promises to continue her support of Marianne, but in fact fully adopts her as her daughter (p. 173). And, finally, in a strongly symbolic gesture of acceptance, Mme. de Miran, with little prodding, acquiesces to the marriage of her son to Marianne with no compunction whatsoever, convinced as she is by that time of the girl's worth. Marianne, through the adroit use of her mask of honesty and innocent virtue, had won Mme. de Miran completely to her side.

Marianne soon discovers that her most appealing virtue

as far as Mme. de Miran is concerned is her apparent honesty. Honesty seems to befit the interior nobility that she feels separates her from those around her. At the same time she is applying the lessons that her first foster mother taught her concerning the rarity of virtue in the world. There are several scenes where this frankness in telling Mme. de Miran the truth gets her out of seemingly impossible situations. The first occurs when Marianne reveals to Mme. de Miran and her friend, Mme. Dorsin, that she is the young "aventurière" of whom her son, Valville, has become enamored. The reaction to this "honesty" is instantaneous: "Voilà une belle âme, un beau caractère!" (p. 180), says Mme. Dorsin. Marianne makes a mental note of the effect her telling the truth has had.

In subsequent episodes of increasing significance, Marianne finds it good policy to tell Mme. de Miran the truth. The second instance occurs when Marianne has to decide whether or not to tell her foster mother that Mme. de Fare has learned that Marianne is nothing other than a seamstress's assistant. This knowledge on the part of an old gossip would injure Mme. de Miran's image with her social world, for she had presented Marianne as the daughter of a provincial cousin visiting Paris for the first time. The situation could in fact make a public liar of Mme. de Miran. But Marianne is still uncertain as to what road to take: "Me tairai-je? C'est assurément le plus sûr, me disais-je; mais ce n'est pas le plus honnête, et je trouve cela lâche. Parlerai-je? C'est le parti le plus digne, mais d'un autre côté le plus dangereux. Il fallait se hâter d'opter, et j'étais déjà devant Mme de Miran sans m'être encore arrêtée à rien" (p. 280). This hesitancy is a fascinating example of how Marianne sometimes sets up a moral problem for the benefit of her reader as well as for herself. It makes her ultimate decision a much more climactic event. Yet the very fact that she hesitates between the options of silence or confession is in itself significant. Marianne knows that society can still exclude her from her rightful place, and she needs Mme. de

Miran's patronage if she is to attain anything at all. Also, Marianne had recently seen that being honest with Mme. de Miran had only strengthened this lady's love for her. So she opts to tell her foster mother the truth.

Marianne vaunts her honesty and sincerity, telling Mme. de Miran that "je ne serais pas pardonnable si j'avais des ruses avec vous, et si je vous dissimulais une chose qui a de quoi vous détourner du dessein où vous êtes de nous marier ensemble" (p. 283). The technique has the desired result. Mme. de Miran is quite impressed by Marianne's action. She attributes it to Marianne's obviously noble background. "Tu es une fille étonnante, et [mon fils] a raison de t'aimer. . . . Notre orgueil est bien petit auprès de ce que tu fais là; tu n'as jamais été plus digne du consentement que j'ai donné à l'amour de Valville, et je ne me rétracte point, mon enfant, je ne me rétracte point" (p. 284). Proud of her adopted daughter's actions, Mme. de Miran asks Marianne to come live with her. Later, she puts into words what Marianne had suspected beforehand and of which she now becomes certain: "As-tu pu croire qu'une aussi louable sincérité que la tienne tournerait à ton désavantage auprès d'une mère comme moi, Marianne?" (p. 286). And still later, Valville reveals to his fiancée that his mother had been very impressed by her frankness, telling him: "Elle m'a tout dit, et je n'en reviens point; je l'aime mille fois plus que je ne l'aimais et elle vaut mieux que toi" (p. 288). This last phrase, although uttered in a teasing tone, is prophetic of the decision Mme. de Miran will make when she learns of her son's infidelity at the story's end.

The final, and most significant, example of Marianne's use of the appearance of honesty toward Mme. de Miran comes at the end of the book, when Mme. de Miran must choose between her son and her adopted daughter. Marianne, in tears as always, tells her foster mother that the marriage between her and Valville must be forgotten. She begs Mme. de Miran not to force her to marry Valville, because it would be unfortunate if Valville, heir to a great family name, had to marry such a girl as she (p. 410). Marianne's reasons for wishing to end her relationship with Valville are obviously lies. Deception is not new to Marivaux's heroine, but in this case she lies from ostensibly noble motives, and Mme. de Miran soon guesses why: "Ma fille, . . . est-ce qu'il ne t'aime plus? Je ne lui répondis que par des pleurs, et puis elle en versa elle-même" (pp. 411–12).

Again, Mme. de Miran's reaction is typical. She will not abandon Marianne, even now that there is no reason for her to protect the young girl. "Allons, ma fille, allons, console-toi, me dit-elle; va, ma chère enfant, il te reste une mère; est-ce que tu la comptes pour rien? . . . Elle est plus ta mère que jamais" (p. 412). And what is her reaction to the infidelity of her son? "Ah! voilà qui est fini, je ne l'estimerai de ma vie" (p. 412). When Mme. de Miran learns that it is to Mlle. Varthon that her son's heart now belongs, she warns her: "Après ce qui arrive à ma fille, je ne vous conseille pas de compter sur le coeur de mon fils" (p. 413). Thus, the mother abandons her son, and Marianne emerges triumphant, with the assured confidence and support of Mme. de Miran. Marianne is herself confident and ready to enjoy the fruits of her victory. It is no wonder that Marivaux felt he could stop his story at this point.

Mme. de Miran's relationship with Marianne serves another and perhaps more significant need of Marivaux's young heroine. There is obviously a great deal of love in *La Vie de Marianne,* but rather than being centered in the Marianne-Valville relationship, it is an essential part of Marianne's liaison with Mme. de Miran. During Marianne's appearance before the minister the climactic scene of the novel, the young girl, when called upon to defend herself, at first does not even mention Valville (an adroit move on her part, to be sure), but rather insists that her only concern is her affection and respect for Mme. de Miran. In addressing herself first to the relative who opposes her marriage, and then to Mme. de Miran, Marianne, in a long harangue, expresses the depth of her feeling for her foster mother. She concludes, affirming that "je ne vivrais point si je vous perdais; je n'aime que vous d'affection; je ne tiens sur la terre qu'à vous qui m'avez recueillie si charitablement, et qui avez la générosité de m'aimer tant, quoiqu'on tâche de vous en faire rougir, et quoique tout le monde me méprise" (p. 335). Marianne has announced to society that her affection for Mme. de Miran is of a kind that surpasses any love for Valville. Not until Mme. de Miran begs her to continue (after she and others have shed numerous tears at the speech they have just heard) does Marianne mention her love for Valville. But never does she approach the passion of the preceding speech where she had spoken of her love for Mme. de Miran.

After the minister has expressed his helplessness in face of such an evident *fait accompli* as Marianne's affection for Mme. de Miran and Valville, Mme. de Miran takes her to her home for the first time and shows what awaits her future daughter-in-law. "Je goûtai tout à mon aise le plaisir de me trouver chez ma mère, et d'y être comme si j'avais été chez moi" (p. 342). She had "arrived." Mme. de Miran expresses her satisfaction at what Marianne said before the minister, her friends and family, and Marianne basks in the glory of her victory. Seated at her foster mother's feet, she says: "Voilà M. de Valville, il m'est bien cher, et ce n'est plus un secret, je l'ai publié devant tout le monde; mais il ne m'empêchera pas de vous dire que j'ai mille fois plus encore songé à vous qu'à lui. C'était ma mère qui m'occupait. . . . Le principal est que vous m'aimez; c'est le coeur de ma mère qui m'est le plus nécessaire, il va avant tout dans le mien" (p. 343).

Finally, after Marianne learns of Valville's infidelity and has the interview with him in which she confronts him with her knowledge, she begs him not to hurt his mother through a quarrel (p. 405). Again, she has an ulterior motive for making such a statement—her wish to convince Valville of her superior character. But, underlying this possible ploy, there is also the idea that she does not wish to hurt Mme. de Miran, nor to lose her as well as Valville. After she acquaints Mme. de Miran with Valville's newly established liaison with Mlle. Varthon, Marianne lets her benefactress know that as long as she is with her, she will be happy. "Ma mère, lui dis-je d'une voix encore faible, je ne connaîtrai jamais de plus grand plaisir que celui d'être avec vous, j'en ferai toujours mon bonheur, je n'en veux point d'autre, je n'ai besoin que de celui-là. . . . Quand M. de Valville aura pris un parti, quand il sera marié, je ne prends plus d'intérêt à la vie que pour être avec ma mère" (p. 413). It is at this point that Mme. de Miran asserts that "tu es pour jamais ma fille, et . . . je te porte dans mon coeur" (p. 414).

Marianne's relationship with Mme. de Miran must be considered the most complex of the novel. Beginning on the most pragmatic level, Marianne *needs* Mme. de Miran if she is to have support in her attempts to storm the ramparts of established social opinion. She discovers early that Valville's mother is greatly impressed by her frankness and uses this knowledge accordingly. The relationship is one based on mutual admiration and respect, as will be seen in the discussion of the concept of *reconnaissance.* But because of a psychological and emotional need on the part of Marianne (and perhaps on the part of Mme. de Miran also, who is, after all, a widow), this relationship deepens into one of real affection or love. Although the emotion is most likely genuine, it must not be forgotten that Marianne had not always acted sincerely with Mme. de Miran. So this relationship, like so many others in Marivaux's universe, is still based on a certain amount of subterfuge and deception. By the end of the novel, Marianne has obtained the love that every Marivaudian character needs. The fact that it is her adopted mother who furnishes this love only serves to underline the originality of Marivaux's approach to the psychological implications of one person's affection for another, and the modernity of his attempt to dissolve the traditional limitations on the proper subjects of narrative fiction.[12]

Marianne is in quest of love, and her quest partially ends when she becomes Mme. de Miran's daughter. Any student of Marivaux must conclude that love and the ambiguous relationship it establishes between two characters is an integral part of Marivaux's view of the world. A Marivaudian character defines himself in terms of others ("Nous avons tous besoin les uns des autres; nous naissons dans cette dépendance, et nous ne changerons rien à cela," p. 221), and it is therefore not only to his benefit, but a *need*, that he enter into a serious liaison with others. Although one would be tempted to see Marianne's professed love for Mme. de Miran as another act of subterfuge on her part, Marivaux goes to great pains to insist on the validity of this emotion. There is no doubt that Marianne is aware of the advantage that such a relationship has for her, but this is only a part of the affection between the two women. Both are in quest of love, of recognition, and both find security in their love for each other. This situation, according to Marivaux's rather cynical view of love and *coquetterie* in his society, is probably a more genuine relationship than any that could have been established between lovers. For Marivaux, friendship and filial devotion (the latter is especially applicable to some of his comedies[13]) are more sincere, and thus preferable, to the *galanterie* in the guise of love he saw around him. Climal's lechery and Valville's infidelity are so effectively contrasted with Mme. de Miran's sincerity and faithfulness that Marianne's affection for the latter is expected and justified.

12. As I have pointed out, Marivaux knew and was inspired by Challe's *Les Illustres Françaises*. Challe hints at a similar filial relationship in the second of his stories, "Histoire de M. de Contamine et d'Angélique," p. 70 of Deloffre's edition.

13. *La Mère confidente* (probably written in early 1735, in the middle of his composition of the *Paysan* and *Marianne*) treats another mother-daughter situation, but, in contrast to the one under discussion, it is the mother who deceives her daughter in order to retain her love. This play can be seen as a reaction to the stock love stories of dramatic tradition, as well as a commitment (to be continued as the *drame bourgeois* developed) to a new sensibility for a new theater.

III

Although most of Marianne's adventures occur within the rather limited confines of the Climal family, she does move in other social contexts. A look at these episodes likewise reveals the consistency of Marivaux's themes of subterfuge and deception. Marianne soon learns to use her talents to manipulate public opinion, much as she manipulated Climal, Valville, and Mme. de Miran. Again, with one or two exceptions, the world in which she moves is a limited one, less so than that of a family, but still an elite society that offers little aid to those who lack the arbitrary qualities that it has established as prerequisites for entrance. Of course, Marianne's ultimate success is all the more exhilarating because of these impediments.

Marianne makes her social debut in perhaps the best-known scene of the book. Her preparations (pp. 49–52) are as revelatory of her character as is her appearance itself (pp. 57–64). It will be remembered that Marianne had finally consented to accept Climal's gift of clothing. The scene that follows, as she tries on her new clothes, is reminiscent of the one in the *Spectateur français* where Marivaux showed us another young coquette at work (*Journaux*, pp. 117–18). Says Marianne: "J'essayai mon habit le plus modestement qu'il me fut possible, devant un petit miroir ingrat qui ne me rendait que la moitié de ma figure; et ce que j'en voyais me paraissait bien piquant. Je me mis donc vite à me coiffer et à m'habiller pour jouir de ma parure; il me prenait des palpitations en songeant combien j'allais être jolie: la main m'en tremblait à chaque épingle que j'attachais; je me hâtais d'achever sans rien précipiter pourtant: je ne voulais rien laisser d'imparfait" (pp. 49–50). The obvious pleasure that Marianne receives on first seeing herself in a mirror, well-dressed and groomed, is one of the most sensually explicit scenes that Marivaux has in his novel. The physical reaction of this young girl is her first real awakening to the possibilities that her attractiveness will afford her in her quest.

The sweet remembrance of this scene causes the narrator to digress again and to analyze the "science de bien placer un ruban" that she learned so well as a novice coquette. "Si on savait ce qui se passe dans la tête d'une coquette en pareil cas, combien son âme est déliée et pénétrante . . . ; cela ferait peur, cela humilierait les plus forts esprits. . . . C'est moi qui le dis, qui le sais à merveille. . . . Il faut lire dans l'âme des hommes." (p. 50). Marianne the elder leaves little doubt in the mind of her reader that she was a coquette, and proud of it. She knew all the rules of *coquetterie*, the paramount of which was to search out the weaknesses of others that would best serve her purposes. Although there is an attempt on her part to speak lightly, there is also an undercurrent of seriousness, almost a sinister tone in her reflection ("cela ferait peur"). A few sentences later, Marianne sums it all up in the following way: "Je me jouais de toutes les façons de plaire, je savais être plusieurs femmes en une. . . . Je fixais l'homme le plus volage; je dupais son inconstance, parce que tous les jours je lui renouvelais sa maîtresse, et c'était comme s'il en avait changé" (p. 51).

Within the relatively few pages of the first part of Marianne's life, Marivaux succeeds in establishing his primary themes and in giving an almost complete portrait of his protagonist. Marianne has progressed from her obscure birth through her provincial childhood to a position of confidence necessary for a successful confrontation with the society she wants to penetrate. Marianne is not happy in Mme. Dutour's establishment ("Il valait mieux qu'une fille comme moi mourût d'indigence que de vivre aussi déplacée que je l'étais," p. 45), and feels that her blood and her *physionomie* demand something better for her. It is with this certainty of purpose that she walks alone to church to test her charms. A close analysis of this episode will reveal some of the recurrent motifs of Marianne's adventures in society.

In this scene at the beginning of Part II, Marianne pits

her wits and attributes against those of high society. From the beginning, she knows why she has gone to church, decked out in her newly acquired finery. "Je vous ai dit que j'allai à l'église, à l'entrée de laquelle je trouvai de la foule; mais je n'y restai pas. Mon habit neuf et ma figure y auraient trop perdu; et je tâchai, en me glissant tout doucement, de gagner le haut de l'église, où j'apercevais de beau monde qui était à son aise" (p. 58). This short paragraph is a resumé of the action of the entire novel. Marianne is unwilling to remain with the crowd because of her attributes, both natural and acquired, which she feels entitle her to a higher station in life. Thus, she advances quietly and furtively ("en me glissant tout doucement") through the crowd to the front of the church where she sees the people whom she wishes to join. She is instantly aware of her equality with, even her superiority over, the beautifully dressed women who are there in the church (p. 60).

Marianne's awareness of the effect she has had on her "audience" reinforces her confidence. Marivaux's female characters are constantly attempting to pierce each other's masks of superiority. Not wishing to appear too interested in other women, they do want to see what effect their own appearance has on others. The church scene is a perfect example of the hide-and-seek that goes on among these sensitive and coquettish characters. "Voilà donc mes coquettes qui me regardent à leur tour, et ma physionomie n'était pas faite pour les rassurer" (p. 61). Marivaux uses scenes like this one to underline another facet of Marianne's rapid rise to social prominence: though she resorts to subterfuge in her search for acceptance, she is not entirely undeserving of such recognition. At dinners where she is surrounded by Mme. de Miran's friends, she concludes that "moi qui m'imaginais qu'il y avait tant de mystère dans la politesse des gens du monde, et qui l'avais regardée comme une science qui m'était totalement inconnue et dont je n'avais nul principe, j'étais bien surprise de voir qu'il n'y avait rien de si particulier dans la leur, rien qui me fût si étranger, mais seulement quelque chose de liant, d'obligeant et d'aimable" (p. 213). Marivaux thereby implies that there is an innate nobility about her that transcends any arbitrary social barriers. Marianne herself soon becomes aware that there is some personal element that enables her to fit into such a society, and her resultant self-confidence allows her to continue her quest for acceptance.

The next social advance that Marianne makes is when she is invited to spend some time at the country home of friends of Mme. de Miran, Mme. de Fare and her daughter. Mme. de Miran, it will be remembered, intimates that Marianne is the daughter of an old acquaintance, and, for a short time, Marianne plays the leisurely role of a noblewoman, rising late, and being served and dressed by her own chambermaid. She finds that she can "naturally" accommodate herself to such luxuries (p. 262). It is because of such scenes that Leo Spitzer's argument that Marianne is not an ordinary girl seems especially relevant. In speaking of the concept of *coeur* as explored by Marivaux, Spitzer says: "Courage, coeur—orgueil, l'éternelle épine dorsale du caractère de Marianne! . . . C'est par sa nature, son innéité qu'elle a de la perspicacité psychologique, du goût, de la politesse du coeur, du savoir-faire, la capacité de tenir tête à des situations inattendues."[14] The whole theme of the innateness of Marianne's feeling of superiority is made consciously ambiguous by Marivaux's use of the word *naître*. Marianne feels that she was *born* superior, but it is her very lack of *naissance*—of respectable birth, of a past—that excludes her from the world she wishes to enter. Marivaux uses both interpretations of *naissance* consistently throughout his novel, fully aware of the paradox that he establishes.

The older Marianne, who is narrating the story, wishes to impress on the reader that she was indeed an exceptional

14. "A Propos de la *Vie de Marianne*," *Romanic Review* (1953) pp. 108, 110.

person. Not only was she beautiful, intelligent, and apparently virtuous, but she also had an important quality that set her on an equal level with Mme. de Miran and her friends: her "sensibilité," manifested in her pride and amour-propre, which did stamp her as being of a superior bloodline (the French word *race* is particularly applicable here). Marivaux, the novelist, would cause Marianne to undergo several more trials before she could finally claim her rightful place in society (e.g., Mme. Dutour enters the home of the de Fares immediately after the scene where Marianne is being dressed, and reveals who Marianne really was). But, as far as the reader is concerned (as well as for Mme. de Miran, Mme. Dorsin, Mlle. de Fare, and even Valville), Marianne had already illustrated that she was what she believed she was. Her psychological make-up enables Marianne to justify more easily the wearing of masks in order to attain what she felt was hers anyway.

The last important confrontation between Marianne and high society is when she is kidnapped and taken before a minister of the court for judgment of her actions and plans to marry Valville. She is visited by a relative of Mme. de Miran, who tells her only that "c'est dommage que vous portiez vos vues un peu trop haut" (p. 289). She is then abducted and brought to another convent, whose abbess informs Marianne that Valville's relatives are opposed to his marriage to her because of her "naissance qu'on ne connaît point et dont vous savez tout le malheur" (p. 297). The abbess insists several times on Marianne's virtue and intelligence, but says that this is not enough: "J'avoue qu'il est fâcheux que le monde pense ainsi; mais dans le fond, on n'a pas tant de tort; la différence des conditions est une chose nécessaire dans la vie, et elle ne subsisterait plus, il n'y aurait plus d'ordre, si on permettait des unions aussi inégales que le seraient la vôtre, on peut dire même aussi monstrueuses, ma fille" (pp. 297–98).

Marivaux was no social revolutionary. He did believe in a social hierarchy, but he also believed that this hierarchy should be based on merit as well as on *naissance*. He ironically played with this concept (as Spitzer has shown), but was serious when he held that only those who merit it should be allowed to succeed. It is because we, the readers, *know* that Marianne the narrator is a countess, and that Marianne the young heroine is beautiful, wise, and virtuous that Marivaux feels safe in advocating her interruption of the pattern of existence heretofore enjoyed by the privileged few. Marivaux lets us know that had Marianne *not* been what we all know she is, her marriage to Valville would really have been monstrous. We see this when the abbess ironically refers to the same forces, "raison" and "Dieu," that Mme. de Miran had previously cited in justifying Marianne's action: "Il n'y aura . . . que les hommes et leurs coutumes de choqués; Dieu ni la raison ne le seront pas" (p. 205). It is through such analyses of accepted social prejudices that Marivaux, through Marianne the narrator, in effect justifies the subterfuge and deception that Marianne practices. The reader is made aware of Marianne's exceptional qualities, and thus enjoys watching her break down barriers. After all, everyone else wears a mask in Marivaux's world, so why should one fault Marianne simply because she is more adept at it than others? Marivaux forces his reader into partial collusion with Marianne the coquette, adding to her appeal as well as revealing the subtlety of her techniques.

While in the convent, Marianne anxiously awaits the chance to defend herself before those responsible for her incarceration. Soon she is led before the official himself, after having first been presented to a proposed suitor chosen for her by the former, and whom she immediately refuses, at least partially because he is a *petit bourgeois*. There follows a scene that Marivaux had been planning and preparing his readers for throughout his novel, and had already previewed in the *Paysan parvenu* (written the year before): his heroine's final triumph over the prejudices of the high social circles. Marivaux describes the minister in a long portrait, which emphasizes his characteristics of wisdom and sincerity (pp. 314–16). And again, the narrator uses the literary portrait not only to present a character, but also to penetrate that character's social mask. From the portrait, we learn that the minister is a just and intelligent man who will doubtless realize the validity of Marianne's plea for understanding. No reasonable and good person has yet refused to admit that Marianne is a worthy recipient of Valville's love, and the narrator's portrait allows for no other possibility. It remains only to see how Marianne will control and benefit from the situation.

Marianne is first alone with the minister and the family of Mme. de Miran, but her foster mother suddenly bursts into the room to protect her young charge (p. 318). Marianne had already categorically refused to consent to the marriage offered her by the minister to M. Villot, the young bourgeois he had chosen for her. "Je ne changerai point de sentiment, monseigneur, repartis-je; je ne me marierai point, surtout à un homme qui m'a reproché mes malheurs. Ainsi vous n'avez qu'à voir dès à présent ce que vous voulez faire de moi; il serait inutile de me faire revenir" (p. 318). It is at this time that Mme. de Miran arrives, but Marianne had already set the tone of the interview, and established the fact that she is a proud, virtuous, and sincere young girl.

Mme. de Miran warns all present that, no matter what the outcome of this meeting, she is going to continue to protect Marianne. She refutes any charge that Marianne is unworthy of Valville's attentions: "Je puis vous assurer que, par son bon esprit, par les qualités de l'âme, et par la noblesse des procédés, elle est demoiselle autant qu'aucune fille, de quelque rang qu'elle soit, puisse l'être. . . . Il faut que cela soit dans le sang; et voilà à mon gré l'essentiel" (p. 329). Mme. de Miran's impassioned pleas for "justice" have the desired effect on those listening, silent and increasingly sympathetic as they watch Marianne's tears. The minister tries to reason with Mme. de Miran, reminding her that although he agrees with her on Marianne's charms, their mutual agreement is not solving the problem before them, that is, the contested marriage. He reasons that "un sentiment généreux," no matter how justified, cannot combat the "usages" of the rest of society. That is why the minister had offered Marianne the opportunity to marry the young M. Villot, a chance any young girl of the people would have desired.

It is at this point that Marianne recites the long speech in which she puts to use all of her abilities as a mask-wearer. She reminds her reader that not only was she careful to say the right thing, but also to notice the effect her discourse was having on her audience. She describes herself as presenting "un air triste, respectueux, mais ferme". She tells her reader that, while giving her story, "je sanglotais" (pp. 333–34). However, about midway through her speech, Marianne reminds us that she is keeping a cool head although the tears were flowing: "Ici, à travers les larmes que je versais, j'aperçus plusieurs personnes de la compagnie qui détournaient la tête pour s'essuyer les yeux. Le ministre baissait les siens, et voulait cacher qu'il était ému. Valville restait comme immobile, en me regardant d'un air passionné . . . ; et ma mère laissait bien franchement couler ses pleurs, sans s'embarrasser qu'on les vît" (p. 335). Marianne had been aware of the power of her tears from the very beginning of her adventures. Speaking of their effect on Valville early in their relationship, she said: "[Les pleurs] viennent d'ennoblir Marianne dans l'imagination de son amant; ils font foi d'une fierté de coeur qui empêchera bien qu'il ne la dédaigne" (p. 80). She had not forgotten this lesson.

All the way through the recounting of her story, Marianne follows the theme that her benefactress had set when she had previously told the assemblage that Marianne was not interested in any financial or social advantages that might come from her marriage to Valville (pp. 323–24). Marianne consistently reminds those present that she is concerned only with her love for Valville, and as we saw

earlier, especially for Mme. de Miran: "Le monde me dédaigne, il me rejette; nous ne changerons pas le monde, et
il faut s'accorder à ce qu'il veut. Vous dites qu'il est injuste;
ce n'est pas à moi à en dire autant, j'y gagnerais trop" (p.
336).

Finally, Marianne uses a stratagem that her reader knows
almost certainly to be a falsehood. She offers to go live
forever in a convent if she can but see Mme. de Miran from
time to time. This offer to cloister herself comes only hours
after she had told the abbess of the convent to which she
had been taken that she did not want to become a nun (p.
301). Also, earlier in her story, she had suggested the same
sacrifice to Mme. de Miran and was happy when her benefactress did not remember it (pp. 199–200). Marianne has
no intention of cloistering herself, and her suggestion is
made only because she knows that no one will seriously
consider it.

Marianne tells us that "un torrent de pleurs termina mon
discours" (p. 337), and the minister's reaction is immediate: "L'autorité n'a que faire ici. . . . La noblesse de vos
parents est incertaine, mais celle de votre coeur est incon-
testable, et je la préférerais, s'il fallait opter" (p. 337). Marianne, in a by now familiar gesture, throws herself at the
minister's feet. The action was calculated: "Il me releva
sur-le-champ, d'un air qui témoignait que mon action le
surprenait agréablement et l'attendrissait; je m'aperçus
aussi qu'elle plaisait à toute la compagnie" (p. 337). Ever
watchful, Marianne is aware of her success.

The impressed minister ends the interview with the
words: "Je vous rends justice. . . . Faites comme vous
pourrez, ce sont vos affaires" (p. 338). And, in effect, Marivaux ends his novel. Marianne had achieved what she had
been seeking throughout her story. Her acceptance by the
representative of the State and, by implication, of God,
only underlines the significance of her victory. All the relatives present (except for the one who had instigated the
plot) sympathize with Marianne and agree with the minis-

ter's final judgments. And Marianne bears no grudges: "Je n'en abusai point; j'avais trop de joie, je sortais d'un trop grand triomphe pour m'amuser à être maligne ou glorieuse; et je n'ai jamais été ni l'un ni l'autre" (p. 340). "Triomphe" is not a misused word.

It is at this point that Marivaux inserts the episode of Valville's infidelity. This infidelity is significant in that it in no way affects Marianne's victory and her newly acquired social stability. Marianne's story ends, in fact, with a scene that completely eradicates the immediate and future consequences of Valville's actions: she is proposed to by an old friend of Mme. de Miran, a retired, middle-aged army officer (p. 418). He had heard of Marianne in conversations with Mme. Dorsin and Mme. de Miran, and uses a pretext to meet her at her convent, where she was remaining until her future was more certain. As soon as she is seated, the older man tells her what is on his mind: "Je suis connu pour un homme d'honneur, pour un homme franc, uni, de bon commerce; depuis que j'entends parler de vous, votre caractère est l'objet de mon estime et de mon respect, de mon admiration. . . . J'ai vingt-cinq mille livres de rente, et je vous les offre, mademoiselle; elles sont à vous, quand vous voudrez, sauf l'avis de Mme de Miran, que vous pouvez consulter là-dessus" (p. 421).

The novel, "la vie de Marianne," has come full circle. There could be no better place, no better way to terminate her memoirs. At the end of her story she is proposed to by a gentleman, a nobleman, and she, as any young nobleman would have done, tells him that she must have a week to consider his flattering offer. Just a few months before, and at the beginning of her story, another gentleman had tried to seduce her in the traditional way, by offering a young girl the material things she could obtain in no other way. But, luckily for her, and thanks to, or in spite of, the tutoring of the curate's sister and Mme. Dutour, she refuses to compromise her virtue (although she does get the best advantage out of the situation), and her reward will be a final, and irrefutable, reversal of her social status. Climal told Marianne she should be honored by his propositions: "Vous êtes une orpheline, . . . ignorée pour jamais de votre famille . . . , sans parents, sans bien, sans amis, moi seul excepté . . . , qui suis le seul qui s'intéresse à vous. . . . Je suis riche, soit dit en passant, et je puis vous être d'un grand secours, pourvu que vous entendiez vos véritables intérêts, et que j'aie lieu de me louer de votre conduite" (p. 111). The attitude of the officer is the exact opposite. He has money (ironically, even more than the sum Mme. de Miran had said that Marianne must have in order to marry Valville [p. 184]) and position, but offers them only as a corollary to his own love and respect for Marianne. When Marianne, in her inimitable and natural way, asks: "Mais vous êtes un homme de condition, apparement?" (p. 421), the officer says yes, adding that he is likewise an "honnête homme," a quality more worthy, he thinks, of Marianne's favors than either his social position or his fortune (p. 422). Although money is mentioned by both men (a significant early eighteenth-century socio-economic element in the novel), the difference is that one is "honest," while the other is not. And perhaps their honesty is not so much determined by the differences in their morals or personalities as by the difference between the social status of Marianne at the beginning and at the end of the novel. What this scene does illustrate is Marianne's final, irrevocable, and just entrance into the social circles that she first sought as she tried, "en me glissant tout doucement, de gagner le haut de l'église, où j'apercevais de beau monde qui était à son aise" (p. 58).

Through her fortuitous meeting and relationship with the Climal family, Marianne attains to the pinnacle of social acceptance, overcoming numerous obstacles, both natural and unnatural. She is an extraordinary young girl who uses her beauty and wit to their best advantage in beating the establishment at its own game. Her triumphant interview with the minister, topped by the unexpected and favorable proposal of the officer, are both manifestations of the success that Marianne has in gaining what she believes is rightfully hers. She had used the mask in many ways and with varying success to arrive, and it is this success and what leads up to it that form the narrative structure of the work. The reader is fascinated as Marianne climbs the ladder, and cannot wait to find out how she becomes "madame la comtesse de * * *," although, unfortunately, he never does.

But Marivaux's heroine plays the game of subterfuge and deception for other reasons, the ones we have just seen are but the most obvious. Marianne was also protecting or defending herself while she attacked. She was protecting the one thing that she held dearer than all else: her *moi,* her amour-propre, that curious Marivaudian type of self-consideration which propels so many of his characters, and which adds so much of the tension necessary to the dramatic fulfillment of his plays and novels.

4

Marianne's Other Quest

I

THE READER OF *La Vie de Marianne* IS AWARE, FROM THE FIRST
few pages of her story, of Marianne's well-developed
amour-propre. Most of Marivaux's fictional characters are
self-centered; they have great faith in themselves and in
their ability to convince others of their superiority. Occasionally this self-concern gets out of hand, as in the case of
the young coquette of the "Lettres contenant une aventure." The reader will remember how she explained to a
friend that she felt an unquenchable need to win new admirers. As a final comment on what makes a coquette act
in such a manner, Marivaux's heroine says somewhat plaintively that this continual desire to subjugate others, her
ability to get herself out of difficult situations, to hide her
coquettish talents, all of these "avantages" are due to her
"insatiable envie de sentir que je suis aimable, et à un goût
dominant pour tout ce qui m'en fait preuve" (*Journaux*, p.
96). This coquette, like many of Marivaux's characters,
looks on love and its requisite use of the mask solely as a
means to give her own existence meaning.

Yet, Marivaux felt that, if well controlled, amour-propre
could be a constructive element in social relations. Realiz-

147

ing the danger and power of their amour-propre, Marivaux's characters know that they must somehow regulate it, and the most prevalent form of control was often a mask —of sincerity, of virtue, or of humility. Such a compromise marks Marivaux as a Modern who lacked the basic pessimism of the seventeenth-century moralists. He was a social realist, and although the words of Marivaux and his predecessors often seem akin, their world views are based on their personalities, and Marivaux, though somewhat cynical, was definitely not the moral absolutist that Pascal and Nicole were—no matter how "misanthropic" he considered himself. He recognized clearly the moral injustices of his society, but did not believe that it should be destroyed, with only the promise of a better one emerging. His characters, as he was himself, were full members and active participants in the world that surrounded them. They act to convince others of their worth, while at the same time parrying the attacks of others. Neither Marivaux nor his characters sit on the sidelines, pointing out the weaknesses and evils of social living. They are interested in effecting some sort of *modus vivendi* until something better appears.

It is here that Marivaux presents the mask as a defensive as well as an offensive device, and that one of the basic ambiguities of Marivaux's moral world view emerges. We have seen that Marivaux believed in the smooth functioning of the machine of society. Though, like most Moderns, he also had respect for the individual, especially in terms of taste and judgment, he did feel that some accommodation between the individual and society had to be made. The question then becomes, up to what point does an individual submerge his originality to ensure the success of modern society? And if the individual is indeed exceptional, as in the cases of Marianne and Jacob, how serious, in psychological and moral terms, does this accommodation become? These are the questions that I will try to answer in this essay on Marianne's other quest, and later, when the similar predicament of Jacob is analyzed.

The fact that Marianne accepts responsibility for her actions weakens still further the often-proffered argument that she is a passive character. She is constantly watchful and ready to thwart any attack on her self as she uses the masks of sincerity and virtue to help hide her true personality from others. She advances on the premise that as long as one's true self is hidden from the public eye, one is free to feint and actually attack others, who, similarly, are protecting their inner selves. Marianne is always careful to parry or neutralize any attack—real or supposed—on her pride, and this characteristic of hers forms one of the consistent themes of *La Vie de Marianne.*

From her earliest adventures, Marianne had realized that the only truth of which she could be certain was herself. And for Marivaux and Marianne, one's personality or ego was expressed by one's feelings. ("Je pense, pour moi, qu'il n'y a que le sentiment qui nous puisse donner des nouvelles un peu sûres de nous, et qu'il ne faut pas trop se fier à celles que notre esprit veut faire à sa guise, car je le crois un grand visionnaire," p. 22). We first see the movements of her amour-propre when she is introduced to M. de Climal by Father Saint-Vincent: "Le coeur me battait, j'étais honteuse, embarrassée; je n'osais lever les yeux; mon petit amour-propre était étonné, et ne savait où il en était" (p. 27). As the story progresses, Marianne's amour-propre will attain more and more importance.

When Climal offers her the chance to be a lady's maid, Marianne reacts to this suggestion with all the pride that a well-bred young girl can muster. The episode is significant in that it establishes what will be one of Marianne's more common strategies: the presentation of the image of a young girl of mysterious birth, but of noble character and worthy of respect. The offer made her blush, she tells her reader, and she refuses it, so that Climal will know that, although an orphan, she still has pride. Climal's answer gives Marianne one of her earliest victories: "Eh! mon enfant, me dit-il, tranquillisez-vous; je vous loue de penser comme cela, c'est une marque que vous avez du coeur, et cette fierté-là est permise" (p. 28). Marianne, in this first of her many tearful speeches, has succeeded in setting in motion all of the particulars of her personal myth. But Climal warns her that though she has shown nobility of heart, the way will not be easy for her. Her pride is commendable, but "il ne faut pas la pousser trop loin, elle ne serait plus raisonnable: quelque conjecture avantageuse qu'on puisse faire de votre naissance, cela ne vous donne aucun état, et vous devez vous régler là-dessus" (p. 28).

His warning, coupled with his condescending tone, causes Marianne, for the first time in the novel, to analyze her feelings about being dependent on others. In a long passage (pp. 29–30), marked by a tone of indignation and bitterness, Marivaux's narrator expounds on the humiliating aspects of accepting charity from those who do not know how to give it gracefully, that is, without offending the amour-propre of the recipient. "Les bienfaits des hommes sont accompagnés d'une maladresse si humiliante pour les personnes qui les reçoivent!," exclaims Marianne. Climal's maladroit attempts at helping the young girl had severely wounded her pride ("j'avais l'âme un peu fière"), and most probably strengthened her resolve to remove herself from such a position of social subordination.

This passage introduces the question of *reconnaissance* that plays a dominant role in *La Vie de Marianne*. Not only must a proud girl undergo the "interrogatoire" that accompanies charity, but she must think of how and when these kindnesses are to be repaid. La Rochefoucauld summed up the whole process in another of his observations: "L'orgueil ne veut pas devoir et l'amour-propre ne veut pas payer" (no. 228). But Marianne, again because of the uncertainty of her origins *must* owe and eventually *must* pay back. The agonies that this causes her pride to undergo form another of Marivaux's favorite leitmotifs. At one point, Mme. Dutour says to Marianne: "Vous êtes d'un naturel soupçonneux, Marianne; vous avez toujours l'esprit au guet" (p. 99). Correctly, she has understood that her young assistant is forever analyzing her relationship with others as well as the advantages or disadvantages that may devolve from them. As her "friendship" with M. de Climal progresses, she realizes that her obligations to him are based on recognition of his charity to her. She also concludes that she can never love Climal, and may even come to hate him, because of the humiliation she suffered when he first offered his help to her. "Il n'y a plus de sentiment tendre à demander à une personne qui n'a fait connaissance avec vous que dans ce goût-là" (p. 38).

In Marivaux's universe, love is based on mutual respect and admiration. And the game of love, of *coquetterie* (both male and female), has for its end to obtain some sort of superiority over, or at least parity with, the opponent. If the relationship begins with one participant at too great a disadvantage, there is no hope that the outcome will be love. Ever watchful, ever sensitive, the heart will brook no attack on its amour-propre, which will become the eternal and implacable enemy of whoever it may be who bruises it. And charity will always bruise it, no matter how honestly it is offered.

As in every other aspect of human endeavor, there is a duality in virtue. There is a mask to be worn constantly so as to hide our true feelings and to protect our amour-propre. As Marianne points out, continuing her reflection: "Est-il rien de si doux que le sentiment de reconnaissance, quand notre amour-propre n'y répugne point? On en tirerait des trésors de tendresse; au lieu qu'avec les hommes on a besoin de deux vertus, l'une pour empêcher d'être indignée du bien qu'ils vous font, l'autre pour vous en imposer la reconnaissance" (p. 38).[1] Neither the giver nor the receiver enjoys the benefits of his actions because of the

---

1. This passage is reminiscent again of one of La Rochefoucauld's most astute observations: "Il y a une certaine reconnoissance vive qui ne nous acquitte pas seulement des bienfaits que nous avons reçus mais qui fait même que nos amis nous doivent en leur payant ce que nous leur devons" (no. 438).

sensitivity of his amour-propre. For Marivaux, this was another example of the constant battle for position between two persons. The question of "reconnaissance" especially intrigued him, because it presented a very tricky problem for his young heroine. How was she best to acquit herself insofar as her obligations to others were concerned? And she had to so acquit herself for at least two reasons. One is that it was expected of a virtuous and sincere young lady, and, second, until the debt was paid back, the recipient was under a continual obligation to the donor.

Perhaps the key to this question lies in the word itself. *Reconnaissance* clearly implies the act of recognition, and thereby an expression of gratitude. But more important than the idea of gratitude is that of *reconnaître*. This is the basis of the Marivaudian character's uneasiness when he is the recipient of someone's charity. To recognize is to give existence to someone else, and thereby to lessen the impact of oneself on the world. We give definition to others and we ourselves are defined *in terms of others,* and our primary duty is to impose ourselves on the world, not to recognize the equality or superiority of others. It is for this reason that Marianne is so upset when she has to accept Climal's money and gifts. Under no circumstances must she ever allow herself to become "stupide de reconnaissance" (p. 45). The very word *charity* repulses her: "Il était un peu cru pour un amour-propre aussi douillet que le mien" (p. 43).

This preoccupation with protecting one's amour-propre when it comes to accepting charity and expressing gratitude, is not Marianne's alone. It plays such an important part in the lives of most social beings that we see others and interpret their actions according to how aware they may be of the services they render us. Marianne tells us that a generous person who is intelligent is less desirable than one who is of "un esprit médiocre." The reason is that men do not like to be reminded of their indebtedness to others. The more intelligence one has, the more aware he is of the favor he is doing for you, and the more humiliated the recipient feels (pp. 220–21). The psychological intricacy of this logic illustrates the concern that a person with a well-developed amour-propre has that he never be placed at any disadvantage vis-à-vis another person. It must be remarked that Marianne's portraits of Mme. de Miran and of Mme. Dorsin had occasioned this little essay on "reconnaissance" and pride. Marianne concludes: "Or, Mme de Miran était de ces bonnes personnes à qui les hommes, en pareil cas, sont si obligés de ce qu'elles ont l'esprit médiocre; et Mme. Dorsin, de ces bonnes personnes dont les hommes regardent les lumières involontaires comme une injure" (p. 221). Marianne's "ingrate délicatesse" will not be bruised so easily, for Mme. de Miran's somewhat "mediocre" personality does not attempt to make the most of her generosity. But Marianne must still be "reconnaissante." How does she rationalize this "unnatural" emotion with her exacerbated amour-propre?

She continues to reason about the problem, and arrives at the conclusion that gratitude for charity received can be turned to an advantage in one's relationship with the benefactor. Marianne realizes that all men need each other, or at least society has to be based on interdependence, and this relationship must be maintained, though we are all victims of our pride. Should one wish to be "modestly" above one's benefactor, then one must learn to use gratitude adroitly, humiliating in turn the charitable friend. Careful, subtle use of gratitude (ingratitude will only place the debtor forever in the service of the benefactor) can be a very effective weapon, concludes Marianne (pp. 221–22). The act of "reconnaissance" thereby becomes a mask because its original meaning has been subverted to fit the needs of the recipient of charity. Pride, revenge, and subterfuge become integral components of a heretofore moral obligation on the part of recipients of charity, and yet another weapon is added to Marianne's defensive arsenal in protection of her amour-propre.

Before Marianne makes her initial appearance in real

society, she comments for the first time on the close relationship between *coquetterie* and amour-propre. The narrator interrupts her story to inform the reader of how her vanity, when she was younger, caused her to use *coquetterie* to enhance her beauty and to take advantage of its effect on her admirers: "Je me jouais de toutes les façons de plaire, je savais être plusieurs femmes en une. Quand je voulais avoir un air fripon, j'avais un maintien et une parure qui faisaient mon affaire; le lendemain on me retrouvait avec des grâces tendres; ensuite j'étais une beauté modeste, sérieuse, nonchalante" (p. 51). The older Marianne again is reveling in the memory of days gone by, when she was the center of so much attention, and when her vanity played its dominant role in her relationships with gentlemen. She wants her reader to understand that hers is not the story of an ordinary girl, while at the same time developing an essential theme of her autobiography. Even though her present state no longer allows her to be a coquette with her charms, the older Marianne *remains* the proud coquette by her frequent reference to what used to be. And she also relies on her excellent prose style, which she repeatedly denigrates (another form of *coquetterie*), to draw the reader's attention to her myth.

Our desire to be recognized, admired, and respected demands that we do everything in our power to convince others that we are worthy of such attention. If subterfuge is necessary, and it most often is, then it is justified. After she enters the church at the beginning of Part II, Marianne is quick to notice that the other women there are playing the same game as she. It would seem that Marianne was watching a play, enjoying it, learning from it, but at the same time constantly aware that she was only watching actors and actresses. "Et moi, je devinais la pensée de toutes ces personnes-là sans aucun effort; mon instinct ne voyait rien là qui ne fût de sa connaissance et n'en était pas plus délié pour cela; car il ne faut pas s'y méprendre, ni estimer ma pénétration plus qu'elle ne vaut" (p. 59). Again, as Spitzer pointed out, Marianne is revealed as "noble d'instinct," and completely at home playing all the games of high society. Marianne the narrator intervenes at this point and underlines the usefulness of *coquetterie* as an important tool in one's attempts at drawing attention to oneself:

> Nous avons deux sortes d'esprits, nous autres femmes. Nous avons d'abord le nôtre, qui est celui qui nous recevons de la nature, celui qui nous sert à raisonner, suivant le degré qu'il a, qui devient ce qu'il peut, et qui ne sait rien qu'avec le temps.
> Et puis nous en avons encore un autre, qui est à part du nôtre, et qui peut se trouver dans les femmes les plus sottes. C'est l'esprit que la vanité de plaire nous donne, et qu'on appelle, autrement dit, la coquetterie. (p. 59)

This essential component of her psychological make-up is an "enfant de l'orgueil qui naît tout élevé," and needs to be protected as it sets out to accomplish its goals. The reason that Marianne knows all this is simple: "Avec une extrême envie d'être de leur [others'] goût, on a la clef de tout ce qu'ils font pour être du nôtre, et il n'y aura jamais d'autre mérite à tout cela que d'être vaine et coquette" (p. 60). The adroit use of this "key" is what makes Marianne so fascinating, and the reciprocity described here is what makes society function so smoothly.

Returning to the passage where Marianne takes her place in the church, we see that she has entered into serious combat with other women (her most worthy opponents) and has emerged victorious. However, Marivaux points out that to attack or injure someone's amour-propre is serious business, and he does not let his heroine off easily. There follows a relatively long episode where Marianne's own pride is pitilessly exposed and threatened. She is psychologically tortured in an episode that covers more than twenty pages of her story (pp. 69–90). Valville takes her to his home to be examined by his doctor after Marianne's near accident. At first pleased and flattered with the attention (and with the occasion to show off her pretty foot),

Marianne soon becomes dismayed as she realizes she must tell Valville her address at Mme. Dutour's so that he may have her driven home. She cannot bring herself to do this: "Mme Dutour choquait mon amour-propre; je rougissais d'elle et de sa boutique" (p. 70). She does not care if Valville knows that she is an orphan, or poor, but to be known as an assistant in a linen shop would do irreparable injury to her pride. She would even have Valville think her independent enough to be roaming the streets alone, rather than divulge her address: "C'était bien mal conclure, j'en conviens, et je le sentais; mais ne savez-vous pas que notre âme est encore plus superbe que vertueuse, plus glorieuse qu'honnête, et par conséquent plus délicate sur les intérêts de sa vanité que sur ceux de son véritable honneur?" (p. 71).

There follows a battle of wits between the two young people; the result is a rarity in *La Vie de Marianne*, a relatively funny scene, which the narrator tells us lasted a half-hour, as Marianne fights desperately to keep the truth from being known. She curses her "misérable vanité," her "vanité inexorable," her "vanité haïssable que je condamnais intérieurement moi-même, qui me paraissait ridicule, et qui, malgré tout le tourment qu'il me causait, ne me laissait pas seulement la consolation de me trouver à plaindre" (p. 79). For one of the few times in her adventures, the young Marianne is confused, and completely at a loss as to how to extricate herself from the situation. Too proud to admit that she is a shopkeeper's assistant, she is equally afraid of losing Valville.

She blames the entire episode on the independence and strength of her amour-propre. "On va d'abord au plus pressé; et le plus pressé pour nous, c'est nous-même, c'est-à-dire notre orgueil; car notre orgueil et nous, ce n'est qu'un, au lieu que nous et notre vertu, c'est deux. N'est-ce pas, madame? Cette vertu, il faut qu'on nous la donne; c'est en partie une affaire d'acquisition. Cet orgueil, on ne nous le donne pas, nous l'apportons en naissant; nous l'avons tant, qu'on ne saurait nous l'ôter; et comme il est le premier en date, il est, dans l'occasion, le premier servi. C'est la nature qui a le pas sur l'éducation" (pp. 86–87). This is a significant commentary on the independence of our pride. It is a passion that demands all of our attention, and over which we have little or no control. It is based on the fact that "dans la vie, nous sommes plus jaloux de la considération des autres que de leur estime, et par conséquent de notre innocence, parce que c'est précisément nous que leur considération distingue, et que ce n'est qu'à nos moeurs que leur estime s'adresse" (p. 87). The "considération" of others means simply that they observe us and that they are aware that we represent a possible danger to their well-being. Their recognition of her worth is much more important to Marianne than their "estime," which will come later. "Nous nous aimons encore plus que nos moeurs," she admits (p. 87). People may admire her for her qualities, but the only thing Marianne wants is that people admire *her* first, no matter *why*. She even goes so far as to say that "pour parvenir à être honoré, je saurais bien cesser d'être honorable" (p. 87).

This passage establishes clearly the dichotomy between outside appearances ("moeurs") and the real self ("soi") that forms one of the unifying principles of Marianne's life, as well as of most of the remainder of Marivaux's work. One's *self*, his amour-propre, is a separate, autonomous entity that demands attention and feeds on what Marivaux calls "considération." In several of the passages quoted in this study of amour-propre, it will have been noticed that Marianne is ever conscious of the independence of her pride and of its demands on her own actions (see especially pp. 59–60, 71, 78, 79). There are many others throughout the work, and they all illustrate the independence of vanity over one's will, over even such a powerful force as love. The protection and nourishment of her vanity causes Marianne to wear the mask at all costs. As she says at one point: "Adieu le plaisir d'avoir de l'amour, quand la vanité d'en inspirer nous quitte" (p. 92).

At one of the most critical moments of her existence,

immediately after she learns of Valville's infidelity, Marianne is very close to despair. She is confused about Valville's action, and uncertain as to what to do. A succession of thoughts runs through her head concerning her present state, the results of Valville's infidelity, her future. Suddenly she is pulled up from her self-pity. She takes stock of her advantages, mentally reasserts her superiority over her unfaithful lover, and decides to confront him and Mme. de Miran with the truth: "En un mot, je me proposai une conduite qui était fière, modeste, décente, digne de cette Marianne dont on faisait tant de cas; enfin une conduite qui, à mon gré, servirait bien mieux à me faire regretter de Valville, s'il lui restait du coeur, que toutes les larmes que j'aurais pu répandre, qui souvent dégradent aux yeux même de l'amant que nous pleurons, et qui peuvent jeter du moins un air de disgrâce sur nos charmes" (p. 386). Thus, pride pulls her from her depression, and amour-propre sets her back into motion. Marianne is seen once more donning the masks of virtue and honesty in order to protect herself and her pride. (Marianne's apparent aversion to tears should be noted here, mainly because of her shameless use of them throughout the book in order to sway her audiences.)[2]

Marivaux's belief that amour-propre was at the base of most of social man's actions was not overlooked by his contemporaries. Probably the most original contemporary critique that exists of Marivaux's novel is the continuation of La Vie de Marianne that Marie-Jeanne Riccoboni composed around 1750. It first appeared in 1760–61 and was advertised as a "continuation de la vie de Marianne."[3] Most

2. The reader should refer to the discussion in chapter 1 of the interpolated episode about Tervire, the young girl who is, in many ways, an anti-Marianne. She has many of the same characteristics as Marianne, but not the sustaining force of a well-developed amour-propre. The result is that she ends her days sequestered in a convent, a fate that Marianne refuses to accept.
3. The "Suite" may be found in F. Deloffre's edition of Marianne, pp. 581–627. See also my article "Parody and Truth in Mme. Riccoboni's Continuation of La Vie de Marianne," SVEC 81 (1971): 163–75.

critics and the public believed that they were being presented with a continuation authored by Marivaux himself.
It is revealing to examine Madame Riccoboni's Marianne
and see what traits her creator insisted on and how they
mirrored, in some way, those of Marivaux's heroine. There
is certainly an attempt to parody Marivaux in parts of the
continuation, but, on the whole, this second Marianne is an
obvious descendant of Marivaux's heroine. Madame Riccoboni's reading of Marivaux's novel was not at variance
with the rest of his public, and her creation is also a young
girl who wishes to protect her amour-propre at all costs,
even that of happiness, and does so through the use of all
the tricks—or *coquetterie*—at her disposal.

Marianne is a perfect example of a person who defines
herself in terms of others, an essential cohesive element in
the making up of society. She was, as was her creator, a
social animal, and felt that she could protect her individuality only by donning a mask of *coquetterie*. Her amour-propre
had to be protected against the attempts of others to injure
it, but, at the same time, one must be careful not to irrepa-
rably harm the amour-propre of others. A *détente cordiale* is
established and the boundaries of good taste and mutual
respect are seldom overstepped. Marianne becomes a part
of this masked society, and becomes increasingly adept at
its rites and rhythms. Her ultimate success makes her a part
of the myth that established the eighteenth century as a
period of individuality that retained an intense interest in
the mechanics of social living.

II

We have seen how Marianne uses the mask to arrive, as
well as to protect her sensitive and well-developed amour-
propre. The mask also serves to protect another action of
Marianne: her quest for self-identification. For although
Marianne has an extremely active amour-propre, she still
does not know who she is, or why she exists. It is her search

for answers to these questions that leads the critic into one of the most original areas of Marivaux's genius. The theme of self-discovery is a pervasive one, appearing in all of his major works. "Je ne sais plus où je suis" (p. 199). "Pourquoi suis-je venue au monde, malheureuse que je suis? Que fais-je sur la terre?" (p. 145). These plaintive cries of Marianne illustrate the confusion in which she often finds herself when left alone to analyze her situation. She does not know of her origins, thus, on another level, she does not know the truth of her own identity. All of Marivaux's characters, at one time or another, attempt to discover some standard of truth on which they can base their lives. Marianne and Jacob are not only searching for acceptance by an established social group; they are in quest of a point of equilibrium that will afford them stability and security. Georges Poulet bases his article on Marivaux on this premise. He sees in Marivaux's work an "absence de toute espérance" as well as the "absence de toute vérité." Speaking of Marivaux's characters, Poulet says: "Ce sont des comédiens qui jouent leur comédie, qui promènent leur mensonge."[4] The only sure thing for the Marivaudian character is that he exists, while the most unsure state of all is existence. This is where the significance of amour-propre becomes so clear: it reminds the Marivaudian character that he *is*, even though he does not know who or why he is. To lose sight of one's amour-propre is dangerous: "Se perdre de vue, c'est perdre de vue le champ de sa propre existence" (Poulet, p. 9). The Marivaudian character must protect his amour-propre, for it is the only certainty he knows.

Both Marianne and Jacob are without roots. Marianne is an orphan and Jacob is a displaced peasant. They are also both essentially loners in a society where gregariousness was the order of the day. The mystery surrounding Mari-

---

4. "Marivaux," in his *Etudes sur le Temps humain*, II, *La Distance intérieure* (Paris: Plon, 1953), pp. 3–4.

anne's birth leaves her a character with no past and uncertain of her future. She repeats often that she is alone on the earth with no one to turn to. All of Marivaux's characters are in an incessant state of motion, never in one place or one state of mind for too long. Marivaux often uses the metaphor of physical displacement in order to underline this theme of uncertainty and instability. This is true not only for Marianne and Jacob, but for most of his other major fictional characters. All of the protagonists in *Les Effets surprenants de la sympathie* (1712–1713) travel from one end of the world to another. They go by sea, by land, and in whatever vehicles they can find. They are in quest of lost sweethearts, lost brothers, lost fathers, lost identities. *La Voiture embourbée* (1713) is about a group of travelers in a stagecoach who tell stories to pass the time. In *Pharsamon, ou les Nouvelles folies romanesques* (1713), the hero travels around his neighborhood looking for worlds to conquer for his Dulcinea. Finally, the *Télémaque travesti* (1714) is the story of a young man in search of his lost father.

This picaresque theme of the quest was increasingly internalized by Marivaux, until, in *Marianne* and the *Paysan*, it became one of his dominant psychological motifs. We will see in the last chapter how successful it was in Jacob's story. Marianne herself first appears in the novel in a carriage on its way to Bordeaux (p. 10). She never reaches her destination, knows nothing of her place of departure, and is left in between because of the robbery of the coach. The remainder of the story will be an attempt to discover from whence she came and where she is going. Because Marivaux never finished his novel, we cannot know whether or not Marianne ever discovered her true identity. As the book was left us, she never did. It is thus revealing to look on the older Marianne's composition of her autobiography as an attempt, through art, to recreate her past or to at least discover a means by which she may know of her origins.

We have already discussed how the older Marianne enjoys retelling her story. Affecting indifference, Marianne the narrator is as intriguing a personage as is the younger Marianne. She repeatedly tells her reader that she does not know how to write ("Où voulez-vous que je prenne un style?," p. 8; "Mais peut-être que j'écris mal," p. 57; etc.), or that she is really not interested in what she is doing (at one point, she says she left off her story "à cause que je m'endormais," p. 219). These protestations are masks, similar to those she wore as a young girl. The narrator's apparent disinterest is belied by the extraordinary detail she indulges in when she analyzes even her most minute sentiments as well as by the pains she takes to convince her readers that everything she did as a young girl was to a virtuous end.

There are several passages where the older Marianne's nostalgia shows itself temporarily. These few brief moments are enough to give her story a more serious, perhaps pathetic, tone, which once again belies the apparent joy she experiences in retelling it. At the beginning of her story, after having discussed her past successes with men, Marianne tells us: "Car à cette heure que mes agréments sont passés, je vois qu'on me trouve un esprit assez ordinaire et cependant je suis plus contente de moi que je ne l'ai jamais été" (p. 9). This is hard to believe when one considers the young coquettish Marianne, whose amour-propre was always her first concern. The narrator is aware that her beauty is past and can no longer serve to set off her other qualities. Marianne had opened her memoirs with the brief tale of the beautiful young woman who had been considered so witty and intelligent, but who, after having contracted smallpox, had lost that wit. "Voyez combien auparavant elle avait emprunté d'esprit à son visage! Il se pourrait bien faire que le mien m'en eût prêté aussi dans le temps qu'on m'en trouvait beaucoup. Je me souviens de mes yeux de ce temps-là, et je crois qu'ils avaient plus d'esprit que moi" (p. 8). "Je me souviens": this is the key to Marianne's reasons for reliving her life through the composition of her memoirs. Unhappy in the present, she searches for happiness in the past.

Later, in another brief aside, Marianne the narrator again uncovers her nostalgia: "J'ai eu un petit minois qui ne m'a pas mal coûté de folies, quoiqu'il ne paraisse guère les avoir méritées à la mine qu'il fait aujourd'hui: aussi il me fait pitié quand je le regarde, et je ne le regarde que par hasard; je ne lui fais presque plus cet honneur-là exprès" (p. 51). The remainder of the passage is a recounting of how, when she was younger, Marianne knew how to be "plusieurs femmes en une." There is little doubt that the older narrator is sorry that those days are now gone. But although her beauty may be diminished, there remains her ability to write well and to her own advantage. From the first, she insists that there is no art to what she is writing, so therefore her reader(s) should accept everything she says at face value: "Je parlais tout à l'heure de style, je ne sais pas seulement ce que c'est. Comment fait-on pour en avoir un? Celui que je vois dans les livres, est-ce bon? Pourquoi donc est-ce qu'il me déplaît tant le plus souvent? Celui de mes lettres vous paraît-il passable? J'écrirai ceci de même" (p. 9). Although the flesh is weak, the spirit remains strong. There is little difference between the younger and the older Marianne when it comes to deceiving others. The older Marianne is still in search of her past, and this is why she reconstructs her life. The book itself becomes her past.

The younger Marianne wears an impenetrable mask of naiveté and *coquetterie* throughout her story to hide and protect herself from others while she attempts to find the truth concerning her identity. In the *Cabinet du philosophe* (1734) Marivaux pointed out the confusion many feel about their existence in a passage where he questions man's search for the answers concerning his soul and its salvation. There are so many things that we cannot know, "dont la première est Nous, qui sommes une énigme à nous-mêmes" (*Journaux*, p. 354). The desire to clear up this enigma becomes one of the underlying themes of Marivaux's two greatest novels. Approached from a metaphorical point of view, Marianne's quest for acceptance by high society is in reality a quest for self-knowledge. The ambiguity between a well-developed self-awareness and a lack of self-knowledge is quite real here. Marivaux is saying that amour-propre is only one step in his characters' ultimate quest; self-awareness does not necessarily bring with it the confidence that is bred of self-knowledge. And he who so actively protects his ego is often doing it in order to ensure the one thing of which he can be certain, and not because of a confident awareness of who and what he is. It is not a point that Marivaux belabors, but it is present, and a close look at some of Marianne's remarks and actions as a young girl will illustrate it.

The older Marianne tells us very little of her childhood —only that which directly concerns her impression on those around her. She tells us that "ma naissance devint impénétrable, et je n'appartins plus qu'à la charité de tout le monde" (p. 13), and that she soon found that she would have to rely on her charms to make her way in the world. If she learned one thing during her childhood in the country, it was that "j'avais des grâces et de petites façons qui n'étaient point d'un enfant ordinaire; j'avais de la douceur et de la gaité, le geste fin, l'esprit vif, avec un visage qui promettait une belle physionomie; et ce qu'il promettait, il l'a tenu" (p. 15). The attention that she received as a child served to give birth to the belief that she was, and remains, an extraordinary girl.

But Marianne's story does not actually begin until, at the age of fifteen, she reaches Paris, where she experiences a sort of rebirth. She feels an instantaneous affinity for the city, and realizes that her quest must begin and end there. "Je ne saurais vous dire ce que je sentis en voyant cette grande ville, et son fracas, et son peuple, et ses rues. C'était pour moi l'empire de la lune: je n'étais plus à moi, je ne me ressouvenais plus de rien; j'allais, j'ouvrais les yeux, j'étais étonnée, et voilà tout" (p. 17). Paris serves to make her remember her solitude and encourages her to seek the truth of her existence. When her adopted mother is dying, the sense of solitude is reinforced: "Je tombai dans l'égarement; je n'ai de ma vie rien senti de si terrible; il me semble que tout l'univers était un désert où j'allais rester seule" (p. 21). Later, after the death of the good woman, Marianne recognizes the difficulty of her position: "J'ouvris les yeux sur mon état, et je pris de l'inquiétude de ce que je deviendrais; cette inquiétude me jeta encore mille fantômes dans l'esprit. Où irai-je . . . , je n'ai personne sur la terre qui me connaisse; je ne suis la fille ni la parente de qui que ce soit! A qui demanderai-je du secours? Qui est-ce qui est obligé de m'en donner? Que ferai-je en sortant d'ici?" (pp. 24–25). Thus, in the first few pages of the novel, Marivaux reiterates Marianne's sense of aloneness, of "statelessness." She has no roots, no identity, no future; nothing is certain in her world. That is why she is in constant movement and why she has to protect herself with her various masks while she searches for some certainty.

Marianne, in quest of this prize, takes refuge in herself. She attempts to establish some norm by which she can judge her actions and those of others. Ironically, in hiding behind the mask, she separates herself even more from those around her. *Marivaudage,* or the mask of language, is the clearest example we have of how the Marivaudian personage, because of his fear of others, separates himself from them. The irony is, of course, that he wants more than anything to become a member of the society he hides from. There is a paradox here from which the Marivaudian character never fully extricates himself. Psychologically, Marianne convinces herself of her superiority vis-à-vis her rivals, and is obviously possessed of an *esprit revendicateur:* "Je devrais sans comparaison être mieux que je ne suis" (p. 43). She continually refers to herself as being "déplacée," out of her element, and seems confused by the discrepancy between her obviously superior qualities (beauty, wit, intelligence, etc.) and her social status: "Dites-moi d'où cela venait? Où est-ce que j'avais pris mes délicatesses? Etaient-elles dans mon sang? Cela se pourrait bien; venaient-elles

du séjour que j'avais fait à Paris? Cela se pourrait encore"
(p. 33).

Paris does seem to offer her all she wants. And, although
alone and without any resources, she feels confident because of her innate feeling of equality with the people of
high society she sees riding around in the streets of Paris:
"Quand je les voyais, c'était comme si j'avais rencontré ce
que je cherchais" (p. 33). There is an affinity between Marianne and the better elements of the exterior world that
causes her to believe that she is somewhat superior to her
present social status. It is as though, during the few months
before she was orphaned, she had been a member of the
social level she dreamed of, and that the memory of these
months, no matter how faint, remains with her. Throughout the first part of the novel, she builds a system of rationalization that convinces her finally that she is definitely a
superior person, and on an equal footing with the higher
class of society. She dreams of conquering worlds and of
establishing herself in her rightful place: "Je faisais toujours des châteaux en Espagne, en attendant mieux" (p.
49); and the first part of her story ends as Marianne leaves
Mme. Dutour's establishment with high hopes, alone but
confident.

Marivaux laid great emphasis on the discovery of love by
his young characters. "La surprise de l'amour" was a test
to be passed successfully if one was to lead a satisfactory
existence in Marivaux's universe. When Marianne first experiences an attraction for Valville, she undergoes a pro-
found psychological shock, and its effects remain with her
the rest of her life. Re-creating the moment, the narrator
uses such terms as "étourdie," "confuse," "charmée,"
"troublée," "trembler," "confusion," and the like (p. 73),
which signify that, for a few brief moments, Marianne had
lost control of the situation and was frightened. But her
recovery is almost immediate: "Je me retrouvai pourtant; la
présence d'esprit me revint, et la vapeur de ces mouvements qui me tenaient comme enchantée se dissipa" (p.

73). We have seen how this is a turning point in her story, for, from here on, Marianne is a woman and must put on a mask in order to protect herself against her lover and others. It is also at this point that the mask and reality begin to become confused.

Whereas, in her relationship with Climal, Marianne had attempted to keep her "virtuous self" separate from her deception of the *dévot*, she now will find it increasingly difficult to separate her "self" from the mask that she must wear. It will be remarked that the intricate *réflexions* that are found in the first two parts of Marianne's story are not so prevalent in the remainder of the novel. Most critics have speculated that this change in narrative style was occasioned by the criticism of the first two parts or was a result of the more restrained style of *Le Paysan parvenu*, most probably written between the second and third parts of *Marianne*. But there is almost certainly a thematic reason for the difference, based on the fact that after Marianne meets Valville and experiences love for the first time, she finds it incumbent upon herself to don the mask almost incessantly. It becomes increasingly difficult for her, as well as for the narrator, to distinguish between "truth" and "reality," and she ceases her attempts to establish a distance between the "real" Marianne and the mask-wearer.

Marianne, in effect, remains alone throughout most of the novel. Although she comes closest to establishing a sincere relationship with Mme. de Miran, she spends much of her time searching for security. Paris and all its attractions, which earlier had excited her to action, now remind her of her solitude: "Plus je voyais de monde et de mouvement dans cette prodigieuse ville de Paris, plus j'y trouvais de silence et de solitude pour moi: une forêt m'aurait paru moins déserte, je m'y serais sentie moins seule, moins égarée. . . . Je ne sais où aller, on ne m'attend nulle part, personne ne s'apercevra que je lui manque; je n'ai du moins plus de retraite que pour aujourd'hui, et je n'en aurai plus demain" (pp. 134–35). She is separated completely from all those around her and wanders "inconnue sur la terre, où j'ai la honte de vivre pour y être objet, ou du rebut, ou de la compassion des autres" (p. 135). Marianne will remain on the edge of desperation throughout most of her story, and, again, the fact that this narrative has no formal terminus can but underline its pervasive tone of dissatisfaction and the theme of an unresolved quest.

The question now presents itself as to whether Marianne and Jacob succeed in their quests for identity. What price do they pay when they don the masks of *coquetterie* and subterfuge? Does their search for stability in an unstable world have a happy ending? The answer must be no. The irony of Marianne's mask-wearing is that it separates her from herself as well as from others. She loses rather than maintains her individuality. Jean Starobinski, remarking on La Rochefoucauld, explains the danger of mask-wearing: "L'homme nous était présenté [chez La Rochefoucauld] comme un malfaiteur masqué. Le voici devenu victime des forces masquées qu'il porte en lui. De simulateur, il passe à la condition de l'ignorance et de l'aveuglement. Non sans qu'il y ait sournoisement consenti: à force de se masquer devant les autres, il devient un inconnu pour lui-même."[5] Slowly, but very surely, as the Marivaudian character makes his way into the society that he so desires to conquer, he loses his individuality, if not his identity. Society continues to function in a civilized way, but a price has been paid, as is always the case when compromise is necessary.

Marianne is never fully integrated into the society that Marivaux depicts in his novel. She remains alone, separated from and unsure of her self down to the last page. The majority of the action in the novel is concerned with how Marianne attempts to define herself in terms of others. As we have seen, the Marivaudian character must be recognized in order to recognize himself. This recognition pro-

---

5. "La Rochefoucauld et les morales substitutives," *La Nouvelle Revue française*, no. 163 (1966), p. 23.

cess is never-ending, and thus the protagonist must cease-
lessly search.

Success has its price, and Marianne and Jacob pay it.
Propelled by their amour-propre and their sense of justice
(or of vindication), they attack the prejudices of their time
only to discover that they become one of the pack. They are
forced to become actors (as all social men are). They subsequently become depersonalized. Once the mask is donned
it is difficult to remove, and the longer it remains on, the
more difficult is its removal. Ironically, both Marianne and
Jacob become part of the vast social comedy without really
realizing it. Their claims to originality—their beauty, wit,
freedom of spirit, intelligence—become lost as they strive
to obtain what they desire. The mask frees the wearer, but
at the same time it imprisons him, and concretizes the
vitality of existence. "Le masque ne rougit point." It thus
dehumanizes the individual who wears it. Appearance and
reality tend to become confused and truth disappears, or is
impossible to find. The coquette who dons the mask in
order to deceive becomes herself deceived. The best example of this is the older Marianne, who attempts to dupe her
reader, and thereby dupes herself, as to why she is composing her memoirs. When the mask-wearer looks into a mirror, the mask and not reality is reflected. This is the real
comedy in Marivaux's works: the human comedy of self-
deception.

Marianne is a combination of the Tartuffe and Don Quixote heroes, two types with whom Marivaux was very familiar. The hypocrite and the idealist are both present in Marianne's actions. She feels justified in her *coquetterie* because
of her innate belief that she is a superior person. This
feeling of superiority gives her the courage to confront the
almost insurmountable obstacles that oppose her desire to
rise to her rightful social station, and she confidently sets
out to battle the prejudices of society. Her strategy is a
composite of *coquetterie* and her reliance on the gullibility of
her fellow men. She uses deception because she sees it

being used successfully by others. Only, in using it as well, she loses more than she gains. As I have remarked, there is a plaintive tone in the authorial interruptions of the narrator, which leads the reader to believe that she is not happy as "Madame la comtesse de * * *." In many ways, Marianne's victory is a hollow one, for at the end of her story, she knows no more about herself than she did at the beginning. She knows only that she is capable of deceiving those around her, and that by so doing she had achieved social prominence and recognition. However, once she has been recognized by those people she has fooled, her quest does not end. She must still find out about herself, a task made more difficult because, in deceiving others, she has simultaneously deceived herself. And she slowly disappears from the reader's view, her unfinished story standing as testimony of her fruitless quest.

In several ways, Marivaux introduced, in *La Vie de Marianne*, subtle changes in the traditional novel. He had sympathetically and seriously treated a heroine of uncertain social origins as she made her way from a village curate's home to the rank of countess. He had likewise shown, as Prévost had done in *Manon Lescaut*, that individual actions are often determined by mundane events—for example, Climal's gift of a dress and the offers of money—rather than idealistic ones. Finally, Marivaux took a long step toward the successful assimilation of the subjects of narration and its means. The adroit use of the memoir-novel and epistolary formats and of the first-person narrator in *Marianne* created a complex fictional personality and gave much-needed support and impetus to the novel as a genre.

5

Le Paysan parvenu

I

ONE OF THE PERSISTENT QUESTIONS CONFRONTING CRITICS OF
Marivaux's prose fiction concerns the composition and
publication of Le Paysan parvenu. Why did Marivaux write
the novel? And why did he stop work on La Vie de Marianne
to do so, then leave it unfinished as he took up Marianne
again? Many answers have been offered, none of which is
entirely satisfactory. Gustave Larroumet, Marivaux's first
serious biographer, suggests that Le Paysan parvenu was an
active answer to La Vie de Marianne's more reflective pace
and subject matter.[1] Marie-Jeanne Durry and F. Deloffre
both offer the interpretation that the two novels answer two
tendencies in Marivaux's prose fiction: the burlesque and
romantic, the picaresque and "galante."[2] Marcel Arland
and Robert Mauzi see Le Paysan parvenu as a direct answer to La Vie de Marianne, parodic and serious at the same

1. *Marivaux, sa vie et ses oeuvres* (Paris: Hachette, 1882), pp. 338–40.
2. Durry, *A Propos de Marivaux* (Paris: Société d'enseignement supérieur, 1960),
pp. 130–31. Deloffre, introductions to his editions of *La Vie de Marianne* and *Le
Paysan parvenu*. See also Deloffre's article, "De Marianne à Jacob: les deux sexes
du roman chez Marivaux," *L'Information littéraire* 11 (1959): 185–92, where he
suggests that the two novels are but expressions of Marivaux's tendency toward
a feminine and a masculine style.

time.[3] Claude Roy has one of the most interesting explanations, asserting that the composition of the *Paysan* is proof that "Marivaux avait échoué dans sa tentative de la *Vie de Marianne.*"[4] He is, however, unclear as to whether this failure was in thematic or formal terms. Finally, the most recent critical biographer of Marivaux, E. J. H. Greene, somewhat unconvincingly concludes that "the creative delight [Marivaux] had in representing the quarrel of [the coachman and Mme. Dutour at the end of Part II of *Marianne*] inspired him to treat the theme on a larger scale."[5] Others have suggested that Marivaux was simply tired of *Marianne* or wanted to make more money with another novel.

The most probable explanations are those of Mauzi and Roy. In 1734–35 Marivaux was still interested in experimenting with diverse narrative techniques and forms. (He had already begun to publish his *Cabinet du philosophe* a few months before the appearance of the *Paysan parvenu.*) And, on a thematic level, *Marianne* was causing him to revaluate some of the themes he had been using for two decades, and to reformulate them. More than *La Vie de Marianne*, the *Paysan parvenu* is a meld of previous narrative genres, and yet remains a truly "modern" novel. At times humorous, the novel is essentially a serious treatment of a young peasant's sentimental education in Paris. Marivaux was most likely aware that he was modernizing an established motif —the amorous adventures of a naive rustic—and yet he felt confident enough in his abilities as a novelist and moralist to try to renew this tradition. Seen in these terms, and with reference to the major themes and motifs that he had developed in Parts I and II of *La Vie de Marianne*, the *Paysan parvenu* was not a very fundamental departure from the former novel. A brief comparison will reveal certain affini-

3. Arland, *Marivaux* (Paris: Gallimard, 1950), pp. 72–74; Mauzi, "Marivaux romancier," introduction to Marivaux, *Le Paysan parvenu* (Paris: Union Générale d'Editions [10/18], 1965).
4. *Lire Marivaux* (Paris: Seuil, 1947), p. 90.
5. *Marivaux* (Toronto: University of Toronto Press, 1965), p. 187.

ties between the two works, and perhaps will clarify some of the mystery surrounding the reasons why Marivaux wrote *Le Paysan parvenu* when he did.

There are obvious and subtle similarities between Marivaux's two most famous novels. Although they differ somewhat in tone and style, and much more in length, their main thematic touchstones are analagous. Both of the young protagonists develop an early and insatiable thirst for the better things in life; they both want to "arrive." They are, at the outset, inexperienced, honest, naive, and good-looking. And they both succeed in their initial plans. They are proud and learn early to use all their attributes to the best advantage. In the end, there is little doubt that they have both compromised themselves in terms of their belief in their superiority over the mask-wearers around them. But, although they have "succeeded" in their searches for acceptance, Jacob and Marianne also tarnish their individuality.

Another important similarity between the two novels concerns the process of narration. Both are in the memoir form; however, Marivaux abandons completely the epistolary structure in *Le Paysan parvenu*. There are essentially *two* major characters in each novel: the older narrator, and the younger protagonist. The reader must accept the older narrator, as a norm adjusting his belief in what the narrator is recounting to what he knows of the narrator's reasons for composing his memoirs. As with the older Marianne, the older Jacob is well established socially and financially as he begins to reconstruct his past. It would seem that Jacob had all that he wished, and that through the composition of his memoirs he was only indulging in the pleasure of reliving his struggle to attain social acceptance. But, as with *Marianne,* there is a certain element of nostalgia that permeates the whole novel. Both narrators give the impression that they are searching for something else through the composition of their autobiographies. The book becomes more than a book; its composition becomes a justification of the narrators' lives, and its physical existence becomes proof of the author's own existence.

As in *La Vie de Marianne*, there is a discernible distance between the narrator and the protagonist in *Le Paysan parvenu*. There are many instances where Jacob, naive young peasant, expresses his feelings in a way that would have been impossible had he not had the aid of Jacob the narrator. In other words, the narrator will interpret scenes and analyze feelings with little or no attempt at informing his readers that it is not the younger Jacob who is making the judgments. This is a phenomenon inherent in most memoir-novels, as in fact it is in most nonfictional memoirs. Another important contemporary instance is found in Crébillon *fils' Les Egarements du coeur et de l'esprit* (1736–38), where Meilcour, the narrator, often imputes insights to Meilcour the protagonist that are inconsistent with the latter's status as social initiate. It is Marivaux's own particular genius that used this inherently unrealistic impediment as a thematic as well as technical structure.

Jacob the narrator's interjection of his own feelings and opinions into Jacob the peasant's story forms an essential part of the whole book. Marivaux is in reality presenting us the portraits of two people, and both have their say. The story of the older Jacob is secondary to that of Jacob the peasant, but nonetheless important. It is through his remarks on the adventures of his youth that the reader may slowly evolve a picture of a self-satisfied man who has attained his present social position through the wise use of his attributes and the manipulation of others. The technique and attitude of the narrator are not unlike those of countless self-made men—before and after 1735—who have seen fit to inform the public of their private stories of success.

From the beginning of his memoirs, the author would have us to understand that we are in the presence of an uncommonly honest man who takes pride in his openness: "Le titre que je donne à mes Mémoires annonce ma naissance; je ne l'ai jamais dissimulée à qui me l'a demandée, et il me semble qu'en tout temps Dieu ait récompensé ma franchise là-dessus; car je n'ai pas remarqué qu'en aucune occasion on en ait eu moins d'égard et moins d'estime pour moi" (p. 5). He goes on to explain his strategy, which was to confront people immediately with the truth about his birth, thereby disarming them. "Ils sentent dans ce courage-là une noblesse qui les fait taire; c'est une fierté sensée qui confond un orgueil impertinent" (p. 6).

The older Jacob is giving his readers the benefit of his accumulated experience. Older, somewhat more self-assured, the narrator forgets the humiliations that he had to undergo often as Jacob the young peasant. He has also forgotten that he too found it feasible, on occasion, to at least keep quiet about his birth (see, e.g., p. 264). But, on the whole, the strategy outlined in these paragraphs is the basic one that Jacob follows throughout his adventures. Similar to Marianne's reliance on her naiveté and honesty to effect her goals, Jacob's "openness" about his origins serves to throw his opponents off guard and allows him the freedom to say and do what he pleases. This affected honesty is reproduced as well on a stylistic level; Jacob, not unlike his creator, is eager to inform his readers that he is no author, and thus can be completely trusted and believed. Yet the careful reader soon learns otherwise. The older Jacob has a reason for writing his autobiography that becomes clearer as the story advances. He states his ostensible reasons for reliving his past at the beginning: retirement, time to kill, desire to instruct others. But as with Marianne, who also had retired from public life at the beginning of her memoirs, Jacob is in search of himself, of that other Jacob whom he so fondly describes.

Essentially, then, we may conclude that the similarities between the stories of Jacob and Marianne are more evident than their differences. However, there are some differences that must be mentioned. The most obvious is that Marianne is searching for something that she believes is

hers by right; Jacob is taking something that does not belong to him. It must also be remembered that Marianne was
a woman, and in Marivaux's universe this is very important.
She was more sensitive, more intelligent, prouder, more
cunning, more coquettish than Jacob. Yet it was easier for
Jacob to use sex as a tool to arrive, since he was a male. This
anomaly was one of Marivaux's most persistent themes,
and he used the role of women in society not only to illustrate the hypocrisy of contemporary moral expectations,
but also as an example of the necessity of compromise and
deception as positive social values. Marianne is a prototype
of Jacob; and Jacob is a parody, although a serious one, of
Marianne.

Jacob, as did Marianne, uses a series of masks as a defense as well as a weapon. He too feels that he must be
constantly on the alert against any attack on his amour-
propre. The only truth he knows is himself, and this self
must be protected at all costs. This protective mechanism
also gives Jacob the seclusion and security he needs to
discover who and what he really is. As with any man or
animal that leaves what is familiar to him for unknown
territory, Jacob feels uncertain and confused about his
place in the general structure of things. Again, we are reminded that Marivaux's characters are often in search of
something more important than social acceptance. This
extra dimension in the stories of Jacob and Marianne adds
to the complexity of the novels, and thereby to their status
as masterpieces.

Jacob was not a new character to Marivaux. In fact, he
had been outlined and developed up until the composition
of Le Paysan parvenu itself. Both Pharsamon, hero of the Don
Quichotte moderne (1712), and Brideron, hero of the Télémaque travesti (1714) may be considered precursors in some
respects of Jacob. They possessed the naive honesty and
trust that occasionally characterize Jacob. They were both
country bumpkins, led astray by too little knowledge and
titillated by the prospect of fame and fortune. This, again,

is also true of Jacob. Both Pharsamon and Brideron are part of the burlesque tradition so popular in French literature for a century, and Jacob is, to a lesser extent, a descendant of this same tradition. By the time Marivaux composed *Le Paysan parvenu*, he had developed his character to the point where the Pharsamon-Brideron influence was greatly weakened, although elements of these two early creations were still evident.

In *La Voiture embourbée*, as we have seen, there appears a young peasant, nephew of the curate, who is another prototype of Jacob. Brash, but very intelligent, he is so busy posing and attempting to impress the voyagers, that he cannot find time to eat. The narrator asserts that "la symétrie guindée dont il réglait tous les mouvements de ses mains et même de sa bouche me donna plus d'une fois envie de rire" (*O.J.*, pp. 333–34). Interest in the young man grows as he expresses his approval of the narrator's idea for an oral "roman impromptu." The narrator concludes that "je crus dans ce verbiage remarquer qu'il avait envie d'être de la partie, et comme il ne pouvait que la rendre encore plus divertissante par l'originalité avec laquelle il traiterait son sujet, je lui proposai d'être des nôtres" (p. 334). Thus, this young man, as his descendant Jacob will also do, intrigues his betters and enters, by dint of his originality, into their social circle.

A reading of *L'Indigent philosophe* (1726–27) reveals another antecedent of Jacob, perhaps the most detailed. Marivaux's philosophical hobo meets a fellow bum who takes him to a café for beer. After a few drinks, he begins his story (which covers numbers 2–4). He is the son of a drunken musician who holds that wine is the source of good music. Our bum is no musician, but he enjoys the wine. Having no profession, the musician's son becomes a soldier, a sexton, and finally joins a troupe of provincial actors, first as roustabout, then as actor. The experience makes him aware of the advantages and disadvantages of one's *physionomie*. He believes that his own face has done him a disservice, because "pour être un grand homme, il ne m'en a jamais manqué que l'air; c'est ce qui m'a dégoûté du grand, et ce qui m'a fait embrasser le genre bouffon. . . . C'est ma bouffonne de face qui me fait tort dans le monde, on ne m'a jamais pris que pour un convive. Regardez-la, cette face: si mes souliers n'ont point de semelles, c'est elle qui en est cause" (*Journaux,* pp. 293, 294). This young actor has slowly come to realize that men are judged and judge others by appearances rather than by a man's true worth. It is altogether fitting that he be in the employ of a theatrical troupe as he learns this important lesson.

The narrator, who is telling his story to Marivaux's "philosophical bum," concludes that since people thought he was a ne'er-do-well because of his face, he would then be so. "Si je suis mal chaussé et mal peigné, ce n'est pas à moi qu'il faut s'en prendre, c'est à ces hommes qui vous font perdre ou gagner votre procès sur la mine que vous portez. S'ils étaient aveugles, ils n'auraient fait que m'entendre, et ils m'auraient admiré, car je parlais d'or; mais ils ont des yeux, ils m'ont vu, et ma mine a tout perdu; *ergo,* si leurs yeux n'y voyaient goutte, leur jugement y verrait clair" (*Journaux,* pp. 294–95). So the unhappy man has allowed himself to be fashioned, even defined, by those around him. He has put up little or no resistance. When he meets the provincial lady who is impressed by his naiveté, she says "vous irez loin," thus echoing a similar pronouncement in *Le Paysan parvenu* concerning Jacob (pp. 12, 13).

Unfortunately, and characteristically, Marivaux ends his story of the musician's son here, and we do not know the outcome of his provincial adventures. We do know, though, that he becomes a "bum" and never takes advantage of the innate qualities that would have made him a success. This tale of failure must be contrasted with Jacob's success story. Although there is some doubt as to how successful, in the long run, Jacob really was, his predecessor was a failure. Marivaux was experimenting with the idea that men are defined by other men on a superficial and tenuous basis. The musician's son is incapable of combating this state of affairs; Jacob will relish the battle.

At almost the same time that he was composing *Le Paysan parvenu*, Marivaux was writing *Le Cabinet du philosophe*. In this work, we find the allegorical story of "Le Chemin de la Fortune." It will be remembered that La Verdure, another proto-Jacob, had an important decision to make concerning his future. He must jump the ditch that will lead him to Fortune's palace. But he is too weighed down by his virtues. Fortune appears, and is immediately impressed by the young man before her. La Verdure is asked why he has not jumped the ditch, and he explains that his master wishes him to marry a chambermaid, for which he will be paid a large sum of money. But he has hesitated, for he does not wish to be cuckolded by his master. Fortune's response is immediate: "Ah! le benêt! ah le sot! J'en allais faire mon enfant gâté. Allons, qu'il se retire: je ne veux plus le voir" (*Journaux*, p. 367). Later, at the end of the story, La Verdure has still not jumped, and Fortune has the last word: "Eh bien! cet honnête homme, qu'il saute, ou que le Ciel l'assiste" (*Journaux*, p. 371), but, again, the story ends before we know of La Verdure's decision.

The similarity between La Verdure and Jacob is striking, and the fact that they were contemporaries makes the comparison even more illuminating. Marivaux was again experimenting with the young peasant prototype that he had been creating since his earliest days as a novelist. Jacob would become the ideal for which Marivaux had been searching. He combines all the attributes, weaknesses, aspirations, and realism of his antecedents. With the *Paysan parvenu*, Marivaux proved finally that he was capable of manipulating tradition at will. He had "modernized" his two earlier novels, *Pharsamon* and the *Télémaque travesti*, and the result was a relatively serious treatment of a certain contemporary and realistic social context. Unlike Lesage's Gil Blas, Marivaux's Jacob is an actor as well as a spectator.

He not only moves through society, he also influences it. Unlike Brideron and Pharsamon, Jacob is not under the influence of heroic romances, but of his own personal myth. He exists in relation to others, reacting with them in a given social situation. The composition of the *Paysan parvenu* completed Marivaux's liberation from the past, and allowed him to continue more confidently with *La Vie de Marianne.*

II

The same preoccupation with mask-wearing, subterfuge, and self-deception that we found in *Marianne* is present in the *Paysan parvenu.* Jacob's weapons in his struggle to advance himself socially are numerous, and the story revolves around how he learns of these weapons and how he successfully uses them. Perhaps his most useful advantage is his good looks, for without his "bonne physionomie," Jacob could never have made it. In *La Vie de Marianne,* Marivaux's heroine felt that her noble physiognomy, her evident grace, and her refined behavior were justification enough for becoming a part of another, higher social order. Her appearance also is the best advantage she has in convincing others of what she feels to be the truth about her origins. Jacob, on the other hand, uses his appearance in a much less subtle manner. It will be his country air that first draws the attention of those he wishes to impress. "J'avais alors dix-huit à dix-neuf ans; on disait que j'étais beau garçon, beau comme peut l'être un paysan dont le visage est à la merci du hâle, de l'air et du travail des champs. Mais à cela près j'avais effectivement assez bonne mine; ajoutez-y je ne sais quoi de franc dans ma physionomie; l'oeil vif, qui annonçait un peu d'esprit, et qui ne mentait pas totalement" (p. 9).

A short while after Jacob has moved further up the social scale, he finds himself before another important lady, Madame de Ferval. He is aware that she is impressed with his appearance, and he revels in this knowledge, because there is no willful immorality in pleasing others by one's good looks. "Je crois que je plais par ma personne, disais-je donc en moi-même. Et je sentais en même temps l'agréable et le commode de cette façon de plaire; ce qui faisait que j'avais l'air assez aisé" (p. 135). As with Marianne, physical attractiveness plays an important role in Jacob's rise to the top, but with the important distinction that Marianne's beauty is *proof* of her nobility, and is the basis of self-justification as well as of her attack on society, while Jacob's attractiveness is primarily an entrée into the world of which he wishes to become a member. His pleasant appearance also serves to soothe the sensibilities of the middle and high bourgeois circles he frequents. If he had looked too much the peasant, his phenomenal successes would have been impossible. As Marivaux pointed out continually in his journals, society (high and low) believed that you *could* tell a book by its cover, and acted accordingly. Both Marianne and Jacob profited immensely from the gullibility of their soon-to-be peers.

Marivaux depicts Jacob as being a naive young man, fascinated by all that he sees in Paris. But unlike most young peasants, and similar novelistic heroes, Jacob soon learns to take advantage of his ingenuousness, and to use it as another weapon in his struggle to arrive. The apparently artless honesty of this young man seems to appeal to a society surfeited with mask-wearing and subterfuge. Of course, Jacob realizes this and makes use of the almost pathetic desire of his fellow men for a change in the hypocritical atmosphere of their closed world. His coarse foolish remarks ("bêtises") turn to his advantage, "car à travers l'épaisseur de mon ignorance, je voyais qu'elles ne nuisaient jamais à un homme qui n'était pas obligé d'en savoir davantage, et même qu'on lui tenait compte d'avoir le courage de répliquer à quelque prix que ce fût" (pp. 11–12).

As the novel progresses, Jacob comes to rely more frequently on his naiveté as a defense as well as an offense in his struggle to attain the social acceptance he desires. As in the case of Marianne, whose apparent sincerity proved so valuable, Jacob's ingenuousness, at first real, becomes progressively more structured until it can be turned off and on at will. At times it comes into play so naturally that he falls for it himself. After a scene where he was attempting to convince Mademoiselle Habert that he does indeed love her, Jacob informs his readers that he was so successful that "j'en fus la dupe moi-même" (p. 92). He had developed his naiveté to such a degree that it had almost become an entity unto itself. It is here, as we shall see later, that the mask begins to stick.

Along with his physical, and later-acquired attributes, Jacob has another advantage that enables him to achieve the success he eventually does. Perhaps it is his most important weapon. It will be remembered that Marianne, as well as Marivaux in his journals (where he asserts: "J'examinais donc tous ces porteurs de visages, hommes et femmes; je tâchais de démêler ce que chacun pensait de son lot"), believed herself capable of seeing through the masks, no matter how expertly worn, of her contemporaries. Jacob explains at one point that "cet art de lire dans l'esprit des gens et de débrouiller leurs sentiments secrets est un don que j'ai toujours eu et qui m'a quelquefois bien servi" (p. 86). In a world of mask-wearers, such a gift is invaluable, and Jacob soon becomes expert in its utilization. Marivaux, through the use of certain stylistic devices, continually reminds his readers of Jacob's ability to see through the deceptions of others. In his story "Le Voyageur dans le nouveau monde," which appeared in *Le Cabinet du philosophe*, Marivaux had illustrated how a man learned in the art of removing verbal masks could understand the true motivations of his fellows, and in many passages throughout *Le Paysan parvenu*, Jacob interprets the *truth*, for his readers as opposed to the lies that are so often uttered by his contemporaries. A few examples will suffice to give the gist of this phenomenon:

Couchons-nous, mon fils, il est tard; *ce qui voulait dire:* Couche-toi, parce que je t'aime. Je l'entendis bien de même, et me couchai de bon coeur. (p. 189, italics added)

A cette apostrophe qui me fit rougir, elle jeta un regard sur moi, mais un regard qui m'adressait un si doux reproche: Eh quoi! vous aussi, *semblait-il me dire,* vous contribuez au mal qu'on me fait?
Eh! non, madame, lui répondis-je *dans le même langage,* si elle m'entendit. (p. 207, italics added)

C'était toujours la mère qui répondait la première; ensuite venait la fille qui appuyait modestement ce qu'elle avait dit, et toujours à la fin de son discours *un regard où je voyais plus qu'elle ne disait.* (p. 210, italics added)

Il faut donc que cette dame soit folle: je crois qu'elle nous enferme! me dit alors Mme de Ferval *en souriant d'un air qui entamait la matière,* qui engageait amoureusement la conversation, *et qui me disait:* Nous voilà donc seuls? (p. 222, italics added)

Agathe avait le bras et la main passables, et je remarquais que la friponne jouait d'industrie pour les mettre en vue le plus qu'elle pouvait, *comme si elle avait voulu me dire:* Regardez, votre femme a-t-elle rien qui vaille cela? (p. 247, italics added)

There are various sorts of masks in use in these scenes. People are trying to communicate, and are succeeding, but *through* masks, not without them. No one, in Marivaux's world of subterfuge, is assured enough of his situation to dispense with the mask, and Jacob learns early to differentiate between what people *say* and what they *mean.* Not all masks, as we have seen, are used for hostile purposes, and here the women concerned have recognized that Jacob may be receptive to their *coquetterie,* and flirt covertly with him to make sure. They protect themselves with the same masks that they use offensively as coquettes.

It is clear that Jacob does not go into battle against society and its prejudices unarmed. He is naturally and intellectually endowed in such a way as to lessen the distance that separates him from those he wishes to impress. One final point should not be overlooked. Jacob has a very well-defined and very strong desire to arrive, to establish himself as an important figure in Parisian society. In his study of Marivaux, Claude Roy explains that Jacob's fascination with society is common to much French fiction. Jacob's mask-wearing is "l'attitude de celui qui, acceptant les hiérarchies et les entraves, s'en libère par la duperie, et reconnaissant l'existence des rangs et des positions sociales, s'élève au-dessus de sa situation et échappe à sa condition par la ruse, le mensonge ou la mystification."[6] Jacob *wants* to be a part of the social structure that so fascinates him, and he decides early in his story to make the necessary plans. He is a lucid, extremely imaginative and intuitive young man who does not care to analyze, or go too deeply into the true motives of his actions. He wants to arrive, and recognizes early that the way is made easier for him because of the pride and gullibility of those whom he must impress. Taking a leaf from their book, he joins in their play-acting, with one difference: Jacob knows what he is doing, and admits to his subterfuge. This sets him above those around him. The result of this play between real and feigned sincerity, between honesty and artifice, gives Jacob's story, and thus his life, a richness and excitement that could not have been attained had he remained down on the farm.

Using the mask as a weapon to arrive, Jacob has his greatest success when he confronts, and is confronted by women. The action of the novel can be divided into two major parts: Jacob's relationships with women and his parallel commerce with men (and the rest of society). It is perhaps because this is so that the *Paysan parvenu* has a reputation as a salacious novel. In fact, Jacob's only explicit sexual encounter is with Mlle. Habert, *after* their marriage,

6. *Lire Marivaux*, p. 89.

and Marivaux refers to it only tangentially. Jacob's relationships with women, though highly suggestive at times, never cross the boundary of a rather strict morality. It is a credit to Marivaux's language of suggestion that this sexually moral novel has been so long considered another product of the literary eroticism prevalent in France between 1730–50. Partially in reaction to this misconception, Robert Mauzi offers the thesis that in fact Jacob's friendship and adventures with the women in the novel are only secondary to its central theme: Jacob's social success.[7] Mauzi believes that women, in effect, contribute little (with the exception of his marriage to Mlle. Habert) to Jacob's ultimate success. Essentially, this is incorrect. The women in the novel are not present solely as "une sorte de poésie qui idéalise" Jacob's own story, but form a necessary part of the novel's psychological plot. It is through these relationships that, as Mauzi does point out, Jacob comes to develop his vanity, his amour-propre. He gains confidence and educates himself through his commerce with Mme. de Ferval and Mme. de Fécour, as well as with Mlle. Habert. And there are numerous other female personages in the novel who likewise serve to illustrate some facet of Jacob's character or who serve as guinea pigs for his experiments in using his good looks and personal charm to arrive.

The first women whom Jacob confronts are the wife of the owner of his father's vineyards, and Geneviève, her servant. This episode is worth close analysis, for it introduces the primary tone of the whole novel (and is not unlike the episode in *Marianne* that deals with Climal's gift of a dress to Marivaux's heroine). Sent to Paris to deliver some wine, Jacob enters the world of the capital in much the same way as Marianne had: "J'arrivai donc à Paris avec ma voiture et ma bonne façon rustique. Je fus ravi de me trouver dans cette grande ville; tout ce que j'y voyais m'étonnait moins qu'il ne me divertissait; ce qu'on appelle le

7. Pp. 13–14.

grand monde me paraissait plaisant" (p. 9). Later, his land-lord's wife will advise him to "rester à Paris, tu y deviendras quelque chose" (p. 11). Such a remark causes him to realize the potential advantages of his apparent naiveté and rus-ticity.

Jacob takes a position in his landlord's Paris home. Soon, because of the interest that Madame had shown in him, the young peasant acquires a certain aura of celebrity, easily impressing the servant girls of the house. He specifically directs his attention to one of them, Geneviève, who, as it turns out, will help him rehearse his ultimate conquest of Madame. At first he banters with Geneviève and relies on his apparent naiveté to impress her. He tells her that he loves her, openly and without any affection, thereby prac-ticing his mask of ingenuousness with success. That very evening, he is called to have himself fitted for the clothes of a valet. It was Madame who had ordered them, and when they arrive, Jacob tries on his new "équipage," obviously pleased with the "new" Jacob. But before going to see Madame, he decides to try out his new costume in front of Geneviève. Somewhat cynically, Jacob is willing to play with Geneviève's heart if it will add to his own high opinion of himself. He notices the effect he has had on the servant girl: "Il me parut qu'elle fut surprise de la mine que j'avais sous mon attirail tout neuf; je sentis moi-même que j'avais plus d'esprit qu'à l'ordinaire" (p. 14). (This remark is similar to Marianne's when she tells us that her beauty often aided her wit [p. 8].) Jacob has "surprised" an opponent and is aware of it, yet at the same time, almost imperceptibly, the mask has begun to stick, as the wearer begins to believe the role he is playing.

At this point, Madame summons Jacob, who leaves Gene-viève precipitously, and presents himself to the mistress of the house. Her reaction to his appearance is likewise favor-able, and Jacob immediately takes the initiative: "De sorte qu'il se passa alors entre nous deux *une petite scène muette* qui fut la plus plaisante chose du monde. . . . Je ne saurais dire dans quelle disposition d'esprit cela la mit, mais il me parut que la naïveté de mes façons ne lui déplaisait pas" (p. 15, italics added). This is another instance where the mask is used to protect the wearers, while simultaneously allowing for secretive communication. Neither wants to commit himself verbally, thus the "petite scène muette." Jacob also employs with apparent success the naiveté and rustic simplicity that become his most useful weapons. At this point, Jacob the elder interjects a comment about his youthful innocence, which shows that he has learned his lesson well: "Mes regards n'avaient rien de galant, ils ne savaient être que vrais. J'étais un paysan, j'étais jeune, assez beau garçon; et l'hommage que je rendais à ses appas venait de pur plaisir qu'ils me faisaient. Il était assaisonné d'une ingénuité rustique, plus curieuse à voir, et d'autant plus flatteuse qu'elle ne voulait point flatter" (p. 16). This authorial interjection concerning the difference between "galanterie" and "ingénuité rustique" is not deceit on the part of the elder Jacob. Rather, he is interpreting for his readers the effect, obviously desired, that his appearance had on Madame. Contrasting himself to the everyday *galant,* Jacob reiterates his reliance on the *appearance* of honesty and sincerity as effective in a society surfeited with the insincere commonplaces of *galanterie.*

After Jacob leaves the apartment of Madame, he comes to the conclusion that even though he had professed love to Geneviève, his fortune lies with the mistress of the house, and not with her chambermaid. But Geneviève still presents a problem because she took Jacob's original protestations of love seriously; she had been duped by him. To complicate matters, she allows herself to be compromised by the master of the house so that she may gain money and thus tempt Jacob into marrying her. Yet Geneviève's *coquetterie* regarding her new liaison with the landlord repulses Jacob, and he uses the word "coquetterie" in its most derogatory connotation to define Geneviève's stratagems (see, for example, pp. 17, 18, 19). In describing Geneviève's actions thus, Jacob has allowed himself to be duped once again by his own mask of sincerity and naiveté, as is evident when he solemnly preaches to Geneviève that she should not sell herself to her master. He lies both to his readers and to himself when he tells us that his concern for Geneviève is because "j'avais naturellement de l'honneur" (p. 17).

The lie becomes evident when Jacob takes the money from the servant girl, knowing that she had received it for favors granted her master. His rationalization as to why he took the money is similar to those made by Marianne in her brushes with vice: "Peut-être fis-je mal en prenant l'argent de Geneviève; ce n'était pas, je pense, en agir dans toutes les règles de l'honneur. . . . Mais je ne savais pas encore faire des réflexions si délicates, mes principes de probité étaient encore fort courts; et il y a apparence que Dieu me pardonna ce gain, car j'en fis un très bon usage; il me profita beaucoup: j'en appris à écrire et l'arithmétique, avec quoi, en partie, je suis parvenu dans la suite" (pp. 22–23). This passage typically illustrates the discrepancies that one often finds in the older Jacob's description of past events. He attempts to justify his taking money from Geneviève by saying that he was too naive to make delicate analyses of his behavior. Yet he admits that he was not unaware of the source of the money, and took it anyway. The younger Jacob is not so astute at reflecting on his actions as is the narrator, but he nonetheless is quite capable of making the decisions that will most aid him in his desire to arrive.

The master of the house soon presents Jacob with a dilemma: either he must marry Geneviève and accept a remunerative position in his household or else the master will see to it that Jacob is imprisoned indefinitely. There are two reasons that Jacob gives for not accepting what was a very favorable opportunity for a young peasant. The first, and most obvious, is that Jacob's pride will not allow him to be a cuckold. This is, at least, the reason he professes. But there is another and thematically more important reason. Jacob asks himself why he should have to accept Geneviève under these circumstances when he could have almost any other woman—the master's wife included—under more auspicious ones. After a few weeks in the atmosphere of Paris, Jacob has come to appreciate the endless possibilities that await him if he makes the most of his advantages. He has partially realized that it is possible to go much further in his social desires than a marriage to Geneviève will allow.

Immediately after this interview with his master, Jacob, in a conversation with Geneviève, reveals himself as the practiced mask-wearer that he has become. Geneviève has learned that Jacob turned down the master's offer, and she is disconsolate. But Jacob is unmoved, and tells her, in one of the novel's most ironic phrases, that "il n'y a rien de si beau que la sincérité, et vous êtes une dissimulée" (p. 33). Coming from the man who had almost encouraged her to sell herself for profit, this utterance reduces Geneviève to tears and speechlessness. Jacob continues his masquerade of surprise and indignation by insisting that Geneviève tell him the complete truth about her feelings, so that he may do the same. Geneviève is wary: "Si l'on pouvait se fier à toi. . . ." Jacob answers: "Eh! qui est-ce qui en doute? . . . Allons, ma belle demoiselle, courage," and Geneviève tells him that she took the old man's money in order to attract Jacob. Yet after she tells him that it was only through love that she did what she did, Jacob remains cold toward her: "Ce discours me glaça jusqu'au fond du coeur. Ce qu'elle me disait ne m'apprenait pourtant rien de nouveau" (p. 34). He had known all along what had motivated Geneviève, but had insisted on continuing the deception. "Je cachai pourtant à Geneviève ce qui se passait en moi," and he tells her that unfortunately "il me semble que mon coeur veut changer d'avis" (p. 34). Jacob has not too gently dropped Geneviève and has no intention of continuing their relationship. He leaves her in a state of "inquiétude," and goes to his room to make plans to leave the house if Madame cannot help him.

This episode is perhaps the most outstanding example of

Jacob's overt use of hypocrisy. It stands in contrast to his (and Marianne's) more subtle uses of the mask. There is no way to escape the fact that Jacob acted reprehensively in this matter, and Marivaux seems to have realized that he had almost boxed himself into a moral corner. The only way to extricate Jacob from this situation was through the somewhat obvious use of a *deus ex machina,* that is, the sudden and fortuitous death of the master of the house. Jacob is of course relieved by the event, because it solves his dilemma regarding Geneviève: "Hélas! la pauvre fille, le malheur lui en voulait ce jour-là" (p. 37). With this cynical understatement Jacob brings to an end his relationship with the girl, and leaves the house a free man. If Jacob learned any lesson from his tryst with Geneviève, it was that to trifle with the emotions of others was a serious business, and potentially harmful to both parties. His subsequent "fidelity" to Mlle. Habert, especially the care he takes not to hurt her amour-propre, is proof that the troubles he had had with the young chambermaid had unnerved him somewhat.

Jacob's experiences with Geneviève and her mistress are a relatively minor portion of the action of the novel. But the whole episode, coming as it does at the beginning of Jacob's story, is significant because it introduces many of the themes that will reappear later. Jacob has learned the advantage of being a naive peasant in a world where honesty is unknown. Unlike Marianne, who possessed a feeling of superiority developed after years of being told that she was someone special, Jacob developed the theory of his superiority within the few months that had passed in the house of his father's landlord. During this relatively short period of time, Jacob had reached the point where he realized that his attributes might set him apart from other men, and therefore enable him to better impose himself on them. He had also learned that the games he had decided to play were serious ones.

Perhaps the most significant woman in Jacob's quest for

social success is the younger Mlle. Habert, whom he meets, by chance, on the Pont Neuf. It is through his marriage to this good lady that Jacob is able actually to enter the social stratum immediately above his own—the lower or middle bourgeoisie. In effect, the attention of his love moves from a chambermaid to a middle-class *dévote* (since he never really established any sort of liaison with the wife of his master). And, again significantly, this relationship is consummated and officialized through marriage, although, a few years after the publication of *Le Paysan parvenu*, in 1741, Marivaux wrote a one-act play that gave a different ending to this story. Recently rediscovered in the archives of the Comédie Française, *La Commère*, which has the same characters that we find in Mme. Alain's boarding house, is primarily concerned with the marriage of Jacob and Mlle. Habert.

At the opening of the play, both lovers are planning their marriage, and, alone for a moment, Jacob exults: "Et voilà ma fortune faite!"[8] His confidence grows even more as he flirts with Agathe, daughter of Mme. Alain (the "commère" of the title), and concludes that "tout le monde est amoureux de moi" (p. 560). But things soon become confused for Jacob; a nephew of the Habert sisters (a personage not in the *Paysan parvenu*) appears and advises his aunt: "Ne vous prêtez plus à un mariage aussi riducule ct aussi disproportionné que l'est celui-ci" (p. 579). And later Mme. Alain explains to the two lovers: "Il y a une règle dans la vie; on a rangé les conditions, voyez-vous; je ne dis pas qu'on ait bien fait, c'est peut-être une folie, mais il y a longtemps qu'elle dure, tout le monde la suit, nous venons trop tard pour la contredire. C'est la mode; on ne la changera pas, ni pour vous ni pour ce petit bonhomme. En France et partout, un paysan n'est qu'un paysan, et ce paysan n'est pas pour la fille d'un citoyen bourgeois de Paris" (p. 583; compare this explanation with those that appear in *Ma-*

8. Marivaux, *Théâtre complet*, ed. F. Deloffre (Paris: Garnier, 1969), 2: 559.

rianne, pp. 184–85, 205, 297–98). In the end, the marriage is thwarted through subterfuge; Jacob is maligned and Mlle. Habert banishes him from her sight forever.

The similarities between the novel and the play are obvious; it is the differences that deserve the most attention. The Jacob of the play is almost a caricature of the Jacob of the novel: he is one-dimensional, obviously conniving, and interested solely in securing his position in society for material gain. None of the subtlety of the novel's hero is evident in this play. Why did Marivaux choose to write such a piece? There are two possible answers: first, to counter the moral criticism against the novel's rather mild licentiousness and the suggested victory of subterfuge over the standards of society; and second, to attempt a reformulation of one of his favorite themes, the role of prejudice and superstitious hypocrisy in thwarting the legitimate desires of low-born men to make something of themselves. In the play, Jacob loses his battle with the artificial values of society, but Marivaux cheats somewhat by removing much of the uniqueness of the novel's peasant, making it easier for society to triumph. Still, the lesson is clear: it takes an accomplished mask-wearer to beat hypocrisy successfully at its own game. A reading of *La Commère* only makes more salient the originality and success of *Le Paysan parvenu.*

To return to the novel, Mlle. Habert is a somewhat sympathetic creature who, next to Jacob, is the best delineated personage of *Le Paysan parvenu.* As soon as Jacob meets her, he analyzes her character through a study of her *physionomie* (p. 42), and discerns immediately that she is a "femme à directeur." This is useful knowledge (although it is uncanny that a peasant can so quickly divine this), because it lets Jacob know that Mlle. Habert is susceptible to flattery and deception, two tools of the *directeur de conscience.* An occasion soon arises that allows Jacob to use his talents to enter the good graces of this lady. She asks him what he does in Paris, complimenting him and accompanying the question with a "grand air de douceur." Jacob notices her interest and decides that "mon histoire était très bonne à lui raconter et très convenable. J'avais refusé d'épouser une belle fille que j'aimais, qui m'aimait et qui m'offrait ma fortune, et cela par un dégoût fier et pudique qui ne pouvait avoir frappé qu'une âme de bien et d'honneur. N'était-ce pas là un récit bien avantageux à lui faire? Et je le fis de mon mieux, d'une manière naïve, et comme on dit la vérité. Il me réussit, mon histoire lui plut tout à fait" (p. 44).

This recourse to "honesty" and Jacob's faith in the success of his "histoire" reminds one of Marianne's belief that her story—no matter how many times told—would cause her listeners to believe that she too was an exceptional person. And Marivaux would use this technique often when he returned to *Marianne*. Jacob, although not so often, exposes the "truth" of his situation for the same reasons. He knows that the appearance of honesty is a difficult defense to breach, and it is a most effective one. Yet, as Marianne would sometimes "orner un peu la vérité," so does Jacob in this instance. It makes his story that much more touching, and the effect is as expected. "Le Ciel, me dit [Mlle Habert], vous récompensera d'une si honnête façon de penser, mon garçon, je n'en doute pas; je vois que vos sentiments répondent à votre physionomie" (p. 44); and later, "mon enfant . . . j'aperçois une sincérité dans ce que vous me dites" (p. 45). And, finally, "je crois que votre physionomie et vos discours ne m'ont point trompée" (p. 57). The mask had succeeded once again.

By the end of the first part of his story, Jacob has not only devised a system of mask-wearing that will enable him to attain the social heights he desires; he has also applied his newly developed skills, and has succeeded. He has tasted life as it is in the city and recognized the opportunities open to him. Through an acute sensitivity to the subterfuge and play-acting that surrounds him, Jacob hopes to succeed in obtaining a station in life commensurate with his abilities. It is this extraordinary sensitivity that separates Jacob and Marianne from the other mask-wearers around them. Everyone participates in the games of Marivaux's society, yet some are more adept at it than others. Their awareness of the opinions of others as well as their loyalty to themselves often necessitate justification of their actions, and this characteristic plus the talented use of their charms make Marianne and Jacob superior to the most successful of those who would impede their progress.

As they leave the Habert home after having had a dispute with the elder sister and Doucin, the spinsters' *directeur de conscience*, Jacob and Mlle. Habert are both happy. The *dévote* has a young and handsome man who has shown an interest in her, and Jacob looks forward to the advantages inherent in such a relationship. Feeling gratitude ("reconnaissance") for the new life being offered him, Jacob puts on a mask of affection to please his friend. Eventually, he feels confident enough to speak to her of love. Again, his confidence is based on his reliance on the mask of naive rusticity that had served him so well previously. But the mask has begun to stick, as is seen when Jacob tells himself that nothing should stop him from telling Mademoiselle of his affection for her because "j'ignorais l'art des détours" (p. 76). This is just not so, and Jacob is beginning to see himself as others see him: naive, sincere, humorously honest. Continuing the use of his rustic manner as a mask, Jacob tells us that "je ne mettais pas d'autre frein à mes pensées qu'un peu de retenue maladroite, que l'impunité diminuait à tout moment, je laissais échapper des tendresses étonnantes, et cela avec un courage, avec une ardeur qui persuadaient du moins que je disais vrai, et ce vrai-là plaît toujours, même de la part de ceux qu'on n'aime point" (p. 76).

Jacob and Mlle. Habert take lodgings at Mme. Alain's boarding house. (This is where the action of *La Commère* begins.) They tell the landlady that they are cousins, and in this way Jacob enters as an initiate into the world of the middle bourgeoisie. He leaves, or attempts to leave, his peasant origins behind him. Jacob the narrator explains how this symbolic break with his past occurred. He is still dressed in the suit that his landlord's wife had purchased for him, and is subsequently taken for a relative of Mllé. Habert (p. 78). He does not dissuade Mme. Alain from thus deceiving herself. Jacob, although he professes innocence as to Mlle. Habert's intentions for him, is aware that his future is bright. It must be realized that he is no longer a social inferior, but has become an equal of Mlle. Habert, mostly through a combination of his *physionomie* and his dress. Mme. Alain treats them as though they were cousins, and Jacob is no longer a valet. Later, Mlle. Habert tells her young protégé to "régler tes manières sur les miennes" (p. 79) so that they may fool Mme. Alain even further. Jacob is thus wearing two masks here: one to fool Mme. Alain and one to deceive Mlle. Habert. He soon adds a third mask, and changes his name to M. de la Vallée, thus breaking completely with his past. The mask becomes more and more permanent as he takes his role-playing more seriously. He begins to change his speech: "Jusqu'ici donc mes discours avaient toujours eu une petite tournure champêtre; mais il y avait plus d'un mois que je m'en corrigeais assez bien, quand je voulais y prendre garde, et je n'avais conservé cette tournure avec Mlle Habert que parce qu'elle me réussissait auprès d'elle, et que je lui avais dit tout ce qui m'avait plu à la faveur de ce langage rustique; mais il est certain que je parlais meilleur français quand je voulais. J'avais déjà acquis assez d'usage pour cela, et je crus devoir m'appliquer à parler mieux qu'à l'ordinaire" (p. 85). He provisionally gives up the mask of rusticity for the greater potential of being a bourgeois, aware that he has passed an important hurdle in his quest for social acceptance and all that it entails.

While at the boarding house with Mlle. Habert, Jacob had already flirted with Mme. Alain, and his attentions had been well received. Now, at supper with Mme. Alain, her daughter, Agathe, and Mlle. Habert, there occurs one of the best scenes of the novel (pp. 86–87). Jacob manages to confront and control three women at once, all on different levels and in different ways. He has several reasons for doing this. Jacob, the *coquet*, must let no woman pass within his ken without making sure that she recognizes his presence. Only in this way can his amour-propre be satisfied. Yet there is another, more immediate purpose, too. Mlle. Habert still represents his best chance of obtaining what he wants, and he must make sure that she does not lose interest in him, but not so much as to cause her to become certain and, subsequently, angry at his deception. "De sorte que j'eus l'art de la rendre contente de moi, de lui laisser ses inquiétudes qui pouvaient m'être utiles, et de continuer de plaire à nos deux hôtesses, . . . de les maintenir dans ce penchant qu'elles marquaient pour moi, et dont j'avais besoin" (pp. 86–87). In a few short months in Paris, Jacob has learned quite a bit. His use of a woman's love for him has become more subtle, but no less deceptive.

Jacob continues to disguise his true feelings behind a mask of ingenuousness and honest sentimentality. As did Marianne, although not so often, he uses tears, or the appearance of tears, to effect a desired response in his listener. Yet, once more, as had happened before with Marianne and with Jacob himself, the mask deceives the wearer: "Je fis si bien que j'en fus la dupe moi-même" (p. 92). The word "dupe" is used with all its connotative power here, for the elder Jacob intends for his readers to know that what happened was quite serious. The confusion continues to grow between mask and reality. But Jacob has not yet overcome all obstacles to his intended marriage to Mlle. Habert, and the union is temporarily thwarted by the elder Habert sister and Doucin, her *directeur de conscience* (pp. 105–9). As a consequence, Jacob is called to appear before an important Parisian magistrate, *M. le président de* * * *. Like Marianne, Jacob must pass the supreme test of acceptance by an arbiter of social respectability. He realizes the necessity for this appearance, and calms his lover's fears: "Non, mademoiselle, lui dis-je alors, je ne crains rien (et cela était vrai)" (p. 122). (By this point in his memoirs, the narrator obviously deems it necessary, through such parenthetical expressions, to assure the reader whenever Jacob is *really* being honest.)

The first thing the young peasant does on entering the room where he will be judged is to survey, quickly and expertly, all those present. His eyes go first to the magistrate's wife, whose composure reassures him. He approaches the *président* himself, and answers his first questions simply and calmly, though he adds that "je m'observai un peu sur le langage, soit dit en passant" (p. 126). The mask has been placed on once again. There follows a lengthy exchange between the magistrate, his wife, the elder Habert sister, and others as sides are drawn up. During these preliminaries, Jacob remains mostly silent, and with reason: he is gathering his forces for the summation of his cause. He is also trying to win his audience before he makes his plea: "J'avais jeté de fréquents regards sur la dame dévote, . . . qui y avait pris garde, et qui m'en avait même rendu quelques-uns à la sourdine" (p. 129). Then he turns his eyes again on the magistrate's wife "d'une manière humble et suppliante. J'avais dit des yeux à l'une: Il y a plaisir à vous voir, et elle m'avait cru; à l'autre: Protégez-moi, et elle me l'avait promis; car il me semble qu'elles m'avaient entendu toutes deux, et répondu ce que je vous dis là." And, finally, he turns his attention to the curate, who was also present: "M. l'abbé même avait eu quelque part à mes attentions; quelques regards extrêmement honnêtes me l'avaient aussi disposé en ma faveur; de sorte que j'avais déjà les deux tiers de mes juges pour moi, quand je commençai à parler" (p. 130). Jacob has played three roles in this brief scene, all in preparation for his final speech: he has been coy with the *dévote*, humble with the wife of the magistrate, and sincere with the priest. It is an outstanding performance, amusingly reminiscent of the supper scene with the three women discussed above, revealing that by this time Jacob is fully confident of the success that the "honest" retelling of his tale will have.

Yet another weapon that Jacob uses in his summation is

substituted for the mask of rustic honesty that served him
so well previously. This is his knowledge of the origins of
most of those present. Mlle. Habert has already told him
that her father had been a *paysan parvenu* also. Addressing
himself to the elder Habert sister, who vehemently opposes
the marriage, Jacob naively asks if this is not true. And, if
so, then were not his daughters just as guilty as Jacob of
"arrivisme"? Jacob has willingly removed his mask of rus-
ticity, and has ostensibly presented himself to his judges as
just another *arriviste* who is trying to make his way in their
inhospitable world. Speaking of his affair with Mlle. Habert, he says: "J'allais être mendiant sans elle [Mlle Habert];
hélas! non pas le même jour, mais un peu plus tard, il aurait
bien fallu en venir là ou s'en retourner à la ferme; je le
confesse franchement, car je n'y entends point finesse" (p.
132). Yet, here again, he is in effect lying, for he is developing this frankness about why he befriended Mlle. Habert
into another mask, which he uses to remove the masks of
his opponents. This straightforward approach is successful,
and, as Jacob finishes, "la compagnie se tut, personne ne
répondit," and the magistrate almost plaintively asks: "Que
voulez-vous que je fasse en pareil cas?" (p. 133). There is
really nothing that anyone can do, for Jacob, with enviable
prescience, has found his bourgeois audience's most vul-
nerable secret, changed his tactics accordingly, and come
away victorious. This brief vignette of the sensibilities of
the upper-class bourgeoisie is indicative of the modernity
of Marivaux's novel.

   This scene occurs almost exactly in the center of the
novel, and is analagous to a similar scene, written about
two years later, in Part VII of *La Vie de Marianne*. Yet,
whereas Marianne's brilliant defense of herself would serve
as the culmination of her quest for social acceptance, Jacob's speech before the magistrate and Mlle. Habert's
family is but the beginning of his most difficult social tests.
This is one of the essential differences between the two
novels: Marivaux wanted to show that even with the im-

primatur of society, Jacob's success is dependent just as much on chance and circumstances as on his savoir-faire. Marianne's universe was much more closed than Jacob's. In fact, the majority of her dealings were with one family, whereas Jacob moves back and forth through several layers of society. Marianne, being a virtuous young woman (unlike Manon Lescaut or Moll Flanders), could not so easily move through society, and Jacob becomes thereby an attempt on Marivaux's part to impart a certain universality to the character of the *parvenu.*

The remainder of the novel's action is almost frenetic compared to the first half. Jacob's possibilities are unlimited, but so are the potential dangers. There are no longer only *directeurs de conscience* like Doucin in his way, but noblemen and more experienced men of the world. In this second half of the book, Jacob undergoes much more humiliation and knows more acutely the fear of being unmasked as he makes his way to success and acceptance. And the novel ends somewhat more ambiguously than would *Marianne,* as Jacob realizes the tenuous nature of his apparent success.

Jacob's continued rapid rise to social prominence, after his successful "trial," begins with a new liaison that he establishes with Mme. de Ferval, the *dévote* he had been flirting with during his interview. She tells him that he is as good-looking as she had heard, and in a tête-à-tête, the two new lovers carry on a complicated series of maneuvers that end with Jacob's verbal infidelity to Mlle. Habert. Mme. de Ferval asks bluntly if Jacob really loves Mlle. Habert, or is he only being friendly to her because of what she has done for him? Jacob is presented temporarily with a moral problem here. He wants to keep Mme. de Ferval interested, but at the same time he does not wish to be unfaithful to Mlle. Habert, "car j'aimais Mlle Habert, du moins je le croyais" (p. 136). But how was he to continue his game with Mme. de Ferval if he did not forsake Mlle. Habert? Should he tell her that he loves the old spinster?" Comme je n'étais pas de caractère à être un effronté fripon, que je n'étais même tout au plus capable d'un procédé faux que dans un cas de cette nature, je pris un milieu que je m'imaginai en être un, et ce fut de me contenter de sourire sans rien répondre, et de mettre une mine à la place du mot qu'on me demanderait" (p. 136). And Mme. de Ferval is pleased with his nonresponse.

This passage illustrates the tenebrous world of virtue and vice in which Jacob and Marianne live. Jacob has in fact duped three people in this scene. He is obviously being unfaithful to Mlle. Habert, whether she knows it or not. Even though he admits that he *may* love her, Jacob still recognizes that Mme. de Ferval is interested in him and he wishes to make the most of a promising situation. He is also duping this latter *dévote*, for though she is primarily interested in Jacob sexually and takes pleasure in seducing him, the peasant hides the pleasure *he* receives from having such an influential woman flirt with him. Clearly, although Jacob is giving Mme. de Ferval what she wants, he is getting much more in return. Finally, Jacob is duping himself into believing that he is in full control of the situation. He uses what he calls a "milieu" that will allow him to tell Mme. de Ferval what she wants while at the same time remaining faithful to Mlle. Habert. But his "milieu" soon gets out of hand and he becomes the "effronté fripon" that he did not wish to believe himself to be. Finally, he contractually kisses her hand, thereby establishing another liaison based on a combination of sexual attraction and *reconnaissance.*

Notwithstanding this new affair, Jacob soon marries Mlle. Habert, a scene only briefly described by Marivaux (p. 162), a writer who very rarely depicts the marriage ceremony in either his prose or dramatic work. The first gift Jacob wants, and receives, from his new wife is clothing. He asks for a sword and a *robe de chambre,* the two items that the still somewhat naive peasant identifies with men of the world. He receives even more than he hoped for: "Cette soie rouge me flatta; une doublure de soie, quel plaisir et quelle magnificence pour un paysan! . . . Le coeur me battait sous la soie" (pp. 166–67). Before going down to dinner, our narrator exults: "J'eus la joie de voir Jacob métamorphosé en cavalier" (p. 167). Jacob is certain now that he has it made, and that the clothes, another mask, will help him even further in his constant quest for more recognition, for, as he says, "j'étais bel homme, j'étais bien fait, j'avais des grâces naturelles, et tout cela au premier coup d'oeil" (pp. 167–68).[9] Dressed in his new clothes, Jacob goes to visit Mme. de Ferval again to convince her of his willingness to have an affair with her.

Before leaving Mme. de Ferval's apartment, Jacob meets the last woman who will be of direct service to him in the novel: Mme. de Fécour. She can be of great aid to Jacob in his search for social and financial security, as Mme. de Ferval explains (p. 179). In a very detailed portrait (pp. 179–81), Jacob again proves himself an excellent interpreter of social types. He penetrates her social disguises, and through a series of nuances, hints, and gestures, Mme. de Fécour eventually becomes the "dupe de [la] mascarade" of Jacob (p. 183), agreeing to aid him through her influence at court. When he leaves the two women, Jacob is supremely self-confident and feels that he has changed completely into a respectable bourgeois gentleman (pp. 187–88).

However, after a few upsetting adventures, which expose his vulnerability to those more accomplished than he at the games of society, Jacob concludes that his "métamorphose était de trop fraîche date" (p. 241), and that he must be more careful in future confrontations if he does not wish to lose all that he has so far gained. To compound this feeling of helplessness and insufficiency, Jacob had also lost Mme. de Ferval, for whom he had in fact some feeling (pp. 229–30), through a series of faux pas, as well as Mme. de Fécour, whom he leaves in the final stages of a serious illness. So

9. This scene is reminiscent of the one in Part I of the novel where Jacob tries his new livery on Geneviève before appearing in Madame's chamber.

he returns home to his trusting wife to regroup his forces and to continue to imitate "la contenance d'un honnête homme chez soi" (p. 250).

Jacob had decided to play the role of *honnête homme* to the hilt, and his innate imitative ability became reality. As happens so often in Marivaux's works, his characters confuse —"successfully"—reality with role-playing. Jacob wears the costume of another social level and he has become someone else—M. de la Vallée. After having used not a small number of women to satisfy his ego and to help him in his quest for social acceptance, Jacob has, in fact, arrived. As we shall see later, the sword that Mlle. Habert had given him will serve to open even more doors for him. Each woman—the *seigneur*'s wife, Geneviève, Mlle. Habert, Agathe, Mme. Alain, the *président*'s wife, Mme. de Ferval, and Mme. de Fécour—has whetted his taste for public approbation and wealth. On this one level, it can be said affirmatively that Jacob arrives through his manipulation of women and of their desires, although in so doing he eventually becomes equally a victim of the deception he so artfully practices.

Most of Marivaux's major characters are aware of the tenuous nature of their holds on society. They are aware that mask-wearing is dangerous, for the mask can be removed by the adept, or can fall without warning. Although they are generally confident of their abilities to fool others, Marianne and Jacob are constantly on the defensive, protecting what they have gained and hiding their real selves from those who deal with them. This is especially true in Jacob's case whenever he confronts those who are not so easily swayed by his rustic charm and insinuating sexuality. When Jacob meets the landlord of his village for the first time, he is intimidated. Although he has experienced some success with the landlord's wife, he is aware that this man controls the money and much of the power of the home. And, in fact, he does offer Jacob an attractive proposition: marriage to Geneviève and financial support from him, as long as he retains the *droits de seigneur* (this latter point being hinted at instead of openly mentioned). This offer presents Jacob with his first, and most important, moral choice. His reaction is understandable: "Je savourais la proposition: cette fortune subite mettait mes esprits en mouvement; le coeur m'en battait, le feu m'en montait au visage. N'avoir qu'à tendre la main pour être heureux, quelle séduisante commodité! N'était-ce pas là de quoi m'étourdir sur l'honneur?" (p. 26).

Jacob, during his brief stay in Paris, had by now learned that he had certain advantages that enabled him to impress women. He had almost seduced the master's wife, as well as Geneviève. He has smelled success and its possibilities, and knows that a marriage to Geneviève would not take him so far as he wanted. Thus, Jacob had made up his mind before even seeing his master, and although so much real money tempts him, he resists. The narrator ostensibly explains why, saying that it was his pure peasant honor that kept him from accepting the *seigneur*'s proposition (p. 27). This is obviously not true; Jacob in fact tells us soon after that honor is useful only when it is evident to others ("c'est avoir de l'honneur en pure perte que de l'avoir à l'hôpital; je crois qu'il n'y brille guère," p. 27). His reliance on "honneur," then, in his long conversation with the master, is mainly an excuse to avoid having to marry Geneviève. Just as Marianne would often do with frankness, Jacob has subverted honor to his own purposes, and the technique partially succeeds. (This episode also reveals the ambiguous position of the narrator, that is, how to continue his affected mask of disinterested honesty, while simultaneously, and nostalgically, justifying his actions as a youth.) Luckily, the master dies before his threat of marriage or jail can be effected, and Jacob is safe. He will learn from this experience that one mask is often not enough to deal with the complications of social commerce.

His subsequent dealings with those elements of society impervious to his physical charms are similar in that they all illustrate stages in Jacob's education as a man of the world. One scene is especially significant because Marivaux uses a similar episode later to illustrate Jacob's metamorphosis into an *honnête homme*. Passing through an alley, Jacob notices a man running past him in a great hurry. The man drops his sword at Jacob's feet. The peasant almost mechanically picks it up, performing one of the key symbolic actions of Jacob in the novel (p. 144). Only gentlemen or adventurers wore swords as a normal part of their attire during Marivaux's time, and Jacob is obviously not among the former. A crowd of bystanders, on seeing him emerge from an alley, sword in hand, suspect him immediately of being a thief or a murderer, and he is immediately arrested and incarcerated by the police, who were chasing the original owner of the sword. This scene is in obvious contrast to the one at the end of the book where Jacob, sword in hand again, leaps from a carriage and runs to the aid of a nobleman in distress. Marivaux uses the first episode to illustrate the fact that Jacob is not yet "educated" enough to wear a sword nor to hide the "air effaré" that he had—that is, his mask has not yet become permanent. He is still a peasant, and has not yet assumed completely the role of *honnête homme*. The time will come soon, though, when Jacob does attain the necessary savoir-faire. When Mlle. Habert buys new clothes for him, he will ask for a sword ("avec cela, tous les honnêtes gens sont vos pareils," p. 165). The mask will become almost inseparable from the real Jacob. But his first experience with a sword had been almost disastrous, and once again he must have realized that carelessness on the part of a mask-wearer could be fatal to his attempts at subterfuge.

The scene also serves to illustrate another favorite theme of Marivaux: his belief in the basic gullibility of all men. As seen above, when Jacob first appeared with a sword, everyone considered him a miscreant. After he is freed from prison (with the aid of Mme. de Ferval), he asks to be returned to the same neighborhood so that he may rehabilitate himself. Jacob, Mlle. Habert, and Mme. de Ferval take the latter's coach to the street where Jacob had been arrested. All those who had formerly believed him to be a thief now see him in a different light, since he is riding in a handsome coach with two ladies at his side. Such comments as "il a la meilleure physionomie du monde," "si jamais quelqu'un a eu la mine d'un innocent, c'était vous assurément" (p. 159) form a contrast to what the same people had thought only a few hours before. Marivaux thus returns to his favorite theme of man's reliance on external appearances as an indication of truth. This basic inability of men to distinguish between truth and appearance is what enables such adept mask-wearers as Marianne and Jacob to succeed so well in their deception.

Another key scene that describes Jacob's relations with the hostile forces of society takes place during the trip that he makes to Versailles to have an interview with Mme. de Fécour's brother-in-law. Jacob is uncomfortable, and not sure how to act in the coach with his three male companions: "Comme je n'étais pas là avec des madames d'Alain, ni avec des femmes qui m'aimassent, je m'observai beaucoup sur mon langage, et tâchai de ne rien dire qui sentît le fils du fermier de campagne; de sorte que je parlai sobrement, et me contentai de prêter beaucoup d'attention à ce que l'on disait" (p. 190). This is the remark of a man unsure of himself. He must be constantly on his guard so that the occasion would not arise where he had to talk at any length. The very rigid mask of appearances must remain firmly in place. Garrulous with women, Jacob realizes that what passed for naiveté with them may be considered only ignorance by his present companions. He succeeds in speaking little and listening well until the coach reaches Versailles, where Jacob hastens to present to M. de Fécour the letter his sister-in-law had written. He finds his potential benefactor a vain, busy, and impolite man who pays little attention

to Jacob's request for employment. The peasant is very ill
at ease, once again uncertain how to react. To make things
worse, M. de Fécour has guests whose manners are similar
to those of their host. They stare at Jacob as if he were a
curiosity, and Jacob confesses that "j'étais pénétré d'une
confusion intérieure." Although he acquits himself well
before these Versailles hangers-on, Jacob is again reminded of the differences that separate him from the world
he wishes to join.

These differences are aptly underlined in a subsequent
scene. Just as Jacob is about to consummate his plans to
seduce Mme. de Ferval, a gentleman enters unexpectedly.
Jacob, at first indignant, places his hand on his sword and
threatens the intruder. But the nobleman (who knew Jacob
from the *seigneur*'s house) looks at him as if he recognized
him. Suddenly he cries out, remembering Jacob as a former
valet (p. 226). This scene demonstrates very well the confusion and sense of vulnerability that arise when one is unmasked. Jacob is at a complete loss for words, and acts
mechanically in response to the nobleman's remarks:
"Pour moi, je n'avais plus de contenance, et en vrai benêt
je saluais cet homme à chaque mot qu'il m'adressait; tantôt
je tirais un pied, tantôt j'inclinais la tête, et ne savais plus
ce que je faisais, j'étais démonté. . . . Tout cela m'avait
renversé" (p. 226). It is a very serious situation, and, as we
shall see later, brings Jacob to question his very identity. He
forgets who he really is, so abrupt is his unmasking.

As for Mme. de Ferval, she is no better off than Jacob, for
she has been caught in a compromising situation with a
former valet. Jacob leaves immediately, but she must remain alone with the unscrupulous gentleman. Marivaux, in
a not-too-clever but quite traditional way, allows us to witness the ensuing scene. It would seem that the thematic
importance of the conversation between Mme. de Ferval
and the intruder outweighed any concern for the obviously
contrived situation whereby Jacob is allowed to spy on the
couple from a peephole in an adjoining room. Mme. de

Ferval, now that she can no longer sustain her mask as a *dévote*, must replace the mask of devotion with other masks, and it is this process that Jacob witnesses. In a relatively lengthy scene, she plays the role of an accomplished coquette, lying to and flirting with the nobleman (pp. 233– 40). Although she speaks lightly and scornfully of the peeping Jacob, he cannot but admire her agile success in turning a difficult situation into a very favorable one. Again Marivaux's hero is reminded that the accomplished maskwearer must always be on his guard, and must never allow himself to be put at a disadvantage by another person.

Jacob's struggle receives an incalculable lift in the last pages of his story. Returning from a visit with a woman whom he had met at Versailles, Mme. d'Orville, Marivaux's hero is offered the occasion to use his newly acquired sword. The chance presents itself after Jacob had gone through a period of intense self-examination. He had met several more people who had shown their interest in him and in his character. He is well ensconced in his role as an *honnête homme*, enjoying the pleasures of middle-class living. He had met and wooed Mme. d'Orville, a young, beautiful, and influential woman, who, although remaining faithful to her husband, has shown Jacob that a woman does not have to be a fifty-year-old *dévote* in order to fall for his charms. Jacob had become more sure of himself, more vain, and more convinced of his own superiority.

As he is leaving Mme. d'Orville's home, Jacob notices a young man beset by three others in a sword fight. He tells us that his reaction was almost immediate: "Le danger où je le vis et l'indignité de leur action m'émut le coeur à un point que, *sans hésiter et sans aucune réflexion*, me sentant une épée au côté, je la tire, fais le tour de mon fiacre pour gagner le milieu de la rue, et je vole comme un lion au secours du jeune homme en lui criant: Courage, monsieur, courage!" (p. 251, my italics). He jumps into the fray, and, even though he had never held a sword before in battle, acquits himself well through courage and a sense of duty.

The two men, after having chased away the others, are followed by a crowd who had watched the battle, and Jacob is bursting with pride: "Oh! c'est ici où je me sentis un peu glorieux, un peu superbe, et où mon coeur s'enfla du courage que je venais de montrer et de la noble posture où je me trouvais. . . . Je n'étais plus ce petit polisson surpris de son bonheur, et qui trouvait tant de disproportion entre son aventure et lui. Ma foi! j'étais un homme de mérite, à qui la fortune commençait à rendre justice" (p. 252). This time he had used a sword, and was being admired, rather than chased, by another crowd.

Almost unable to believe it himself, he tells his readers that the man whose life he saved is the nephew of the prime minister. Although he is really surprised at his good fortune, it would be well to look more closely at Jacob's reasons for acting as he did. He has said that he went to d'Orsan's aid "sans hésiter et sans aucune réflexion," and that it was for him almost a natural thing to do. F. Deloffre, in his introduction to *Le Paysan parvenu,* comments on this action, concluding that "plus qu'en refusant d'épouser Geneviève ou de succéder à d'Orville, c'est en secourant sans calcul un homme attaqué dans la rue [que Jacob] se distingue du lot des arrivistes trop prudents, qu'il se rend en un mot digne de son destin" (Introduction, p. xxi).

There is an element of intuition in both of Marivaux's major characters that separates them from others in their class. But Jacob does not act by intuition alone, and Deloffre's moral judgment that such an action reveals a basic goodness in Jacob's character does not give full credit to the peasant's savoir-faire. Before he jumped into the fray, Jacob had clearly noticed that the young man he was to aid had "une très belle figure" and was "fort bien mis" (p. 250). Later, he remarks that he must assuredly be an "honnête homme" because he looked so much like one. Jacob, therefore, knows that he is helping someone who is a gentleman. Also, Jacob, at the time of the fight, was at a certain

psychological point of self-confidence in his own abilities
and was anxious to prove finally that there was a difference
between Jacob and M. de la Vallée. Thus, although Deloffre's observations are correct, they only go so far. One must
take into account that *nothing* that Jacob or Marianne does
is without reason. The results of their actions may often
bring temporary setbacks, but they continue to analyze every situation and possibility before acting. Their actions
generally reflect the results of a concentrated desire to
succeed, to receive something worthwhile for their efforts.
Jacob's decision to aid d'Orsan is not entirely an "acte
gratuit," as Deloffre suggests, but the result of a series of
decisions and an intuition that have enabled him to advance
as far as he has.

D'Orsan tells Jacob that henceforth he will aid the young
man in whatever endeavor he wishes to undertake. Jacob
realizes the possibilities open to him: "Me voilà donc côte
à côte de mon ami de qualité, et de pair à compagnon avec
un homme à qui par hasard j'aurais fort bien pu cinq mois
auparavant tenir la portière ouverte de ce carrosse que
j'occupais avec lui" (pp. 261–62). Later, he adds, "la hau-
teur de mon état m'éblouit" (p. 262). But, in ending the last
part of his novel, Marivaux is not to leave Jacob on this
plateau of security. The story of Jacob will end on an ambiguous note, concomitant with the whole theme of ambiguity that characterizes both novels.

D'Orsan wants to take Jacob to the Comédie. On the way
to the theater, he questions Jacob about himself. Once
again, as in the carriage scene on his voyage to Versailles,
Jacob feels insecure, so he decides to speak as little and as
simply as possible:

> Je remerciai donc dans les termes les plus simples; ensuite:
> Mon nom est la Vallée, lui dis-je; vous êtes un homme de
> qualité, et moi je ne suis pas un grand monsieur; mon père
> demeure à la campagne où est tout son bien, et d'où je ne fais
> presque que d'arriver dans l'intention de me pousser et de

devenir quelque chose, comme font tous les jeunes gens de province et de ma sorte (et dans ce que je disais là, on voit que je n'étais que discret et point menteur) (p. 264).

But Jacob has lied, and he knows it. He has again "decorated the truth" ("orné la vérité"), and thus placed himself in the same category as those who lie not only to others, but also to themselves. A similar example of Jacob's tendency to deceive some people concerning his origins had taken place at Versailles. M. Bono, a bourgeois who offered to help him, had asked the *parvenu* who he was. Jacob answered: "Le fils d'un honnête homme qui demeure à la campagne, répondis-je. C'était dire vrai, et pourtant esquiver le mot de paysan qui me paraissait dur" (p. 216). His admonitions to those who hide their origins, so confidently expressed at the beginning of his memoirs, become meaningless, and the deceptions of protagonist and memorialist merge temporarily.

When Jacob and d'Orsan reach the Comédie, Jacob becomes even more unsure of himself. He tries to hide his uneasiness behind a mask of indifference, but he is uncertain of his ability to do so, so frightened is he. Putting it succinctly, Jacob realizes that "j'y avais sauté trop vite" (p. 265). He is convinced that d'Orsan's friends have seen behind his mask of apparent disinterest; he does not know how to answer even their simplest questions; he ridicules himself for having the effrontery to pass himself off as anyone else but Jacob. He is experiencing the fear common to all those who wear masks, that they will be unmasked and humiliated before everyone. Marivaux is saying that there is never absolute security for the one who chooses to join the game of mask-wearing. The art becomes increasingly subtle, more and more layers of masks must be donned, and there can be no reneging on the commitment to subterfuge that Jacob had willingly made. As his story ends, Jacob is led onto the stage of the theater to take his seat. There could be no more appropriate ending to Jacob's memoirs. The actor has come home.

At the conclusion of this study of how Jacob arrives, we realize that Jacob had indeed achieved most of what he set out to obtain on his arrival in Paris. He had acquired money and all it brings: position, a wife, and important friends. He had also become more self-confident and more assured of his own worth. He had used subterfuge and a certain amount of boldness to confuse and convince those whom he wished to impress. He had used the mask to arrive. But the use of the mask also had its price, and Jacob had paid it.

III

As the analysis of Marianne's story showed, the mask can be used for other reasons than to dupe others. Although mask-wearing is the primary offensive weapon in Jacob's arsenal, it is also important as a defense. And though Marivaux's main story line in *Le Paysan parvenu* is how an extraordinary peasant breaks all social barriers to achieve acceptance by those who arbitrarily fix those artificial barriers, there are, likewise, corollary themes that he wished to examine.

Jacob uses the mask to defend himself, to hide his true feelings and thoughts. As we saw in the last pages of his story, he was making an immense effort to disguise his apprehension: "C'était une confusion secrète de me trouver [à la Comédie], un certain sentiment de mon indignité qui m'empêchait d'y être hardiment, et que j'aurais bien voulu qu'on ne vît pas dans ma physionomie, et qu'on n'en voyait que mieux, parce que je m'efforçais de le cacher" (p. 265). This fear that all of Marivaux's characters have that they are on the verge of being discovered is the reason for the extreme care that Jacob (and Marianne) takes to protect his amour-propre. Since his story is shorter than Marianne's, and since the emphasis of the memoirs is on *how* he arrived, we find less direct reference to the significance of this phenomenon in Jacob's personality, but it is still present.

From the beginning of his story, we find that Jacob is not unaware of the role that pride plays in the lives of his fellow men (pp. 5–7). But unlike Marianne, Jacob was not educated from birth in the belief that he was an extraordinary person, perhaps even of noble birth. He must *educate himself* —before the readers' eyes—as to his own superiority, and he does so. His encounters with Geneviève and her mistress give his ego its first sense of superiority. He realizes that people are impressed by him and by his ways. Later, he even comes to his own defense when M. Doucin, the *directeur de conscience* of Mesdemoiselles Habert, tells him that he should leave their service. Doucin attempts to flatter Jacob (who had previously overheard the priest's denunciation of him) so that he will leave of his own free will, but Jacob resists, although somewhat heavy-handedly (p. 69). He had already gained enough confidence to fight back, and to protect himself from the attacks of those who would deprive him of what he wants. As his social position becomes more and more secure, his sense of pride, that indelible mark of nobility, becomes more developed. He learns to blush whenever his cover is removed, while always managing to respond to the attempts of those who would injure his pride. Soon, Jacob is as adept at protecting his amour-propre with a mask as he is at using the same mask to fool others.

After he has been assured of Mlle. Habert's love, of her financial support, and of her hand in marriage, his vanity causes him to turn to others for affection. His affairs with Mesdames de Ferval and de Fécour, although somewhat helpful in his quest for social acceptance, feed his amour-propre and give him more confidence in his abilities. As he says, concerning Mme. de Fécour's advances: "En fait d'amour, tout engagé qu'on est déjà, la vanité de plaire ailleurs vous rend l'âme si infidèle, et vous donne en pareille occasion de si lâches complaisances!" (p. 136). Again, there is a reminiscence here of La Rochefoucauld's dicta that even such strong feelings as fidelity and love are subjugated when one's amour-propre demands to be heard.

As we noticed with Marianne, Jacob is a person whose amour-propre, after it becomes more developed, needs constant satisfaction and attention. Many of the actions of Jacob and Marianne are invented to obtain recognition of their worth by others. Perhaps one of the most puzzling actions of Jacob is his apparently gratuitous act of generosity at Versailles. It will be remembered that Jacob had gone to Versailles with a letter of recommendation from Mme. de Fécour to her brother-in-law. Jacob is given a job, which turns out to be that of a certain M. d'Orville. D'Orville had been ill for a long time, and his wife appears on his behalf before Fécour, begging that her husband be reinstated. Fécour is unmoved, and dismisses the case. But Jacob intervenes and offers not to take the position offered him if it means making the d'Orvilles (and especially Madame) unhappy. Jacob then leaves a surprised Fécour in the company of a grateful Mme. d'Orville.

There is no evidence that this act of generosity was in any way intended to impress Mme. d'Orville so that Jacob could use her as he had other women. After all, Fécour was in a much better position than the wife of a minor court functionary to aid Jacob. Yet this action is not entirely out of character, for it helps restore Jacob's self-confidence. As we have seen, the whole trip to Versailles had been traumatic for him, and after arriving at court, he once again had felt completely out of place. He was almost openly scorned by Fécour and his friends. The former, before offering Jacob the position, mockingly commented to his friends: "Voilà le cinquième homme, depuis dix-huit mois, pour qui ma belle-soeur m'écrit ou me parle, et que je place" (p. 205). Blushingly, Jacob finally accepted the promise of a job, learning from the experience once more that there is never any respite for the insecure mask-wearer.

When the occasion suddenly arose for Jacob to perform a generous act, he did so almost without thinking. He noticed that M. de Fécour had been completely unmoved by Mme. d'Orville's story, and thus Jacob's act of generosity becomes proof of his own superiority over Fécour and his friends. Speaking of Mme. d'Orville's plea, Jacob tells us: "Je ne doutai pas un instant que M. de Fécour ne se rendît; je trouvais impossible qu'il résistât: hélas, que j'étais neuf! Il n'en fut pas seulement ému" (pp. 206–7). And when Jacob offers to relinquish his newly won position, he notices that M. de Fécour is not at all pleased, but somewhat shocked: "Il trouva mauvais que je me donnasse les airs d'être plus sensible que lui" (p. 208). Yet Jacob had succeeded in impressing—and surprising—those who believed themselves superior to him. His amour-propre had been appeased, and after the humiliation he had just undergone, Jacob was satisfied with himself and with his action: "Il y a de la douceur à se sentir vertueux; de sorte que je suivis ces dames [Mme. d'Orville and her mother] avec une innocence d'intention admirable, et en me disant intérieurement: Tu es un honnête homme" (p. 209). This generous act, no matter how freely given, was in fact another subtle mask put on to protect as well as to assuage Jacob's sensitive amour-propre.

The prominence of amour-propre in the personalities of Jacob and Marianne is the primary reason why there is a lack of love in Marivaux's novels: *amour-passion* is replaced by *amour-reconnaissance.* Jacob reiterates that he is not sure whether he really loves Mlle. Habert or whether he is actually only *reconnaissant* toward her. The same is true regarding his liaison with Mme. de Ferval, whose hand he kisses with a "vive et affectueuse reconnaissance" (p. 139). Mme. de Ferval herself had said, only half-teasingly, after Jacob had too quickly blurted that he loved her: "Prenez garde, . . . je parle d'amour, et vous n'en avez pas pour ces personnes-là [like Mlle. Habert], non plus que pour moi; si vous nous aimez, c'est par reconnaissance, et non pas à cause que nous sommes aimables" (p. 139). This is true. Jacob is not being hypocritical when he says that he feels a certain affection for Mlle. Habert, but this affection is not love. None of Marivaux's characters are really capable of love; they are too caught up in trying to discover and sustain their own identities. The closest that Marianne and Jacob get to true love is the surrogate invented by Marivaux that he called *reconnaissance.*

Jacob even goes so far as to admit that he was attracted to Mme. de Ferval especially because of her social position. Love becomes only a function of self-interest: "Je voyais une femme de condition d'un certain air, qui avait apparemment des valets, un équipage, et qui me trouvait aimable; qui me permettait de lui baiser la main, et qui ne voulait pas qu'on le sût; une femme enfin qui nous tirait, mon orgueil et moi, du néant où nous étions encore; car avant ce temps-là m'étais-je estimé quelque chose? avais-je senti ce que c'était qu'amour-propre?" (p. 140).

Jacob continues to explain that even though he was going to marry Mlle. Habert, he considered himself her equal now and could not be proud of having won her. Thus, in his inimitable way, Jacob has succeeded in confusing reality and appearance, to the point of basing subsequent actions on what he had made others believe. But with Mme. de Ferval, there was an enormous social difference, and the fact that she is interested in him does no end of good to his amour-propre: "J'aimais donc par respect et par étonnement pour mon aventure, par ivresse de vanité, par tout ce qu'il vous plaira, par le cas infini que je faisais des appas de cette dame. . . . De sorte que je m'en retournai pénétré de joie, bouffi de gloire, et plein de mes folles exagérations sur le mérite de la dame" (p. 141).

After he has had time to savor his new liaison with Mme. de Ferval, Jacob, through a revealing recapitulation, reflects on his extraordinary luck and what it has done for his ego: "Voyez que de choses capables de débrouiller mon esprit et mon coeur. . . . Aussi étais-je dans un tourbillon de vanité . . . flatteuse; je me trouvais quelque chose de rare" (p. 187). He is at the point of no longer recognizing himself: "Je retournai donc chez moi, perdu de vanité, comme je l'ai dit, mais d'une vanité qui me rendait gai, et non pas superbe et ridicule; mon amour-propre a toujours été sociable; je n'ai jamais été plus doux ni plus traitable que lorsque j'ai eu lieu de m'estimer et d'être vain; chacun a là-dessus son caractère, et c'était là le mien. Mme de la Vallée ne m'avait encore vu ni si caressant, ni si aimable que je le fus avec elle à mon retour" (p. 187).

"L'âme se raffine à mesure qu'il se gâte": this pessimistic maxim is the result of Marivaux's extensive study of his fellow men, and especially those who are enjoying the luxury of the easy life so avidly defended by many of his contemporaries. Jacob has changed, or rather his potential has been awakened, and he realizes that one of the most exquisite pleasures of social man is to have his amour-propre caressed. Soon it becomes a means of communication between people of a certain rank and awareness: "Nous nous connaissons tous si bien en orgueil, que personne ne saurait nous faire un secret du sien; c'est quelquefois même sans y penser la première chose à quoi l'on regarde en abordant un inconnu" (p. 203).

Jacob, unlike Marianne, develops his amour-propre during his story. The *esprit revendicateur* that characterized Marianne's quest for social acceptance is not present in Jacob's considerations until toward the end of his adventures. He feels that he must earn the approbation of others, whereas Marianne felt that such recognition was owed her. But as Jacob's vanity becomes more defined, it plays an increasingly significant role in his machinations. Soon it even determines which courses of action he will follow. For instance, if he is virtuous, it is because "il y a de la douceur à se sentir vertueux" and "on se plaît avec les gens dont on vient de mériter la reconnaissance" (p. 209). The mask that he wears and uses as a weapon serves also to protect his slowly emerging vanity, and acts to disguise it from those who would attempt to injure it. And, like most masks, this one too has an unfortunate tendency to stick.

While Jacob is scheming and duping his fellows, he is also suffering from an identity crisis. Like Marianne, Jacob is a rootless young person who finds himself in Paris without friends or money. He has a family (unlike Marianne), but it is in the country, and Jacob realizes that if he is to make anything of himself he must cut himself off from his past, an ironic situation given the older Jacob's nostalgic desire to re-create it. Like Marianne, his origins too become only a mask, a tool that he uses to arrive; they no longer offer him the security that one's family should provide. A peasant in eighteenth-century Paris who associated himself with the bourgeoisie and the nobility was not in the most secure of positions, and Jacob must find some plane of stability. While in search of this psychological equilibrium, he too wears a mask as a *defensive mechanism* to hide his uncertainty and anxiety.

A corollary of this attitude is the theme of the quest, which is prevalent in most of Marivaux's prose fiction. His characters are all in search of something: Pharsamon looks for his Dulcinea, Brideron for his father, La Verdure for Fortune, and so on. Marianne and Jacob are in quest of several things: fame, fortune, security, and themselves. Marianne looks for a family because she lost it; Jacob's quest is more hectic because he had wittingly severed his past from his present. And Jacob's quest has two levels, which further distinguishes it from Marianne's and makes his a somewhat more complicated story. On the narrative level, Jacob is in many ways a picaresque hero, thoroughly enjoying his adventures. Gil Blas and Jacob have much in common when it comes to their rapid and tumultuous movement through society. But, on a different level, Jacob's quest for identity and security is much more open-ended. In fact, when the novel ends, Jacob is suspended between the worlds of the mask and of reality, uncertain of his existence, and very unhappy. This unhappiness is mirrored in both Jacob's and Marianne's search for the love that they cannot reciprocate. Since, as I have emphasized, love is a form of recognition (of *reconnaissance*), neither of these self-centered persons will ever be able to commit himself in terms of love, and thus this aspect of their quests will remain fruitless.

This theme of sentimental confusion, and its corollary themes of rootlessness and a search for identity, are best exemplified in *Le Paysan parvenu* when Jacob becomes M. de la Vallée. In order to continue their masquerade that Jacob is Mlle. Habert's visiting country cousin, the two lovers have to find a name for Jacob. As Jacob points out: "Il faut encore ajuster une autre affaire; on pourra s'en qùêter à moi de ma personne, et me dire: Qui êtes-vous, qui n'êtes-vous pas?" (p. 79). Mlle. Habert sees the good sense in this argument and agrees: "Prends le nom de la Vallée, et sois mon parent; tu as assez bonne mine pour cela" (p. 80).

By taking her advice, Jacob in effect changes his identity. He believes that by taking a new name, he can form and sustain a new existence, but, as we saw in his dealings with several people, he remains uncertain and even more insecure. This new mask proves to be even more cumbersome than the one he wore as a simple peasant. Yet he remains M. de la Vallée, "il ne sera plus question que de monsieur de la Vallée" (p. 84), and the remainder of the book's action will center around how he protects his newly acquired nobility while simultaneously trying to find some firm ground on which he may stand in his quest for identity. This uncertain state of affairs is reflected in several tableaux where Jacob finds himself having to play some of his masks against others. For instance, when he meets Mme. de Fécour, his last feminine conquest, he thinks that he has fooled her because of a snuffbox that he was carrying. The lady had asked for some tobacco, and playing the role of a gentleman, Jacob offered her some. However, a few minutes later, another person present at this little scene suddenly reveals that she is *au courant* as to his story, his marriage to Mlle. Habert, and so forth. On hearing himself thus unmasked, Jacob blushes. "Pour moi, il était naturel que je fusse honteux," he explains, since Mme. de Fécour had been "la dupe de ma mascarade" (p. 183). Yet he soon discovers that the lady had chosen to be duped, that she had known all along who Jacob was, and that it had made little difference to her. His confidence restored, Jacob replaces his mask of an *honnête homme* and continues to banter with the two ladies, even offering some more tobacco to Mme. de Fécour.

And so the rest of his story continues as he is constantly on the defensive, sometimes winning a battle and occasionally losing one. This state of anxiety is exacerbated by the fact that he simply does not know who he is. At one point, Jacob tells of his thoughts as he sits and admires his new acquisitions: "J'y contemplai ma robe de chambre et mes pantoufles; et je vous assure que ce ne furent pas là les deux articles qui me touchèrent le moins; de combien de petits bonheurs l'homme du monde est-il entouré et qu'il ne sent point, parce qu'il est né avec eux?" (p. 248). The contemplation of these physical symbols of his social success (cf. his sword and snuffbox) causes the dichotomy between Jacob and M. de la Vallée to again express itself: "Comment donc, des pantoufles et une robe de chambre à Jacob! Car c'était en me regardant comme Jacob que j'étais si délicieusement étonné de me voir dans cet équipage; c'était de Jacob que M. de la Vallée empruntait toute sa joie. Ce moment-là n'était si doux qu'à cause du petit paysan" (pp. 248–49). Who is Jacob?

The question will have to go unanswered. Jacob, the hero of *Le Paysan parvenu*, does not find the answer. He arrives but, as Claude Roy so aptly put it, "Parvenir (mais où?). Arriver (mais dans quel état?)."[10] He remains, at the end of his story, rootless and confused. Led onto the stage by his benefactor, he is the actor come home, but does not know happiness or peace of mind. The elder Jacob, the narrator, has used the composition of the book as a means through which he hoped to construct an identity. The physical existence of his memoirs, as was the case of Ma-

10. *Lire Marivaux*, p. 89.

rianne, gives him a palpable, if not an actual past. The effort to create an identity, to find a plane of stability on which to settle, has resulted in two unfinished sets of memoirs, which, on one level, are symbolic of an endless quest.

The question that must be asked is whether Jacob gains more than he loses through his mask-wearing and subterfuge. It is a valid moral problem, as I tried to show in the study of *La Vie de Marianne*. Can one succeed if he must practice deception, no matter how muted or justified, to do so? Is there any possibility at all of establishing one's true identity behind a mask? The answer to both of these questions is a half-hearted no. Although Marivaux recognized the prevalence, as well as the social necessity and apparent success of mask-wearing, every day, by everyone, he did not condone it. Unfortunately, and perhaps purposely, he offered no solution to the problem either. His sole aim seemed to be to show that although one gained many things through subterfuge—money, prestige, recognition, security—there was something lost as well. There is an almost pathetic quality to the older Jacob's melancholy contemplation, through reconstruction, of his adventurous past.

The older Jacob is supposedly a well-established, well-respected country gentleman, but he knows no happiness. Although we do not get to know the older Jacob as well as we do the older Marianne, Marivaux hints at the unhappiness of this man who has "arrived." The older Jacob tells us that he is now retired in the country, and that one of the reasons for writing his memoirs is that "je cherche . . . à m'amuser moi-même" (p. 6). Jacob had been an active young man, who seduced numerous women, who climbed rapidly through society to become a friend of the nephew of France's prime minister, yet who now passes his time writing his memoirs. He lives alone with his brother, and one of the first stories he tells concerns his two nephews. They had gained riches and had risen to a certain social level (partly through the aid of Jacob), but had then forsaken their father. "En effet, ils ont quitté leur nom, et n'ont plus de commerce avec leur père, qu'ils venaient autrefois voir de temps en temps" (p. 8). The reason for their absence is that Jacob had reprimanded them because of their affected ways, and, ashamed, they went away, leaving the two old men alone in the country.[11]

Ironically, these two vain and successful young men had done nothing that Jacob himself had not done. Their masks of social superiority and their affected speech were both tools that Jacob himself had used with success. It is not too much to suppose that their actions had in fact resuscitated memories in Jacob of his own youth and thus had occasioned the composition of his memoirs. At any rate, from time to time in the reconstruction of his past, the older Jacob seems to want to explain his actions, to analyze the reasons why he so quickly forgot his own origins, only now to want so much to rediscover that past. What originality he had, he has lost through his lifelong practice of trying to appear something that he was not. This is the pathos of both Jacob and Marianne, so successful in their attempts to breach the barricades of prejudice and hypocrisy thrown up before them, yet failing in their ultimate quests for individuality and self-definition.

The entire strategy of mask-wearing is inadvertently questioned by Jacob at one point toward the end of his story. Describing the young count d'Orsan as an obviously *honnête homme,* Jacob observes:

> Et en effet, ces choses-là se sentent; il en est de ce que je dis là-dessus comme d'un homme d'une certaine condition à qui vous donneriez un habit de paysan; en faites-vous un paysan pour cela? Non, vous voyez qu'il n'en porte que l'habit; sa figure en est vêtue, et point habillée, pour ainsi dire; il y a des

---

11. Cf. the plaintive reasons for writing his memoirs given by a forsaken father who writes to Marivaux in his *Spectateur français:* "Je suis seul, ignoré de tout l'Univers, de mon fils que je regrette, que j'appelle à mon secours, et qui m'ignore comme tout le reste des hommes" (*Journaux,* p. 188). And so he, too, tries to recreate his past.

attitudes, et des mouvements et des gestes dans cette personne, qui font qu'elle est étrangère au vêtement qui la couvre. (p. 254)

And what of a peasant who dons the clothes of a gentleman? Is there any hope that he will be successful? This unanswered question leaves open the possibility that Jacob will find the truth that he seeks, but even he seems to realize that simply wearing a mask in no way assures that one will succeed in his quest. Jacob, like Marianne, loses much more than he gains when he plays the role of a gentleman. The mask destroys the vitality that had distinguished him from his fellows, and Jacob becomes just another of Marivaux's "porteurs de visages."

Conclusion

MARIVAUX'S ARTISTIC EFFORTS LAY IN THREE REALMS; HE WAS a dramatist, a narrator, and a *moraliste*. All of these activities were functions of each other, and they can be shown to have had a reciprocal, salutary effect on one another. On a formal and thematic level, his work was defined by a consistent urge to experiment and a ceaseless search for new things to say and new ways to say them. Yet, to insist too heavily on Marivaux's novelty in any of these fields would risk understating the fact that, not unlike most of his generation, he was obviously a product of the age of Louis XIV, and of the traditions that neo-classicism had codified. The novel was not a new genre; comedy was one of the oldest of dramatic modes; and, the *moraliste* was part of a well-established French literary tradition. Nonetheless, Marivaux's work was not solely a patchwork reconciliation of a sclerotic tradition and new, contemporary ideas.

In one of the most important aesthetic treatises of the first half of the eighteenth century, the *abbé* Dubos makes a prescient observation on the future of art, and reaffirms some of the suspicions of those writers like Marivaux who had learned of new literary possibilities as a result of the Quarrel of the Ancients and the Moderns. The most significant legacies of Dubos's *Réflexions critiques sur la poésie et la peinture* (published in 1719, and reedited in 1733) were its insistence on two theorics. One affirmed that the domain

223

of art was as large as reality itself, and the second warned that art must cease to limit itself to a small élite. The first of these theories did not call for increased "realism" in art, nor did the second suggest that artists write for the masses. Yet such affirmative observations did go a long way in liberating the Modern littérateur from the more limiting aspects of the neo-classical aesthetic. It was an important step, and the most perspicacious of Dubos's contemporaries took his observations quite seriously. The result would be the development, in the eighteenth century, of the opera, of serious melodrama, and of the modern novel.

Marivaux's genius lay in the successful adaptation of older themes and forms to contemporary exigencies and tastes.[1] In a recent study, English Showalter has shown that the history of the post-Renaissance French novel is one of evolution rather than revolution, of gradual accommodation rather than radical change, and a close study of Marivaux's themes and techniques supports this thesis. As Jean Ehrard has pointed out in his own study of the aesthetics of the Enlightenment: "Il est remarquable que la recherche des formes d'art adaptés à l'esprit du siècle évite de rompre brusquement avec les traditions classiques."[2] The same was true of the themes of Marivaux the *moraliste:* the function of amour-propre, social compromise, the use of masks to befuddle and deceive, the often fruitless search for sincerity were not new subjects. Yet Marivaux was a Modern

---

1. For an excellent account of Marivaux's early attempts at formulating, or at least expressing, a new literary theory, even before Du Bos's famous essay, see Oscar Haac's recent article, "Theories of Literary Criticism and Marivaux," *SVEC* 88 (1972): 711–34. Haac carefully outlines the critical atmosphere of the early Enlightenment, places Marivaux in this context, and, through a careful reading of the writer's few theoretical essays, concludes that his "primary objective is the new, the original, the unsuspected" (p. 726). Haac sees Marivaux's theory as an anti-rhetorical one, a truly Modern attempt to emphasize the individual, the distinctive, as opposed to the prescriptive canon of traditional criticism. "More keenly than any of his contemporaries, Marivaux was aware of the newness of his enterprise, of the need for original formulations. . . . He called for new terms to express new concepts" (p. 733).

2. *L'Idée de nature en France dans la première moitié du XVIIIe siècle* (Paris: S.E.V. P.E.N., 1963), p. 314.

moralist who was interested less in perfection than in accommodation, less in uniformity than in individuality. As a result, he presented and analyzed traditional themes within the context of this new individuality that defined most of the early Enlightenment. Like his mentor, Fontenelle, he was fascinated with the possibilities of a new "human science" based on the same faith in reason that had produced "natural science." Again, Ehrard has put it best: "Ennemi du faux romanesque, Marivaux est aussi rationaliste que les 'géomètres' qu'il rencontrait jadis dans le salon de Mme de Lambert."[3]

Marivaux's art caught man in critical moments of his emotional life. It was an attitude that emphasized the transient quality of an individual's search for social acceptance and self-knowledge. As with every great writer, there is an ambiguous note that rings persistently throughout Marivaux's work. Despite his moralistic realism, he remained intrigued and often tempted by the ineffable quality of sincerity. Most of his characters look for it, and often seem to find it, ultimately realizing that in fact sincerity is impossible in the society that they inhabit. Even Marivaux himself, in such works as "Le Voyageur dans le nouveau monde" and his play *Les Sincères* seemed to agree. However, the very absence of sincerity causes the idea, at least, to be present in his works, and subsequently there is a recurring sense of nostalgia and pathos that prevades Marivaux's writings, qualities that have heretofore been misinterpreted as the result of a superficial and precious style.

During the early Enlightenment in France, there was definitely a reordering of artistic priorities. Marivaux must be understood in terms of this fact, and the traditional conclusions that have been drawn concerning his prose work must be revised. There should no longer be any doubt that Marivaux was a hardheaded moralist who saw in the novel the most effective means of communicating his

3. *Ibid.*, pp. 311–12.

new philosophy of social existence, spending over thirty years developing his mastery of the form. A careful study of his plays reveals how he subtly changed the style and direction of French theater, giving respectability and intelligible form to the melodrama and the intellectual comedy. More obviously, and perhaps more importantly, he did the same with prose narrative, though the formal incompleteness of his novels caused him to be studied mainly in terms of his theater. With Prévost, and, to a lesser extent, Lesage, Marivaux played a crucial role in the development of the modern French novel, personifying the early Enlightenment's quest for formal and thematic certainty. It was especially in the latter category that he succeeded. His "common" heroine and her serious introspection, his peasant's movement through various social milieux, described in a serio-comic tone, would prepare the way for Diderot and Rousseau, for Sade and Stendhal.

One of the most astute—and succinct—observations ever made about Marivaux's prose work was jotted down by Stendhal in his *Pensées:* "La Marianne de Marivaux excellent roman à lire en allant dans le monde. Demi-heure avant." The brilliant juxtaposition of the concepts of *monde* and *roman* reflects Stendhal's comprehension of Marivaux's most haunting preoccupation—the successful combination of theme and form. The result of his efforts would be the modern novel which, after years of criticism and hesitancy, would ultimately become an essential tool in the Enlightenment's propagandization of truth. This is the most significant legacy of Marivaux's prose experience.

Bibliography

A. EDITIONS OF MARIVAUX USED

Oeuvres complettes. 12 vols. Paris: Veuve Duchesne, 1781.

Théâtre complet. Edited by Bernard Dort. Paris: Seuil, 1964.

Théâtre complet. Edited by Frédéric Deloffre. 2 vols. Paris: Garnier, 1968.

Romans, récits, contes et nouvelles. Edited by Marcel Arland. Bibliothèque de la Pléiade. Paris: Gallimard, 1949.

Journaux et oeuvres diverses. Edited by F. Deloffre et Michel Gilot. Paris: Garnier, 1969.

Oeuvres de Jeunesse. Edited by F. Deloffre, Bibliothèque de la Pléiade. Paris: Gallimard, 1972.

Le Paysan parvenu. Edited by F. Deloffre. Paris: Garnier, 1959.

Le Télémaque travesti. Edited by F. Deloffre. Paris: Droz, 1956.

La Vie de Marianne. Edited by F. Deloffre. Paris: Garnier, 1957.

B. WORKS ON MARIVAUX

Alembert, Jean le Rond d'. "Eloge de Marivaux." In Marivaux, *Théâtre complet*, edited by B. Dort, pp. 17–38. Paris: Seuil, 1964.

Arland, Marcel. *Marivaux.* Paris: Gallimard, 1950.

Bonaccorso, Giovanni. *Gli Anni difficili di Marivaux.* Messina: Peloritana, 1965.

Brady, Valentini P. *Love in the Theatre of Marivaux.* Geneva: Droz, 1970.

Coulet, Henri. "Marivaux romancier: essai sur l'esprit et le coeur dans les romans de Marivaux," *L'Information littéraire,* 25e année, no. 3 (mai-juin 1973), pp. 103–9.

Crocker, Lester. "Portrait de l'homme dans le *Paysan parvenu,*" *SVEC* 87 (1972): 253–76.

Deloffre, F. "Aspects inconnus de l'oeuvre de Marivaux." *Revue des Sciences humaines* 54 (1954): 5–24, 97–116.

————. "De Marianne à Jacob: les deux sexes du roman chez Marivaux." *L'Information littéraire* 11 (1959): 185–92.

————. *Une Préciosité nouvelle: Marivaux et le marivaudage.* 2d ed. rev. Paris: Armand Colin, 1967.

————. "Premières idées de Marivaux sur l'art du roman." *L'Esprit Créateur* 1 (1961): 178–83.

————. "Sources romanesques et création dramatique chez Marivaux." *Mélanges d'histoire littéraire offerts à M. Paul Dimoff.* Annales de l'Université de la Sarre 3 (1954): 59–66.

Desvignes-Parent, Lucette. *Marivaux et l'Angleterre: Essai sur une création dramatique originale.* Paris: Klincksieck, 1970.

D'Hondt, Jacques. "Hegel et Marivaux." *Europe,* nos. 451–52 (1966), pp. 323–37.

Durry, Marie-Jeanne. *A Propos de Marivaux.* Paris: Société d'Edition d'enseignement supérieur, 1960.

Fabre, Jean. "Intention et structure dans les romans de Marivaux." *Zagadnienia rodzajów literackich* 3 (1960): 5–25.

————. "Marivaux." *Dictionnaire des Lettres françaises: Le Dix-huitième siècle,* 2: 167–88. Paris: Fayard, 1960.

————. "Marivaux." *Histoire des Littératures (Encyclopédie de la Pléiade),* 3: 677–95. Paris: Gallimard, 1958.

Friedrichs, Friedhelm. *Untersuchungen zur Handlungs-und Vorgangsmotivik im Werk Marivauxs.* Heidelberg: Ruprecht-Karl Universität, 1965.

Gilot, Michel. "Marivaux: Homme de lettres 'sans enseigne.' " In *Marivaux,* edited by Sylvie Chevalley, pp. 27–34. Paris: Comédie Française, 1966.

————. "Un étrange divertissement: *l'Iliade travestie.*" *La Régence,*

Centre Aixois d'Etudes et de Recherches sur le dix-huitième siècle, pp. 186–205. Paris: Armand Colin, 1970.

Girard, René. "Marivaudage and Hypocrisy." *American Society Legion of Honor Magazine* 34 (1963): 163–74.

Gossman, Lionel. "Literature and Society in the Early Enlightenment: The Case of Marivaux." *MLN* 82 (1967): 306–33.

Greene, E. J. H. *Marivaux.* Toronto: University of Toronto Press, 1965.

———. "Marivaux's Philosophical Bum." *Esprit Créateur* 1 (1961): 190–95.

Haac, Oscar. "Humour through Paradox." *Esprit Créateur* 1 (1961): 196–202.

———. *Marivaux.* New York: Twayne, 1974.

———. "Marivaux and the *honnête homme.*" *Romanic Review* 50 (1959): 255–67.

———. "Theories of Literary Criticism and Marivaux." *SVEC* 88 (1972): 711–34.

Ince, Walter. "L'Unité du double registre chez Marivaux." *Les Chemins actuels de la critique,* edited by G. Poulet, pp. 131–46. Discussion avec Max Milner, Georges Poulet, Jacques Roger, Jean Rousset, pp. 147–56. Paris: Plon, 1967.

Jaloux, Edmond. "Marivaux." *Tableau de la littérature française de Corneille à Chénier,* pp. 239–44. Paris: Gallimard, 1939.

Jamieson, Ruth K. *Marivaux, a Study in Eighteenth-Century Sensibility.* New York: King's Crown Press, 1941.

Koch, Phillip. "On Marivaux's Expression 'se donner la comédie,' " *Romanic Review* 56 (1965): 22–29.

Larroumet, Gustave. *Marivaux, sa vie et ses oeuvres.* Paris: Hachette, 1882.

Levin, Lubbe. "Masque et Identité dans le *Paysan parvenu,*" *SVEC* 79 (1970): 177–92.

McKee, Kenneth N. *The Theater of Marivaux.* New York: New York University Press, 1958.

Matucci, Mario. "Dagli *Effets* al *Pharsamon* di Marivaux." Part 2 of his *Figure e Aspetti del '700 francese,* pp. 51–92. Naples: R. Pironti e figli, 1960.

———. "Intorno alla narrativa di Marivaux." *Rivista di letterature moderne e comparate* 9 (1956): 17–35.

———. *L'Opera narrativa di Marivaux.* Naples: R. Pironti e figli, 1962.

Mauzi, Robert. "Marivaux romancier." Introduction to Marivaux, *Le Paysan parvenu.* Paris: Union Générale d'Editions (10–18), 1965.

Meister, Anna. *Zur Entwicklung Marivauxs.* Berne: Francke, 1955.

Ménard, Jean. "*Le Paysan parvenu* de Marivaux." *Revue de l'Université Laval* 11 (1956): 40–52.

Nøjgaard, Morten. "Le Problème du réalisme dans les romans de Marivaux. Réflexions sur l'introduction de la *Voiture embourbée.*" *Revue Romane* 1 (1967): 71–87.

Parrish, Jean. "Illusion et réalité dans les romans de Marivaux." *MLN* 80 (1965): 301–6.

Pomeau, René. "La Surprise et le masque dans le théâtre de Marivaux." *The Age of the Enlightenment: Studies presented to Theodore Besterman.* Edited by Barber, Brumfitt, Leigh, Shackleton, Taylor, pp. 238–51. London: Oliver & Boyd, 1967.

Poulet, Georges. "Marivaux." In his *Etudes sur le Temps humain,* vol. 2, *La Distance intérieure,* pp. 1–34. Paris: Plon, 1953.

Proust, Jacques. "Le 'Jeu du temps et du hasard' dans *Le Paysan parvenu.*" *Europäische Aufklärung: Herbert Dieckmann zum 60. Geburtstag,* pp. 223–35. Munich: Wilhelm Fink, 1967.

Rogers, William S. "Marivaux: The Mirror and the Mask." *Esprit Créateur* 1 (1961): 167–77.

Rosbottom, Ronald C. "Marivaux and the Significance of 'naissance.'" *Jean-Jacques Rousseau et son temps.* Edited by M. Launay, pp. 73–92. Paris: Nizet, 1969.

———. "Marivaux and the Possibilities of the Memoir-Novel." *Neophilologus* 56 (1972): 43–49.

———. "Marivaux and the Crisis of Literary Forms in the Early Enlightenment." *The Varied Pattern,* edited by P. Hughes and D. Williams, pp. 97–111. Toronto: A.M. Hakkert, 1971.

———. "Truth and Parody in Mme. Riccoboni's Continuation of *La Vie de Marianne.*" *SVEC* 81 (1971): 163–75.

Rousset, Jean. "Comment insérer le présent dans le récit: l'exemple de Marivaux." *Littérature,* no. 5 (1972), pp. 3–10.

_____ "L'Emploi de la première personne chez Chasles et Marivaux." *Cahiers de l'Association internationale des études françaises,* no. 19 (1967), pp. 101–14.

_____. "Marivaux, ou la structure du double registre." *Forme et signification; Essais sur les structures littéraires de Corneille à Claudel,* pp. 45–64. Paris: José Corti, 1962.

Roy, Claude. *Lire Marivaux.* Paris: Seuil, 1947.

_____. "Un théâtre grave et cruel." *Cahiers Renaud-Barrault* (Jan. 1960), pp. 29–36.

Schaad, Harold. *Le Thème de l'être et du paraître dans l'oeuvre de Marivaux.* Zurich: Juris Druck + Verlag Zürich, 1969.

Schérer, Jacques. "Marivaux," Introduction to Marivaux. *Théâtre complet,* pp. 7–10. Paris: Seuil, 1964.

Séailles, André. "Les Déguisements de l'amour et le mystère de la naissance dans le théâtre et le roman de Marivaux." *Revue des Sciences humaines* 65 (1965): 479–92.

Spitzer, Leo. "A Propos de la *Vie de Marianne* (Lettre à M. Georges Poulet)." *Romanic Review* 44 (1953): 102–26.

Stackelberg, Jürgen von. "Le *Télémaque travesti* et la naissance du réalisme dans le roman." *La Régence,* Centre Aixois d'Etudes et de Recherches sur le dix-huitième siècle, pp. 206–12. Paris: Armand Colin, 1970.

Trapnell, William H. "Marivaux's Unfinished Narratives." *French Studies* 24 (1970): 237–53.

Turnell, Martin. "Marivaux." *Scrutiny* 15 (1947): 36–55.

Walker, Hallam. *"L'Epreuve:* Comic Test and Truth." *Esprit Créateur* 1 (1961): 184–89.

Wrage, William. "A Critical Edition of Marivaux's *Spectateur français."* Ph.D. dissertation, University of Wisconsin, 1964–1965.

C. OTHER WORKS CONSULTED

Adam, Antoine. *Histoire de la littérature française au XVIIe siècle.* 5 vols. Paris: Editions Mondiales, 1949–1956.

232   MARIVAUX'S NOVELS

_____. "Hommage à la mémoire de Fontenelle." *Annales de l'Université de Paris* 27 (1957): 402–405.

Auerbach, Erich. *Mimesis: The Representation of Reality in Western Literature.* 1953; rpt. New York: Anchor Books, 1957.

Bardon, Maurice. *"Don Quichotte" en France au XVIIe et au XVIIIe siècles (1605–1815).* Paris: Champion, 1931.

Barthes, Roland. "La Bruyère." *Essais critiques,* pp. 221–37. Paris: Seuil, 1964.

Booth, Wayne C. *The Rhetoric of Fiction.* Chicago: University of Chicago Press, 1961.

_____. "The Self-conscious Narrator in Comic Fiction before *Tristram Shandy,"* PMLA 67 (1952): 163–85.

Braudy, Leo. *Narrative Form in History and Fiction: Hume, Fielding and Gibbon.* Princeton: Princeton University Press, 1970.

Brooks, Peter. *The Novel of Worldliness: Crébillon, Marivaux, Laclos, Stendhal.* Princeton: Princeton University Press, 1969.

Coulet, Henri. *Le Roman jusqu'à la Révolution.* Paris: Armand Colin, 1967.

Crocker, Lester. *An Age of Crisis: Man and World in Eighteenth Century French Thought.* Baltimore: Johns Hopkins Press, 1969.

_____. *Nature and Culture: Ethical Thought in the Eighteenth Century.* Baltimore: Johns Hopkins Press, 1963.

Deloffre, F. "Une mode préstendhalien d'expression de la sensibilité à la fin du XVIIe siècle." *Cahiers de l'association internationale des études françaises,* no. 11 (1959), pp. 9–32.

_____. *La Nouvelle en France à l'âge classique.* Paris: Didier, 1967.

_____. "Le Problème de l'illusion romanesque et le renouvellement des techniques narratives de 1700 à 1715." *La Littérature narrative d'imagination; des genres littéraires aux techniques d'expression,* pp. 115–33. Paris: Presses Universitaires de France, 1961.

Ehrard, Jean. *L'Idée de nature en France dans la première moitié du XVIIIe siècle.* Paris: S.E.V.P.E.N., 1963.

Frye, Northrop. *Anatomy of Criticism: Four Essays.* 1957; rpt. New York: Atheneum, 1966.

Gillot, Hubert. *La Querelle des Anciens et des Modernes en France.* Paris: Champion, 1914.

Godenne, René. *Histoire de la nouvelle française aux XVIIe et XVIIIe siècles.* Geneva: Droz, 1970.

Goffman, Erving. *The Presentation of Self in Everyday Life.* Garden City, N.Y.: Doubleday and Co., 1959.

Goode, William O. "A Mother's Goals in *La Princesse de Clèves:* Worldly and Spiritual Distinction." *Neophilologus* 56 (1972): 398–406.

Gossman, Lionel. *Men and Masks: A Study of Molière.* Baltimore: Johns Hopkins Press, 1963.

Goubert, Pierre. *Louis XIV and Twenty Million Frenchmen.* 1966; trans. 1970; rpt. New York: Vintage Books, 1972.

Green, F. C. *Minuet: A Critical Survey of French and English Literary Ideas in the Eighteenth Century.* New York: Dutton, 1935.

————. "Some Observations on Techniques and Form in the French Seventeenth- and Eighteenth-Century Novel." *Stil- und Formprobleme in der Literatur,* pp. 208–15. Heidelberg: Winter, 1959.

Hazard, Paul. *La Crise de la conscience européenne (1680–1715).* 1935; rpt. 2 vols. Paris: Gallimard, 1968.

————. *La Pensée européenne au XVIIIe siècle, de Montesquieu à Lessing.* 1946; rpt. Paris: Fayard, 1963.

Krailsheimer, A. J. *Studies in Self-Interest from Descartes to La Bruyère.* Oxford: Clarendon Press, 1962.

Laufer, Roger. *Lesage ou le métier de romancier.* Paris: Gallimard, 1971.

Le Breton, André. *Le Roman au dix-huitième siècle.* Paris: Société française d'imprimerie et de librairie, 1897.

May, Georges. *Le Dilemme du roman au XVIIIe siècle: Etude sur les rapports du roman et de la critique (1715–1761).* Paris: Presses Universitaires de France, 1963.

————. "L'Histoire a-t-elle engendré le roman?; aspects français de la question au seuil du siècle de lumières." *Revue d'histoire littéraire en France* 55 (1955): 155–76.

Monty, Jeanne. *Les Romans de Prévost: procédés littéraires et pensée morale. SVEC* 78. Geneva: Institut et Musée Voltaire, 1970.

Moore, W. G. *La Rochefoucauld: His Mind and Art.* Oxford: Clarendon Press, 1969.

———. *Molière: A New Criticism.* Oxford: Clarendon Press, 1949.

Mylne, Vivienne. *The Eighteenth-Century French Novel: Techniques of Illusion.* Manchester: University of Manchester Press, 1965.

Paulson, Ronald. *The Fictions of Satire.* Baltimore: Johns Hopkins Press, 1967.

Peyre, Henri. *Literature and Sincerity.* New Haven: Yale University Press, 1963.

Ratner, Moses. *Theory and Criticism of the Novel in France from "l'Astrée" to 1750.* New York: New York University Press, 1938.

Raymond, Marcel. "Du Jansénisme à la morale de l'intérêt." *Mercure de France* 330 (1957): 238–55.

Rigault, Hippolyte. *Histoire de la Querelle des Anciens et des Modernes.* Paris: Hachette, 1856.

Sgard, Jean. *Prévost romancier.* Paris: José Corti, 1968.

———. *Le "Pour et contre" de Prévost.* Paris: Nizet, 1969.

Showalter, English, Jr. *The Evolution of the French Novel, 1641–1782.* Princeton: Princeton University Press, 1972.

Stackelberg, J. von. "Le *Télémaque travesti* et la naissance du réalisme dans le roman." *La Régence,* Centre Aixois d'Etudes et de Recherches sur le 18e siècle, pp. 206–12. Paris: A. Colin, 1970.

Starobinski, Jean. *L'Invention de la liberté, 1700–1789.* Geneva: Skira, 1964.

———. *Jean-Jacques Rousseau: La Transparence et l'obstacle.* Paris: Plon, 1957.

———. "Introduction," La Rochefoucauld, *Maximes et Mémoires,* pp. 7–35. Paris: Union Générale d'Editions, 1964.

———. "La Rochefoucauld et les morales substitutives." *La Nouvelle Revue française,* no. 163 (1966): 16–34; no. 164 (1966): 210–29.

Steiner, Arpad. "A French Poetics of the Novel in 1683." *Romanic Review* 30 (1939): 235–43.

Stewart, Philip. *Imitation and Illusion in the French Memoir-Novel, 1700–1750; The Art of Make-Believe.* New Haven: Yale University Press, 1969.

———. *Le Masque et la parole: Le langage de l'amour au XVIIIe siècle.* Paris: J. Corti, 1973.

Trahard, Pierre. *Les Maîtres de la sensibilité française au XVIIIe siècle (1715–1789)*. 4 vols. Paris: Boivin, 1931–33.

Varga, Kibédi. "La Désagrégation de l'idéal classique dans le roman français de la première moitié du XVIIIe siècle." *SVEC* 26 (1963): 965–98.

Wade, Ira O. *The Intellectual Development of Voltaire*. Princeton: Princeton University Press, 1969.

_____. *Voltaire's "Micromégas": A Study in the Fusion of Science, Myth, and Art*. Princeton: Princeton University Press, 1950.

Watt, Ian. *The Rise of the Novel: Studies in Defoe, Richardson, and Fielding*. 1959; rpt. Berkeley and Los Angeles: University of California Press, 1965.

Westgate, David. "The Concept of Amour-propre in the *Maximes* of La Rochefoucauld." *Nottingham French Studies* 7 (1968): 67–79.

Index

Adam, Antoine, 21, 22
Addison, Joseph, 30, 78, 79, 88
Alembert, Jean Le Rond d', 31
Amadis de Gaula, 56
Apologie des femmes, L' (Perrault), 23
Argenson, René-Louis d', 26
Arland, Marcel, 171
Aspar (Fontenelle), 22
Auerbach, Erich, 69

Barthes, Roland, 46n, 99n
Bayle, Pierre, 19
Boileau-Despréaux, Nicolas, 21, 23, 24
Bollogne, Colombe, 27, 30
Booth, Wayne C., 63n
Bossuet, Jacques-Bénigne, 21
Brady, Valentini, 10
Braudy, Leo, 50n
Brooks, Peter, 9, 10, 46, 99n, 124n, 126

Caractères, Les (La Bruyère), 76
Carlet, Nicolas, 25, 29
Carlet, Pierre, 76. *See also* Marivaux
Cervantes, Miguel de, 56, 57, 62
Challe, Robert, 48, 49, 51, 56, 117n, 134n
Chamblain, Jean-Baptiste Bullet de, 26
Comédie Italienne, 41
Coquetterie, 33, 38, 39, 44, 46, 47, 77, 78, 80–81, 83, 125, 134, 136, 151, 154, 155, 159, 163, 168, 169, 183, 187
Corneille, Pierre, 35
Coulet, Henri, 10, 11n
Crébillon, Prosper Jolyot de *(père),* 27
Crébillon, Claude de *(fils),* 51, 174

Dacier, Mme. Anne Lefebvre, 24, 27
Defoe, Daniel, 65
Deloffre, Frédéric, 10, 14, 27, 31, 52n, 56, 57, 58n, 61, 62n, 63, 69n, 73, 116n, 124, 170n, 171, 208, 209
De l'usage des romans où l'on fait voir leur utilité et leurs différents caractères (Lenglet-Dufresnoy), 49
Desvignes-Parent, Lucette, 10
Diable boiteux, Le (Lesage), 56
Diderot, Denis, 48, 226
Don Quixote (Cervantes), 56, 63, 67, 169
Dubos, *abbé* Jean-Baptiste, 24, 223, 224
Dufresny, Charles Rivière, *dit,* 56
Du Plaisir, *sieur,* 49
Durry, Marie-Jeanne, 30–31, 171

Egarements du coeur et de l'esprit, Les (Crébillon *fils*), 51, 174
Ehrard, Jean, 224, 225
Essais de morale, Les (Nicole), 44

Fabre, Jean, 38
Fénelon, François de Salignac de, 24, 28, 51, 56, 66, 69n
Fontenelle, Bernard Le Bovier de, 19, 22, 26, 27, 56, 58, 62n, 225
Friedrichs, Friedhelm, 12
Frye, Northrop, 55, 88

Gassendi, Pierre, 23
Gil Blas (Lesage), 48, 52, 56, 179
Gilot, Michel, 27n, 31
Godenne, René, 10
Goffman, Erving, 42, 43
Goldoni, Carlo, 41
Gomberville, Le Roy de, 56, 58
Goode, William O., 121n
Green, F. C., 10, 101n
Greene, E. J. H., 85n, 172
Guardi, Francesco, 40

Haac, Oscar, 224n
Homer, 20
Huet, Daniel, 49, 50

Iliad, The (Homer), 24, 26, 54, 65
Illustres Françaises, Les (Challe), 48, 56, 117n, 134n

Jansenists, 22
Jesuits, 22
Journal de Trévoux, Le, 22
Journal des Savants, Le, 62n

La Bruyère, Jean de, 21, 56, 76, 80
La Calprenède, Gauthier de, 56, 58
Laclos, Choderlos de, 48
Lafayette, Mme. de, 121n
Lambert, Mme. de, 26, 124
La Motte, Houdar de, 24, 26, 27
La Rochefoucauld, François, duc de, 32, 44, 45, 56, 91, 150, 151n, 168, 212
Larroumet, Gustave, 30, 171
Law's System, 27, 29

Le Breton, André, 10
Lenglet du Fresnoy, abbé, 49
Lesage, Alain-René, 48, 49, 56, 65, 179, 226
Lettre-traité à M. de Segrais sur l'origine des Romans (Huet), 49
Lettres persanes, Les (Montesquieu), 51, 56
Liaisons dangereuses, Les (Laclos), 51, 77
Libertins érudits, 23
Longhi, Pietro, 40
Louis XIV, 11, 19, 20, 21, 26, 223

Malebranche, Nicolas de, 21
Manon Lescaut (Prévost), 93, 170, 199
Marivaudage, 90, 165
Marivaux, Pierre Carlet de Chamblain de: becomes licencié en droit, 30; birth in Paris and youth in Riom (Auvergne), 25; birth of only child, Colombe-Prospère, 29; and collapse of Law's System, 29–30; and comic fiction, 28–29, 62–75 passim, 97; death of his wife, Colombe, 30; decision to become man of letters, 29–30; and the early eighteenth-century novel, 12, 47–53 passim, 84, 170, 172, 225–26; early literary career, 25, 26, 54–57; friendship with Fontenelle, 26–30 passim; and journalistic tradition, 75–92 passim; lack of biographical data on, 11, 30; literary versatility, 11, 94; marriage to Colombe Bologne, 27; and Mme. de Lambert's salon, 26, 124; and moraliste tradition, 12, 32–35, 45, 147–49, 223–26 passim; and Prévost, 79–80; and the Quarrel of the Ancients and Moderns, 20–29 passim, 91, 223–26 passim; renounces claim to father's inheritance, 30; and romance tradition, 55–57; search for

new literary style, 34–36, 94, 172–73, 224; sensitivity to criticism, 28, 31–32; studies law, 25; and themes of *coquetterie*, 46–47, of the mask, 40–44 passim, 60–61, of sociability and compromise, 34–45 passim; view of love, 107–10, 112; works by: *Amour et la vérité, L'*, 29; *Annibal*, 29; *Arlequin poli par l'amour*, 25, 29, 41; *Bilboquet, Le*, 28; *Cabinet du philosophe, Le*, 36, 75, 86n, 87, 88–92, 163, 172, 179, 182; "Chemin de la Fortune, Le" *(Cabinet du philosophe)*, 36–37, 87, 88, 179; *Commère, La*, 191–92, 194; *Double inconstance, La*, 13, 77; *Effets surprenants de la sympathie, Les*, 25, 26, 28, 55, 57–62, 65, 95, 161; *Iliade travestie* (also *Homère travesti*), *L'*, 27, 65; *Indigent philosophe, L'*, 75, 85–86, 88, 177; *Jeu de l'amour et du hasard, Le*, 12, 77; "Lettres contenant une aventure" (also "L'Apprentie coquette"), 29, 76–78, 83, 147; "Lettres sur les habitants de Paris" (also "Les Caractères de M. de Marivaux"), 29, 46, 52–53, 75, 76; "Mémoire de ce que j'ai fait et vu pendant ma vie" *(Spectateur français)*, 82–84; *Mère confidente, La*, 134n; *Paysan parvenu, Le*, 12, 40, 43, 55, 56, 57, 66, 68, 73, 79, 87, 91, 92, 97, 99, 134n, 140, 167, 171–222; *Père prudent et équitable, Le*, 25; *Pharsamon, ou les Nouvelles folies romanesques* (also *Le Don Quichotte moderne*), 25, 28, 58, 62–65, 66, 74, 97, 161, 176, 179; "Réflexions sur l'esprit moderne à l'occasion de Corneille et Racine," 35; "Réflexions sur les coquettes" *(Cabinet du philosophe)*, 88; "Réflexions sur Thucydide," 34; *Serments indiscrets, Les*, 35, 77; *Sincères, Les*, 225; *Spectateur français, Le*, 30, 33, 34, 47, 75, 78–85, 87, 88, 89; "Sur la clarté du discours," 35; *Télémaque travesti, Le*, 28, 65–70, 74, 75, 97, 161, 176, 179; "Veuve et le magicien, La" *(Cabinet du philosophe)*, 87; *Vie de Marianne, La*, 12, 37–39 (Tervire episode), 42, 43, 45, 51, 54, 55, 56, 57, 65, 66, 70, 73, 75, 79, 83, 84, 85, 87, 91, 92, 93–170, 171, 172, 173, 174, 180, 185, 191, 193, 198, 199, 220; *Voiture embourbée, La*, 26, 28, 65, 70–75, 161, 177; "Voyageur dans le nouveau monde, Le" *(Cabinet du philosophe)*, 87, 89–92, 182, 225

Marmontel, Jean-François, 31
Matucci, Mario, 10, 12, 59n
Mauzi, Robert, 171, 172, 185
Maximes, Les (La Rochefoucauld), 44
May, Georges, 9, 49n, 50
Mémoires et aventures d'un homme de qualité, Les (Prévost), 51
Mercure, Le, 29, 75
Montaigne, Michel de, 56
Montesquieu, Charles de Secondat de, 50, 51, 56
Monty, Jeanne, 51n
Moore, W. G., 44

Nicole, Pierre, 44, 148
Nouvelle Héloïse, La (Rousseau), 51
Novelas ejemplares (Cervantes), 56

Orlando Furioso (Ariosto), 56
Orléans, Philippe, duc de, 22

Pamela (Richardson), 56, 101n, 105, 121
Pascal, Blaise, 44, 56, 91, 148
Paulson, Ronald, 88
Pensées (Stendhal), 226
Perrault, Charles, 23, 24
Persiles y Sigismunda (Cervantes), 56, 57

Pomeau, René, 42n
Port-Royal, 44
Poulet, Georges, 110, 111, 160
Pour et contre (Prévost), 51n, 80
Presentation of Self in Everyday Life, The
    (Goffman), 42
Prévost, abbé de, 51, 65, 69, 78, 79, 93,
    170, 226
Princesse de Clèves, La (Mme. de La-
    fayette), 121n
Proust, Marcel, 13

Quarrel of the Ancients and Moderns,
    20, 21, 22, 23, 24, 65, 223

Racine, Jean, 21, 35
Raymond, Marcel, 44n
Reconnaissance, 133, 150–53, 200, 214–
    15, 217
Réflexions critiques sur la poésie et la peinture
    (Dubos), 24, 223
Riccoboni, Mme. de, 37, 116n, 158,
    159
Richardson, Samuel, 56, 65, 81, 101n,
    105, 121
Rigault, Hippolyte, 26
Rousseau, Jean-Jacques, 48, 226
Rousset, Jean, 63n
Roy, Claude, 172, 184, 219

Sade, marquis de, 48, 226

Santayana, George, 42
Scarron, Paul, 28, 56
Scudéry, Mlle. de, 56, 58
Séailles, André, 95n
Sentiments sur les Lettres et sur l'Histoire
    avec des scrupules sur le Stile (Du Plai-
    sir), 49
Sévigné, Mme. de, 21
Sgard, Jean, 51n, 79
Showalter, English, Jr., 10, 48n, 224
Simon, Richard, 19
Sorel, Charles, 28, 56, 62
Spectator, The (Addison, Steele), 30, 79,
    88
Spitzer, Leo, 38n, 138, 140, 155
Stackelberg, Jurgen von, 69n
Starobinski, Jean, 41, 168
Steele, Richard, 30, 78, 88
Steiner, Arpad, 49n
Stendhal, 226
Stewart, Philip, 10, 43n, 52n

Télémaque (Fénelon), 28, 56, 66, 69n
Tiepolo, Giambattista, 41

Villedieu, Mme. de, 56
Voltaire, François-Marie Arouet de,
    35, 50

Watt, Ian, 55, 56